T0319920

First published in Great Britain in 2020 by

Bristol University Press
University of Bristol
1-9 Old Park Hill
Bristol
BS2 8BB
UK
t: +44 (0)117 954 5940
www.bristoluniversitypress.co.uk

North America office:
Bristol University Press
c/o The University of Chicago Press
1427 East 60th Street
Chicago, IL 60637, USA
t: +1 773 702 7700
f: +1 773-702-9756
sales@press.uchicago.edu
www.press.uchicago.edu

© Bristol University Press 2020

British Library Cataloguing in Publication Data
A catalogue record for this book is available from the British Library

Library of Congress Cataloging-in-Publication Data
A catalog record for this book has been requested

ISBN 978-1-5292-0067-6 hardcover
ISBN 978-1-5292-0068-3 paperback
ISBN 978-1-5292-0070-6 ePub
ISBN 978-1-5292-0069-0 ePdf

Cover design by blu inc
Front cover image: Stocksy/Rowena Taylor
Printed and bound in Great Britain by CMP, Poole
Bristol University Press uses environmentally responsible print partners

To Edith

Contents

Acknowledgements   ix

1 Change Is Possible and Necessary   **1**
Points of departure   4
Institutions   4
Power   7
Structure of the book   10
Further reading   12

2 The Political Economy of Everyday Life   **15**
Gender   16
Racism   20
Class   21
Intersectionality   24
Love   25
Reconstructing everyday life   27
Lifestyles and sustainability   31
Ecological footprint   32
Energy return on energy invested   33
Social justice   34
Fighting racism and gender oppression   35
Conclusion   37
Further reading   38

3 Markets Are What We Make Them   **41**
The state as we know it   41
The multilateral institutional system   43
Multilateral economic institutions   44
    The International Monetary Fund   45
    The World Bank   47
    Free trade and growth   49
    The General Agreement on Tariffs and Trade   50
Change in the global economic order   51

	Reconstructive lessons from the 1970s and 1980s	54
	Markets for a sustainable future	55
	Solving problems	55
	Transformation of market structures	60
	Conclusion	61
	Further reading	62
4	**Trade Constructs**	**63**
	The global free-trade regime	64
	The WTO: a victim of its own success	67
	The Battle of Seattle	68
	The Doha Development Round	69
	The Cancun breakdown (2003)	70
	Breakdown in Geneva (2008)	72
	Prevailing free trade?	73
	Reconstructing trade	75
	Conclusion	81
	Further reading	82
5	**What Development?**	**83**
	Overdevelopment in the North	86
	The debt trap	87
	SAP reconstruction	90
	Lessons from the SAP era	96
	The Beijing Consensus	97
	Designing another modern project	98
	Poverties	99
	Addressing poverties	101
	Degrowth and the upper-class problem	109
	Conclusion	111
	Further reading	112
6	**Financial Markets and the Future**	**115**
	Financial instruments	115
	The logic of the whole thing	121
	The actors	122
	The 2008 crisis	128
	The G20 to the rescue	131
	Reconstructing global financial markets	133
	Reconstructing ownership	134
	Money	138
	Debt	140
	Endemic risks	143

Conclusion 147
Further reading 147

7   Globalized Production   **149**
What is a firm? 149
The end of Fordism 150
Post-Fordist political dynamics 156
Clusters and regions 158
Reconstructing global production 161
What's in a firm? 165
Reconstructing the corporation 166
Technology and reconstruction 169
Gender, class and racism 171
Conclusion 175
Further reading 175

8   Do Not Waste a Crisis   **177**
Sustainable finance? 178
Just, sustainable global production 179
Treaties for sustainable trade 181
Post-crisis markets 182
Conclusion 183

Notes 185
References 189
Index 197

Acknowledgements

This book comes from 25 years of thinking, teaching, researching and writing about the global political economy. Since I work as a lecturer at the School of Global Studies at the University of Gothenburg, those most involved in my intellectual process have been my students. Assisting their learning process about the global economy, being challenged and held accountable for theories, data and knowledge in the field of Global Political Economy, and thinking creatively and collaboratively with them in countless seminars and lectures has been a privilege and a great intellectual stimulus. A first thank you therefore goes to my students.

I am also indebted to my editor, Stephen Wenham, who came by my office in November 2016, quickly understood this project and agreed to take it on. His advice and his respectful editing of my style and English-as-second-language writing has been a great support. Vaarunika Dharmapala and Marie Doherty were also a great help in making the manuscript publishable.

I have presented the argument of this book in two seminars. The first was part of the 'Deglobalization' workshop hosted by the Gothenburg Centre of Globalization and Development in early November 2017. The second was to an assembly of economic sociologists at the European Sociological Association conference in Manchester in August 2019. I am grateful to participants in these seminars for their critical comments and questions.

Bristol University Press arranged two anonymous reviews, and these provided valuable advice and criticism, on both an overarching and a more detailed level. Their work helped me clarify and substantiate my arguments.

Parts of the manuscript have received comments from Joe Anderson, Anja Franck, Sofie Hellberg, Olga Stepanova and Fredrik Söderbaum, which were very helpful and encouraging at the very beginning of the writing process.

Edith Brookes provided valuable intersectional language coaching and great comments on the first chapters. Markus Lundin volunteered as student test reader in the middle of the process, and reassured me that the book was interesting and fairly accessible.

My life partner, Åsa Wettergren, has read and commented and discussed and encouraged and cheered me on throughout the writing process. She is a true inspiration academically and spiritually, and the life we build together is far richer than anything all the wealth of Wall Street could possibly buy me.

Thank you all!

Change Is Possible and Necessary

In the summer of 2011, an *Economist* blogpost convinced me that it is absolutely necessary to reconstruct the global economy. The *Economist* online team had arrived at an astounding figure when playing around with historical data on global gross domestic product (GDP). The alarming sentence read: 'Over 23% of all the goods and services *made* since 1 AD were produced from 2001 to 2010, according to an updated version of Angus Maddison's figures' (*The Economist*, 2011). This was in 1990 US dollars, so inflation had nothing to do with it. This was real growth, with a severe financial crisis during the period in question. Many reports from various sources, including the Stern Report, the United Nations Intergovernmental Panel on Climate Change, Al Gore's *An Inconvenient Truth* and Timothy Jackson's *Prosperity Without Growth*, had sounded the alarm before. But this figure – 23 per cent of humanity's production in a single decade – makes it clear that the metabolism of capitalist civilization is running amok and has to be changed. Or, in other words, the global political economy must be reconstructed. We need to start thinking outside the box to achieve this.

From a strictly growth-centred economistic perspective, this exorbitant increase in world output is a good thing. On a planet with seven billion or more inhabitants, we need more stuff and more resources if everyone is to live a good, or at least decent, life. Economics, my old teachers told me, is a discipline about the optimal allocation of scarce resources in a society. Less scarcity is therefore a good thing and makes allocation easier. But as soon as we broaden the perspective, two global problems call for our immediate attention.

The first problem is the ecological consequences of increased output. With our present energy system based on fossil fuels, our globalized production system, profit-driven commercial market allocation of goods and services, and consumption as the end goal and motive force for global economic interaction, the planet is on its way to ecological disaster. Bees are dying; hurricanes and thunderstorms are getting stronger; sea levels are rising; droughts are getting aggravated; antibiotic resistance is increasing; species are rapidly becoming extinct; the list is long. This ecological destruction is all a consequence of our present global economic system. Yes. All of it. Most of these problems are not part of commercial logic in itself, but are 'externalities' – that is, consequences of capitalist and market activities that are not priced into the deliberations of market actors or regulators. If we do not want ecological disaster, we need to change the global political economy.

The second and related problem concerns how unevenly all this wealth and growth is distributed. Of all the growth in the US between 1976 and 2007, about 58 per cent went to the top 1 per cent of the population (Standing, 2014). During this period most of the economic changes and re-regulations that today are lumped together under the term 'globalization' occurred. From Standing's structural perspective, globalization has aggravated capitalist exploitation of the working class and trashed their social fabric. As a result, their working and living conditions today are so uncertain that the term 'precariat' is a more apt description of the new role for most workers in global capitalism than Marx's 'proletariat'. From the liberal economic perspective of the International Monetary Fund (IMF), the fact of increased inequality is also a concern, but the problem is not one of exploitation and injustice, but rather that 'excessive inequality could erode social cohesion, lead to political polarization, and ultimately lower economic growth' (IMF, 2017, p 1). The people who remain poor in this era are metaphorically described by the IMF as having been 'left behind' by globalization, and hence denied an economic stake in it. Deep societal changes have taken place as part of globalization, linking it to an aggravated sense of poverty as a result of increasing inequality. This breeds explosive politics. The polarization that the IMF points to is already exemplified by the spreading of fascism in Europe, the rise of Hindu nationalism in India and the election of Donald Trump as president of the US. The lines of conflict, however, are not drawn according to straight class divisions, and the picture is further complicated by racism and nationalism influencing politics. While the global economy cannot be blamed for all the racism today, austerity, inequality and economic insecurity produce social and political tensions that allow colonial and xenophobic discourses to gain traction. Inequality, therefore, is not only a problem that needs to be addressed for reasons of social justice and fairness. It also needs to be addressed to strengthen the legitimacy of the institutions and principles of democracy and an open global society.

There is a saying that 'global problems need global solutions', which might give the impression that global ecological disaster and social injustice need to be fixed at global summits by heads of states. This makes the project seem daunting, dependent on one quick fix that sweeps away all destructive forces and establishes a sustainable system in one giant global manoeuvre. But history's verdict on the forceful implementation of predesigned utopias is not favourable. Even when a utopian project has wide popular support, the social engineering that is intended to materialize it tends to derail it as it unfolds. Or, in the words of Maurice Merleau-Ponty (1973, p 207): 'Revolutions are true as movements and false as regimes'. If we focus and stop dreaming of a giant silver bullet, the task before us becomes difficult but not daunting, immense but not impossible. It might also be wise to acknowledge the possibility that a new global economic order, a new societal metabolism, can be established in a step-by-step fashion, without predesigning the ultimate utopia. By addressing economic problems and mechanisms themselves, it is possible to gradually achieve beneficial and sustainable systemic effects (and destructive and unsustainable effects too, of course). The globalized economy we have today also came about in this way: through a politically designed global economic institutional order gradually put into operation (Ruggie, 1998; Peterson, 2003), and through similar measures undertaken on the national level that made countries globalize (Helleiner, 1994). This similarity of measures was a consequence of the IMF and World Bank articles of agreement and the trade agreements overseen by the World Trade Organization (WTO), all of which clearly state that their purpose and desired systemic effect is to increase international trade and stimulate GDP growth. When an increasing number of countries ratified these agreements and became members of the institutional order, private entrepreneurial interaction was globalized in only a couple of decades. Economic growth and huge profit accumulation followed. So in its own terms the Bretton Woods Conference in 1944, and the resulting global economic system, was a tremendous success. It is also one among many examples of how the global political economy can be influenced and reorganized. Major political-economic changes have happened many times, as with the US economy's transition to war production after Pearl Harbor in 1942–3, or the building of heavy industry in the Soviet Union during the 1930s, or the establishment of the European Union (EU), or the agricultural restructuring of many European countries in the 19th century, or the political dismantling of the British Empire during the 1940s and 1950s, or the establishment of the Bretton Woods exchange-rate system. There are many more examples, positive as well as horrendous, of massive, politically driven socioeconomic changes throughout history. As these examples indicate, there is no need to succumb to a globalized economy and its problems simply because they are there. If we have problems, these can be solved by undertaking constructive measures based on analysis.

I write this book to present readers with a conceptual toolbox that will allow them to make their own analysis of global challenges and approaches to the political and economic changes they call for. This toolbox is by necessity not limited to that offered by the standard Economics currently guiding the work of global economic actors and institutions. In the following chapters I will first set out what is at stake, and then outline possible pathways to change in everyday economic life, economic institutions, global trade, economic development, financial markets and globalized production. I present these analytical approaches with the aim of facilitating step-by-step analysis of how we might reconstruct the most important socioeconomic phenomena that together make up the global political economy. Before embarking on this presentation, let me briefly explain the perspective and tradition within which I write this book.

Points of departure

When we analyze societal phenomena like the global political economy, we use concepts, models and theories to disentangle complex sets of information with the purpose of highlighting their construction, mechanisms and primary agents (in this book, those terms appear in **bold** text when they are first discussed). When such analysis leads to better understanding of a societal phenomenon, we can design better measures to solve the problems related to it. This is a central motive for most of us working in the social sciences, including in Global Political Economy (GPE). Academics do not, and perhaps should not, run the world or the world economy. But as Naomi Klein (2007), Gillian Tett (2010), Donald MacKenzie (2006) and others have shown in different ways, theories, models and concepts produced by economists and other academics are used to craft economic policies, to design the institutions that regulate economic interaction and sometimes even to provide the knowledge that makes certain markets possible at all. When economic and societal dynamics open up new avenues, applicable academic knowledge is used to legitimize and explain the choices and actions of corporations, investors and politicians. This interweaving of changing economic structures and changing knowledge and norms produces a new situation that is constructed not by ideas or material forces, but by the political and economic interplay between the two. Liberals would say that ideas are the primary drivers of this process, while Marxists would say that material capitalist forces are. Constructivists (such as myself) would say that the dominant driver depends on the specific historical conjuncture and phenomenon in question. I write this book within the perspective that the global economy evolves as an assemblage of knowledge, political struggles, and economic structures and agents, which constantly overlap and interfere and clash with one another. The resulting global political economy then realizes itself in everyday life interaction, which materializes the prevalent knowledge and discourse in one way or the other, depending on how meaningful and legitimate the institutional order is in people's lives (Cox, 1981). If an economic and institutional order is impossible to live in it will not function, and there will then be a need for new knowledge, new political struggles and a different political economy. That is how simple and complex the critical perspective of this book is.

Institutions

The global economy is big. It is impossible to chart and describe it empirically and inductively as a whole. What we can do is approach its different parts, structures and dimensions to find out what the vital mechanisms and relations are and analyze which forces shape economic interaction, what the outcome of this interaction is and how we can influence it.

A concept helpful for such analyses is the **institution**. An economic institution is something that gives societal interaction its specific form and makes social actors behave in a certain way. It can be either a formal institution, such as a law or regulation, or an informal institution like a tradition or morality (North, 1990). Regarding economic interaction, Karl Polanyi (1944) taught us that if we want to understand a specific market, we must understand the formal and informal institutions that regulate behaviour within it. A market does not exist without people buying and selling stuff to each other, and institutions regulate what can be bought and sold and how. This means that there is no such thing in the real world as a 'free market': all market interaction exists within and is formed by institutional frameworks. The behaviour of market participants, therefore, is shaped by the institutions that regulate the market, and this behaviour is what makes the market materialize as a specific socioeconomic phenomenon. As an example, we can take the German market for sexual services, as compared to the same economic interaction in Sweden. In Germany it is legal to buy sexual services, sex workers have trade unions and the business of selling these services is regulated by local and national law. This means that in Germany we have a legal market brought into being and given a specific form by formal institutions. In Sweden, on the other hand, it is illegal to buy sexual services (but not to sell them). This means that there is no institutional regulation that brings a formally legal market into being, but a law that criminalizes the buying of sexual services. The result is that in Sweden there is no formally legal market for sexual services (since buying such services is prohibited), whereas in Germany there is one. Proponents of the laws in both of these countries claim that the institutional order is constructed to protect sex workers, most of whom are women, and yet the results are starkly dissimilar. This difference is an example of how institutions reflect and encompass not only traditions and values in already existing markets, but also what regulators and lawmakers want markets to be and become. Institutions make market actors behave in a certain way, and thereby bring about a certain result. An effective institutional market framework then fosters economic interaction that realizes the values and results that regulators and lawmakers had in mind when they wrote the framework and put it into operation. When we are looking to understand a market, therefore, one way to analyze it is to look at the formal and informal institutions in and around it, how they influence market behaviour and what this interaction results in. A focus on institutions is helpful for understanding the economic interaction that they regulate, on the one hand, and how the regulators would like this interaction to materialize, on the other. The two are almost never coterminous. Regulators and lawmakers are always trying to influence economic behaviour in one way or another, to make it change in one or the other direction. The constant tension and dynamic between what happens in the economy and what politicians, entrepreneurs, workers and consumers would like to happen is a vital force for change in the local and global political economy.

The social and material reality of a political economy is what we conventionally think of as 'economics' – what we see, do and feel as economic actors in everyday life as doctors, cleaners, corporate board members, welders and so on. In this era, global capitalist structures and mechanisms give our economic interaction its historically specific form: a form that is the result of centuries of work, trade, technological development, and public and private investment, but also of power struggles over natural resources, institutions, technologies and money. Struggles that on the one hand have produced wealth and poverty, and on the other hand raise vital questions about the institutional order that maintains this present form. Who owns what and how? Who gets to decide what, and to what degree will the decision be allowed to affect others? Which economic activities are beneficial and which are destructive? And what are the structural and systemic effects of economic interaction after all this has been settled? Questions like these define GPE as an academic field.

There are two overarching ways to understand GPE as a discipline. The first is to look at it as the field where you study the issues that fall between the stools of Political Science and International Economics. From this perspective GPE becomes a rather limited field, characterized by the methods and paradigms of Political Science and Economics. The other way, which Björn Hettne calls 'big IPE [International Political Economy]',[1] is to study the global economy from an interdisciplinary perspective, including the role scientific disciplines have had for its construction and dynamic (Hettne, 1995). This 'big' GPE perspective is unconstrained by paradigmatic and methodological trends in other disciplines, even though it stems from a strand of research within International Relations (IR). Being paradigmatically unconstrained, however, does not mean that 'anything goes'. What it means is that researchers in this field must account for whatever concepts and theories they use in a specific research project, but can choose and combine from a variety of disciplines the most appropriate tools for that project. Ontologically, this 'big' GPE very rarely approaches the global economy as a given empirical thing, but usually looks at it as a political and social construction, an outcome of political-economic and social forces that produce global orders, stable over longer or shorter periods. As a consequence, there are no facts in GPE without political content, and the empirical study of these facts can never be scientifically 'objective' in the traditional positivist sense. Scientific quality in this tradition is achieved through researchers adhering to the principles of good social science.[2]

Robert W. Cox (1981) draws a distinction between different theoretical objectives within GPE. On the one hand, we have theory and research projects that aim to solve problems within existing global political and economic structures – a branch known as 'problem-solving theory'. On the other hand, we have theory and research projects that aim to contribute to the transformation of existing political and economic structures – a branch called 'critical theory'. In this book I will present concepts and research stemming from both of Cox's branches. The aim, as stated earlier, is to present an analytical guide consisting of both problem-solving and critical theories and concepts.

Reconstructive political projects come to an existing social world in which people live and struggle to make a living within economic and cultural structures. At the same time, these structures provide the material and mental conditions for how people construct and understand themselves as meaningful subjects. While society and its historically specific political economy shape us as persons, our actions and interaction simultaneously strengthen or weaken, corroborate or criticize this material and discursive construction (Foucault, 1971). We become products of society while at the same time shaping society. A corollary to this is that political change cannot be engineered from design to implementation without power struggles and conflicts arising along the way. The dynamics in this process will also influence the outcome, so that the final result may (and in most cases will) be different from what was originally intended. Political and economic change always means interference in lives, norms, traditions and resources that are valuable and meaningful to some people, and destructive and incomprehensible to others. Constructing a viable and legitimate new global political economy, therefore, will most probably not be done via peaceful consensus. But if this change is designed based on careful and legitimate analysis, conflicts and power struggles along the way can potentially be handled in a civil and constructive fashion.

Power

If we accept that we shape the society of which we are products, then we also need to accept that we possess and exercise power. We do this to different degrees and in different forms, but we do. From the echelons of high finance to the most squalid sweatshop, relations and mechanisms of power can be found. When analyzing global economic and political issues and problems, it is important to discern and understand which powers, and which forms of power, are at play. In the following chapters I will return to issues of power many times, and in order to make these discussions fruitful and intelligible, I will flesh out the basics of power theory at some length here. This overview will move from structural power to discursive power, then account for agenda power and the control of what is deemed political, and will finish with direct power.

Structural power is the control over others that you gain from a certain position in the economic and institutional order. Corporate CEOs have power over employees of their firms, since the corporate structure places them in a position to make the employees produce as much value as possible during each working hour. The CEO is appointed by the corporation board to run the firm in the interest of the owners. Mid-range bosses in a corporation are powerful by force of their position in the corporate structure, whereas the board and the CEO have the power to change the structure of the firm itself. This distinction between *power in structures* and *power to change structures* is an important feature of structural power that Susan Strange made vital to IPE in her book *States and Markets* (1988). Another feature of structural power is that it gives powerful actors the ability to shape the interests of those below them (Lukes, 2004). This means that structural power does not only allow you to reconstruct, say, how a corporation is organized. If you can make workers perceive the interest of the corporation as congruent with their own personal interests, they will work harder and produce more value during each working hour. If you can make women perceive patriarchal values as their own values, they will treat each other as more or less valuable according to a structure that systematically benefits men. Being selected employee of the month, or the most honourable woman in the neighbourhood, may be a pleasant experience in the short term, but it does not necessarily serve the long-term interests of workers or women, but rather maintains structures benefitting corporate owners or men. To find structural power a good analytical tool, you probably need to accept that there are gender structures and economic structures that subordinate some and serve the interests of others, and that this is a politically charged issue worthy of analysis.

Discursive power is the power of norms, values, knowledge and images. It does not neglect material structures, but these are not the most common focus of a discourse analysis. When you analyze a discourse, you approach it as a system of thoughts, values and the like that informs and regulates social interaction in a given sphere. By means of this influence, a discourse gives this interaction a specific form and makes it produce a result in line with its norms and values (Foucault, 1971; Butler, 1993). Discourses make our life and intersubjective relations meaningful and predictable, so we are both subjected to them and subjectified by them. We become persons by acting in a meaningful way, and meaning always relates to a discourse. The interaction that a discourse regulates and informs can be local or global. There are, for instance, national discourses on parenting, which tend to differ a great deal between countries and their formal and informal parenting institutions. There is a global discourse on (free) trade, which is inscribed in and institutionalized as the agreements of the WTO, and made operative by all member states adjusting their laws and governance in accordance with these agreements. Discursive power operates by dichotomizing and hierarchizing. By dividing and holding one value above another, it embodies and upholds norms for what is good or bad, beautiful or ugly, rational or irrational, valuable or worthless, and so on. Although such a normative dynamic is never completely closed or universal, discourses have a pervasive influence on our actions and self-images. The disciplinary function of norms is both institutional and individual. At the same time as institutions regulate our behaviour to produce a discursively attractive society, we as individuals discipline ourselves because we want to be good, beautiful, rational and valuable persons. A vital part of this dynamic is the production of knowledge, and universities play an important role in the legitimizing of institutionalized disciplinary norms. New laws and regulations are passed and upheld by reference to knowledge produced by university researchers, which makes retributive measures against breaking the norm appear legitimate and rational (which in many instances they are, but not always or in the best way). Discursive discipline is never absolute or absolutely successful. There is always some interaction and knowledge that is unconstrained by the dominant norms and dichotomies; there is always something 'extradiscursive' (Foucault, 1971). This does not mean that the extradiscursive is ugly or irrational, but that it is unconstrained by the boundaries around what is discursively 'normal'. In one sense, this book might be viewed as a means of helping readers to think 'extradiscursively', to analyze how the global political economy can be reconstructed in some alternative beautiful, efficient and rational way.

Reconstructing the global economy will mean that the political agenda is rewritten, and many things not considered political in the present order will be brought to parliaments to be handled as political issues. Here another form of power presents itself: Bachrach and Baratz's (1962) **agenda power**. By controlling which issues are brought to parliaments or to the media, and thus made worthy of political decision- and law-making, you can preserve existing structures and power relations. Think of the unwillingness of all-male parliaments in the early 1900s to discuss and vote on universal and gender-neutral suffrage. By stopping an issue from entering political debate and decision-making, you also preserve what is deemed normal. What is considered normal and apolitical can be left for experts and specialists to decide, especially if it is something complicated. Agenda power will be important for many issues, such as central bank independence, financial markets and their regulation, free-trade policy, corporate ownership, and so on. In Marieke de Goede's (2004) terms, these issues will be repoliticized (see Chapter 6) when discursive normality is challenged.

Robert Dahl's conception of power is perhaps the one most in agreement with our everyday use of the word. His first version (1957) was that 'A has direct power over B if A can make B do something B would not otherwise do'. When he later developed his conception to study power in democratic systems (1961), this notion of **direct power** became more sophisticated. First, he explained that the holders of power could be persons, offices or institutions, who performed power as 'controlling units', while he termed the entities subjected to power 'responsive units'. Second, he elaborated several characteristics of power helpful for our analysis. Power, we learn, is characterized by the magnitude of power that a controlling unit has; the distribution of power among controlling units; the scope of power that can be exercised; and the resources available for this exercise of power, such as skills and money. Another important characteristic is the controlling unit's interest in exercising its power. Rich people, for example, often have power of great potential magnitude, as they control a lot of resources, but many do not exercise this power to achieve anything specific, instead happily trusting these resources to fund managers and bankers. Dahl's conceptualization might be less groundbreaking philosophically than that of Michel Foucault or Judith Butler, but it is nonetheless helpful for analyzing power.

These four forms of power[3] are most often in operation at the same time in the same process, and which one you choose to focus on depends on the analytical task you set yourself. Take the Paris Agreement on climate change, for instance, which was concluded in December 2015. In the preamble of this agreement, the signing parties lay out how they understand the situation and which norms and structures inform the agreement, so this can be used to study the prevailing discourse of the 21st Conference of the Parties (COP 21). After this preamble the specific articles are listed, and here the parties specify what is to be achieved and how. These articles have subsequently been presented to the parliaments of the signing countries, where politicians have voted (or something similar) on whether the articles should define and inform each country's future political agenda on climate change. By examining this process, you can study the ways in which control of the agenda influences how, and if, the Paris Agreement of COP 21 becomes politics. Many nongovernmental organizations (NGOs) at Paris 2015 wanted passages contained in the preamble (such as the passage on 'climate justice') to become articles of the main agreement, which would have forced signing parties to put these passages on their political agendas. When articles of the agreement are made into national politics, new laws may be written, or existing ones changed, and this institutional change will influence how the power of Dahl's controlling units is exercised over citizens and corporations. So if we want to analyze how the Paris Agreement gets realized, we can study if and how national changes make people, organizations and firms behave in a less climate-damaging way. To discern if this changed behaviour is an effect of national adaptation to the Paris Agreement, it will help to specify which form of power we are looking for and analyzing.

An interesting reaction to the Paris Agreement came from the business community, which was generally very positive. To a critical political economist this was a little counterintuitive, but as business leaders explained, the agreement clarified the direction institutional change would take, and thus also clarified the changes in investment and business plans that corporations would need to make to stay profitable during this period of change. In power terms, it clarified which discourse would guide political agendas and decisions in the future, and for which structural changes they should start planning.

Structure of the book

In the following chapters I will discuss a number of pressing issues in the global economy. Each chapter will start with an account of one important issue. After this description the chapter will present analytical approaches to a possible solution to the issue and its related problems. These approaches will consist of concepts and theories that might help design the reconstruction. I will discuss and present both critical and problem-solving theories and concepts. At the end of each chapter I will present a short selection of academic works helpful for further study in that particular area.

Chapter 2 is about how the global economy is made real in everyday life. The items and values that circulate globally are all products of work by everyday people, who also populate the consumer and business markets where items and services are sold and consumed. The materialization of the global economy in everyday life takes place along social variables such as gender, race and class – in other words, the power and values of the world economy weave into everyday life through the 'intersectional matrix'. If we want to change how the global economy affects society and individuals, we need to understand how femininity, whiteness, class origin and the like condition our position in the global economy, and how the interweaving of everyday life and the global economy can be negotiated and influenced by different groups and individuals.

Chapter 3 deals with the institutional structure of the present global economy, in which the state is still the highest sovereign institution in the world. The global economy has outgrown this institutional order, in the sense that financial and corporate strategies today are transnational, with alternative national localities as one variable among many. States, however, retain the power and mandate to do whatever they (or in democracies, the electorate) deem most beneficial in relation to the global economy. It is states that own the multilateral institutional system, consisting of organizations such as the United Nations (UN), the IMF, the World Bank, the WTO, the Bank for International Settlements (BIS) and others, that is used to negotiate and regulate the global economy. At the same time, national institutions are crucial for shaping how the global economy materializes and develops. This chapter presents concepts useful for disentangling how globalization has influenced power structures, and how these structures and institutions can be changed through different forms of power, by different actors, in order to reconstruct the global economy to increase sustainability and social justice.

Chapter 4 focuses on the issue of international trade, noting that what is called 'free trade' has been the multilateral norm, while individual states constantly pursue more mercantilist policies. At the discursive centre of this free-trade norm stands the private entrepreneur, to whose benefit the global trade regime is currently designed. What benefits the private entrepreneur in the 'long run' allegedly benefits all societies and individuals involved. This chapter disentangles the interplay between this norm and actual trade, WTO negotiations and trade policy, and examines how we can develop alternative modes and principles for international trade.

Chapter 5 is about development. The academic discipline of Development Studies used to focus on non-industrialized countries, and how they should design their economic policies in order to modernize and catch up with countries in the Organization for Economic Cooperation and Development (OECD).

This understanding of development is changing and globalizing, especially as the climate crisis exposes the disastrous problems of 'overdevelopment', consumerism and indulgence in rich parts of the world. A paradox is that industrialization in poorer places of the world relies on producing for and contributing to this overdevelopment. Copying and continuing the development path of the OECD countries is ecologically unsustainable from a global perspective, and so far does not seem to be solving the global inequality problem. What we have hitherto understood as 'development', therefore, needs to be rethought and politically redesigned in a reconstructed global political economy.

The theme of Chapter 6 is how today's destabilizing and exploitative financial markets can be transformed into something that serves sustainable global development. A society needs mechanisms for the redistribution of economic value in time and space. But deregulation of financial markets, both on a national level as well as in terms of international financial flows and interaction, has led to the tremendous growth of these markets, and an increasing share of global earnings today ends up in the hands of private actors in the financial sector. The combination of financial growth, deregulation and agglomeration of wealth has made global financial markets an intrinsically destabilizing force for macroeconomic and development policies, as well as for ordinary private and entrepreneurial investment and economic interaction. This is because the financial values in financial markets rest on expectations, and these expectations must be realized in everyday economic interaction.

Chapter 7 starts with an analysis of how industrial globalization has deterritorialized and reorganized production. Today it consists of networks involving many exchangeable firms and countries, rather than the multinational monoliths of the Fordist era. This shift has spurred many other processes: power over industry has tilted from states to business, gender roles are changing, the composition of industrial labour is changing, the nature of bargaining between trade unions and employers is changing, and so on. These processes are reversible and have no predetermined direction or form.

Chapter 8 discusses how thorough global economic change comes about most often in the form of political responses to crises. There will be similar openings for change in coming economic crises, and the chapter discusses how such openings might be utilized to make the global economy more just and sustainable. I return to the theme of each chapter, and discuss how responses to the crises of everyday life, global institutions, trade, financial markets and global production can put local and global development on a trajectory towards increased sustainability and justice.

Further reading

For readers who find this first chapter complicated, or who want a more thorough introduction to GPE, I can recommend Robert O'Brien and Marc Williams' textbook *Global Political Economy* (5th edn, 2016). This book offers a theoretical introduction to the GPE field and a long historical overview of the development of the world economy, and the authors present the key GPE issues and debates in a way that is both in–depth and pedagogically sound. I can also recommend John Ravenhill's edited anthology *Global Political Economy*, which contains well–written contributions by a range of academic specialists on the same issues and debates.

Readers who want to dig into the work of classical IPE scholars are well advised to read Susan Strange's *States and Markets* (1988). In IR, and particularly its neorealist branch, Robert Gilpin had a huge impact with *The Political Economy of International Relations* (1987; and with several books after that). From a structuralist perspective, Immanuel Wallerstein also had a significant influence on GPE and IR with his four volumes on *The Modern World-System* in the mid–1970s and 1980s.

A book worth returning to for inspiration and guidance is Marieke de Goede's edited volume *International Political Economy and Poststructural Politics* (2006), in which several leading critical scholars address pressing theoretical issues within the GPE discipline. In addition, Ronen Palan's edited collection *Global Political Economy: Contemporary Theories* (2013) presents a broad range of perspectives, summarizing the debate around central concepts and theories used in the field. In 2003 Richard Sandbrook gathered a group of renowned critical thinkers in the book *Civilizing Globalization: A Survival Guide*, in which they take turns discussing global reconstruction based on their respective fields of research. Another inspiring book is Adam Smith's *An Inquiry Into the Nature and Causes of the Wealth of Nations* from 1776, still available from several publishers. This classic is equal parts philosophical work and economic analysis, seeking to establish how the British and international economy could be reconstructed at that time. Those looking for inspiration from classics of a more structuralist and historical materialist kind are advised to read Karl Marx's *A Contribution to the Critique of Political Economy* (1859), which may not be his best work analytically, but which presents central parts of his thinking in an energetic and succinct way. This book is available on several sites on the Internet.

If readers are interested in the intellectual tradition that shaped me and led to this book, the works of Björn Hettne are good reads. His last book, *Thinking About Development* (2009), presents a synthesis of his lifelong theorizing about the global political economy and how it relates to and shapes societal development.

2

The Political Economy
of Everyday Life

My anthropologist colleagues often say, "Nothing is global; everything happens somewhere". This is a call to engage with the meaning-making social interaction of actual people, and with the fact that the global economy always takes place as part of local everyday life. I usually reply that the cultural specificity of a Mexican sweatshop as compared to Cambodian one is not an indication that nothing is global, but rather that the global political economy is realized in different ways in different places. The *Encyclopaedia Britannica* states that 'markets cater to national culture as much as national culture mutates to conform to the discipline of profit and loss. It is to this very adaptability that capitalism appears to owe its continued vitality' (Boettke and Heilbroner, 2019). In many instances the analysis stops with this, and assigns differences in the materialization of the global economy to 'culture', and the process itself to the vitality of capitalism.

A conclusion to be drawn from this agreement between my anthropologist friends and Boettke and Heilbroner in *Encyclopaedia Britannica* is that the global economy does not happen somewhere else, above us or some such. On the contrary, our physical, social and mental engagement with everyday life is the very foundation of the global economy. It is here that the global political economy comes to its final fruition, where we make it real, and its meaning and discursive power evolve in the interweaving of global economic processes with our local lives.

If we want to understand and reconstruct how the global economy matters for everyday life around the world, we need to approach this analysis with a set of good, analytical concepts. In this chapter I will focus on how the global economy interweaves with our lives through an intersectional matrix of gender, race and class structures.

I will first discuss gender and sex, and how the global economy is gendered, especially how the values around masculinity and femininity inform traditional economic roles and a certain division of labour, and how economic globalization is changing gender roles. I will then move on to discuss race, and how the discursive and material structures of colonialism still condition everyday life for a majority of the global population. As with gender, the physical construction of our bodies relates to structural and discursive forces, which either enable or close off different versions of everyday life. The problem of skin colour, for instance, is not a problem with white or black skin as such, but a problem regarding what skin colour comes to mean, evoke and make possible in a globalized economy. The third dimension in the intersectional matrix – class – is not inscribed on our bodies at birth, but nonetheless assigns people quite specific relations to power structures in the global economy. These intersecting dimensions get their meaning from a complex set of cultural and moral codes that legitimize the positions of some, and at the same time exclude others from those same positions. To conclude the presentation of these three dimensions, I will briefly discuss how they spill over into and inform each other – in other words, the intersecting power of gender, race and class. The second half of the chapter presents concepts and strategies we can use to analyze how a reconstruction of the political economy of globalized everyday life might be possible.

Gender

When the global economy realizes itself in everyday life, the patriarchal discourse values and orders activities and resources according to what is deemed feminine and masculine. Work performed by women is given less worth than work performed by men, which means that women get paid less than men, or not at all. In a mirror image of this, work assigned high value and high salary is deemed masculine, and is carried out predominantly by men. This is how it has traditionally been, and even though we have seen some change, it is still the prevailing situation. In 2003 the leading American feminist and GPE scholar V. Spike Peterson published a seminal book on gender and GPE titled *A Critical Rewriting of Global Political Economy: Integrating Reproductive, Productive and Virtual Economies*. Everyday life is lived within these three economies, and in her analysis of the relations between them Peterson describes how capitalism and patriarchy interweave to secure global exploitation, and to make it appear natural.

In terms of hours worked and human occupation, the **reproductive economy** is the largest economy of the three. Work in this economy is not monetized, and the human activity not directly subjected to market mechanisms or ordered by market institutions. Here we bring children to life and raise them; it is here we cook and clean and sew, and tend to our homes and vehicles. The principle concerning how we relate to each other's work here is **reciprocity** (Polanyi, 1944): the norm being that if everyone contributes their share of work, the overall effect will be that we reproduce human life and society. We do our share, expecting others to do theirs, and as long as our expectations are realized we continue. What is considered a 'fair share' is based on social norms, of which gender norms are the most pervasive and pivotal to the ordering of the reproductive economy. Normal reproductive work has generally been considered feminine – that is, according to the norm in this economy, should normally be done by women. The origin of this norm is lost far back in history, but for as long as there have been written records patriarchal discourse has **feminized** reproductive work, and in most cases valued it less than work normally performed by men. When money, commerce and capitalist institutions start influencing how work is organized and valued, this predominantly female economy gets no monetary value assigned to its labour. Families (extended or nuclear) are politically and economically constructed as 'the private sphere', secluded from public life and the market, and regulated informally by norms, traditions and material circumstances. This separation of economic gender roles serves to maintain a division and hierarchy between feminine and masculine work that benefits men over women in both social and economic terms. Part of people's socialization is learning how chores, professions, and sexual and other identities are unavailable to them because of their sex, and the gender system and its norms serve to make them perceive this loss as normal and right (Butler, 1993).

The **productive economy** is the economic interaction we are often referring to when we use the term 'economy'. This is where goods are produced by private or public enterprises, shipped to retail stores around the world and sold to consumers in markets in accordance with the price mechanism. The productive economy also supplies services to society. Although there may be elements of reciprocity between firms and people in this economy too, the market price principle of distribution of goods and services is fundamental. A corollary to this market price principle is money, which is a necessary part of all social interaction in this here. Liberal feminists often state that the neutrality of the price mechanism makes gender relations irrelevant in the market. Feminist political economists such as Marianne Marchand and Anne Runyan (2010), Spike Peterson (2003) and Lourdes Benería et al (2016) have found the opposite to be true. Capitalism makes profitable use of the different monetary values ascribed to female and male work, and of patriarchal wage differences between women and men. Globalization has produced a shift in the global labour force in which manual labour has to a large degree been feminized, quite simply because women are paid less than men. In Sweden, a country generally considered gender equal, women in manufacturing earn only 91 per cent of the average male wage. In Japan they earn only 61 per cent as much as men in the same sector (Benería et al, 2016). Additional factors – such as a lower degree of unionization among women, and in many places a continuous exodus from jobs to marriage – make women attractive workers in global value chains (more on these in Chapter 7).

The productive economy is most often pictured as the economy of the masculine breadwinner, who leaves the private sphere during the day and returns home with cash in the evening. Boys are brought up to take on this role, and to assume their entitlement to a position in society where they can perform this economic form of masculinity (Gelfer, 2014). A problem with globalization is that such positions – industrial jobs you can get with general qualifications, such as strength, discipline and dexterity – are becoming increasingly rare, especially in OECD countries. A consequence of this is that patriarchal norms are losing large parts of their economic foundation, and an important motive for and source of traditional masculine (self-) respect is corroding and falling apart (Faludi, 1999; Sennett, 1999). The economic and social insecurity that this process leads to is handled in a multitude of ways by different men, very much depending on the societal position they are in, and the power this position enables them to exercise (Connell and Messerschmidt, 2005; Gelfer, 2014). If we are to understand the full meaning of the globalization of production, we need to analyze the effects this has on the gender system for women, men and others. As Marchand and Runyan (2010) show, these effects differ from place to place, from industry to industry and very often between individuals. The feminization of work has meant a new platform where women in some places can renegotiate unfavourable gender contracts, while the weakening of traditional economic masculinity in many places feeds into neoconservative or fascist political processes which aim to strengthen patriarchal norms. We cannot tell in advance how this rearranging of gender roles will play out; we need to look at each specific place and situation and its gendered economic dynamic.

The relation between the productive and reproductive economies has long been of interest to both Gender and Development scholars. It is generally accepted that the productive economy benefits tremendously from work performed in the reproductive one. Or, to put it differently, the productive economy unremittingly exploits unpaid female work in the reproductive economy in several ways. First (and obviously), all humans originate from reproductive work, and are raised in the reproductive economy. Second, people working in the reproductive economy function as a reserve pool of labour for the productive economy, and in times when additional workers are needed, entrepreneurs hire from this reserve pool – only to send these workers back into it when business slows down, a technical change happens or demand for labour falls for some other reason. The existence of a pool of labour that most of the time supports itself outside the productive economy adds flexibility to the labour force that is beneficial to entrepreneurs by reducing the number of workers they need to employ on long-term contracts, saving them a great deal of money over time. This flexibility itself becomes a source of competition between workers: when employers have the option of hiring low-cost temporary labour instead of unionized permanent workers, this exerts a downward pressure on wage levels. Third, on a macroeconomic level the reproductive economy works as the social security and care sector. In times of business downturn or crisis, those made redundant are expected to return to and survive in the reproductive economy, and when they get old or sick (or both), female reproductive work is expected to provide the care that a shrinking or non-existent public sector otherwise would. All in all, taxes would be higher and profits lower were it not for all the benefits that capitalist production gains from the reproductive economy. You may view the care and reciprocity of the reproductive economy as natural and ethically rational, but its economic effects on the productive economy exist, regardless of whether you consider them exploitation or think this is the natural gendered order of things.

The global financial markets, which Peterson terms the '**virtual economy**', are where the profits from the productive economy end up. What circulates in financial markets are not real products, but digitalized symbols (Peterson, 2003) – hence the virtuality of these global markets. A share in a corporation is a symbol of ownership, which gives the holder a stake in the profits of that corporation, and additionally the opportunity to benefit from increases in the share price. Debt establishes a lender's claim on the future money of the debtor, and the interest rate imposed is compensation for the risk and opportunity cost of the lender. Derivatives are instruments that give you the right to do a specific trade or participate in a financial deal during a specified future period at a price agreed on today. This might seem esoteric and futuristic and hard to grasp, and we will return to financial markets in Chapter 6. The vital point for this chapter, however, is that the expectations that determine the prices of the symbols in the virtual economy must become real. This realization of expectations takes place in everyday life in the productive economy (Andersson, 2016a), and the benefits and additional profits that the productive economy accrues in its relation to the reproductive economy ultimately end up in the virtual economy, as profits to shareholders, lenders and speculators. In order to maintain a steady flow of profits from the productive economy, there cannot be too much change in the social systems that undervalue the work of women, because the low wages of women are part of the basis for corporate profits. If wages push up production costs, low-skilled production is likely to move somewhere else in the world, where women workers can be hired at a lower cost. Critics such as Peterson view this as just another way for capitalism to exploit social inequalities produced by a patriarchal order. Proponents, such as Jeffrey Sachs (2005), see a division of labour that perhaps is unequal today in the economic sense, but also a form of modernization that will produce a higher degree of gender equality in the long run. In its information processing and valuation, the virtual economy seeks primarily to determine how the prices and earnings of its assets and instruments will develop in the future. It generally has no objections to gender equality in the political sense, but wage equality among workers is generally not good for profitability. A future in which gender equality is achieved, therefore, would not be good for the value of the symbols in the virtual economy. In short, there is a complex but profitable and/or exploitative relationship between gender systems of every society and household, via everyday production and consumption, and the virtual economy of the financial markets.

Since gender is so ingrained in our identities and the way we understand our place in society, gendered values and valuations, as well as the economic structuration consequences of the gender system, might appear natural and predestined. Since gender is also very personal, it might appear to be private. In one sense, the individual negotiation of a position within an existing gender system is private, but it is also a global political and economic issue, as every economic order incorporates the gender system. With economic change comes a rearranging of gender roles and valuations. There is therefore very little that is natural or predestined about how gender interrelates with the global political economy. This interrelation is specific to each era and its power struggles, technology, and modes of reproduction and production.

Racism

While 'race' as a concept has lost its explanatory function within scientific analysis, *racism* as a social fact and social mechanism is still important for understanding how modern society and capitalism works. The global economy as we know it arose on the basis of colonialism. Colonialism, in turn, is unthinkable without racism: the classification of people based on their physical and/or cultural features, and the valuing of certain features above others. This discursive power exercise subsequently influences the identities of the related groups and the ideas they have about each other. Ideas and identities historically have often come to shape the formal and informal institutional order, and racist valuations and norms have thus become decisive in social practices (Fanon, 1967). Even though formally institutionalized racism is largely gone today, discourses, norms and practices (or 'informal institutions') often ascribe meaning to physical and cultural differences between groups. When this meaning influences social, political and economic practices, racism becomes important to the way everyday life unfolds in the global political economy.

The first influence of racism on everyday life is discrimination: the unequal treatment of those identified as belonging to a group that differs from a majority group, whose physical and cultural features are regarded as 'the normal'. People might not know that they belong to a specific group, on these grounds, until discrimination hits. In other words, people do not experience race until they are **racialized**. You might be well aware of your skin colour, and also notice that it is darker or lighter than that of your friends, but it is not until this difference is allotted a social, economic and/or political meaning that racism, and your 'race', become a meaningful experience for you (Fanon, 1967). Racism starts when the physical and cultural specificities of a group, as compared to those of other groups, are deemed economically, politically or socially important in a predictable and systematic fashion that discriminates against some of the groups on individual and collective levels.

In the diaries of Christopher Columbus you can find several racist depictions of the people on Hispaniola. This racism was of a naive and ethnocentric nature, similar to the racism of African slave hunters and Chinese emperors: the depiction of one's own people as superior to others, and the conviction that the 'others' were conquered and subjected to one's political or commercial will as a result of one's own superiority. With the Enlightenment and the publication of the *Rights of Man* in the 18th century, this form of racism became politically untenable. Imperialism, however, needed some form of legitimacy for its colonization and subjugation of non-Europeans. This need led to a new form of racism, practised under the banner of 'science' by ethnographers, physicians and anthropologists to the benefit of colonial powers. Class structures, ethnic and cultural specificities, gender roles, physical features, and economic interaction, all of which had changed and developed over centuries prior to colonial rule, were classified and described as ancient and inherent characteristics of each Asian, African or American 'race' (Loomba, 1998). This 'scientific' depiction of colonized peoples as physically, morally and intellectually inferior became the racism of colonial rule in the 20th century. While Phrenology (the measuring of skulls to chart human 'races') has been consigned to the academic scrapheap, Anthropology spent several painstaking decades cleansing itself as an academic discipline from its imperial legacy. The racism of this colonial era still informs everyday life in globalized capitalism, sometimes openly but more often tacitly. Today's racism does not talk of human bodies, but instead of the 'culture' of those regarded as inferior, including their clothes, beliefs, family structures and everything else that may differ from that of the norm-people. 'Culture' as a racist concept depicts those who have been racialized as driven by essential and unchanging norms and beliefs, and their resulting behaviour and interaction as the inescapable consequences of their culture.

Racism is profitable in a similar way to gender discrimination. Like naive racism, colonialism promoted and established a division of labour that allotted heavier, dirtier, more dangerous and more demeaning work to people of colour. According to the racist norms of this division of labour, this work was paid less than work performed by norm-people. As with gender this goes both ways: some jobs are constructed as 'for them', and are paid less than other jobs even when performed by 'us' (Peterson, 2003). Today, after globalization, this process is accentuated, with foreign racialized workers are treated as a reserve army of labour, available for utilization in times of need, and a bargaining chip exerting downward pressure on the wages of domestic workers. Increasing labour mobility and migration – both regular and 'illegal' – means that the reserve labour army is expanding, which gives entrepreneurs increasing flexibility in how they can utilize globalized labour over business cycles.

Class

In traditional Marxism, classes are formed by their members' relations to capital. What signifies the capitalist class is its ownership and/or control of the financial and productive resources of society. Thanks to this control, this upper class also has a stranglehold on the formal institutional structure, also known as 'the state'.

This control of the state is used by the capitalists to maintain and develop their control of society's resources, so as to secure future profits from financial and real assets. The working class, in contrast, are identified by Marx and Engels (1848) as those who have no control over, or ownership of, capital or other assets, and have only their own labour to rely on for their survival. In a capitalist society the working class is forced to sell its labour to those who control the means of production – the capitalists – to get money to buy food and shelter on the market. The need to sell one's labour, while having no control over how, where or for what this labour is used, leads to two distinctly capitalist processes.

The first is the process of **exploitation**, which means that workers are never paid the full value of their work. Since the capitalists control the resources with which the worker produces value, the capitalist can claim a portion of that value for himself (yes, it is most often a 'he'). And since workers have to sell their work, there is not much they can do about it if they want to eat. This combination of capitalist control over resources with worker dependence on wage labour makes exploitation possible. How accentuated, pervasive and harsh exploitation becomes is a matter of historical circumstances and the relation between capital, the state and labour.

The second capitalist process in Marxist thinking is **alienation**, which means that you become a stranger to yourself. A central tenet of Marxism is that personal identity and sense of self are formed through work and other social activities. You become a person by establishing creative relations to other humans and to nature. Freedom is having the power to shape and influence this productive relation, as an individual within a collective. Under capitalism, workers have minimal control over their labour, and this means you also lose control over how you produce yourself as a person. Labouring with machines and resources over which you have no control makes you perform work alien to your true self, and the harder the exploitative capitalist industrial work becomes, the further from your true self you are alienated.

Between the upper class and the working class, we have the middle class, who have some control over their own lives, but little control over society's larger assets or general development. They are not exploited and alienated to the same degree as the working class, but can live good lives as academics or with small businesses, siphoning off or getting allotted a portion of the values exploited from the working class (Marx and Engels, 1848).

A consequence of these relations, according to Marxism, is that class conflict becomes a vital driver of history and economic development. The theory holds that when exploitation and alienation reach a certain degree of severity, the working class (or 'proletariat') must revolt for the sake of their survival and human dignity. Societal development in a broad sense is furthered by these conflicts and crises, through the reinvention of new forms of exploitation and rearranged modes of production, on the basis of which new forms of exploitation can be resurrected and maintain the power and riches of the upper class. Each of these crises will be more severe than the last, and this process will eventually result in revolution and the establishment of socialist rule leading towards a communist society. According to this prophetic element in Marx and Engels' work, the modes of production that will exist under communism will have no need to control the working class with the instruments of the state, since there will be no class structure. The state will therefore dissolve, and the freedom of the individual will be realized as a result of the liberation of everyone from capitalist exploitation and state oppression. Historical attempts to realize this prophecy, such as the Soviet Union and Enver Hoxha's Albania, showed no sign of abolishing either state oppression or the state itself.

Adam Smith (1776) also identified exploitative and alienating processes – including the desperation of workers leading to legitimate and logical reactions to secure their collective survival – but valued them completely differently. His objective was to explain 'the nature and causes of the wealth of nations'. This objective made him view the division of labour, and the technological and economic development that led to productive changes in this division, as beneficial to the wealth of nations. Organized protests, he said, seldom improved the lot of workers. The only thing that led to higher wages was the increasing wealth of a nation, since the 'masters' of the workers needed their share of the revenue in order to finance the development of society´s productive resources. As a moral philosopher Smith looked with similar disdain on labour riots as on the 'follies of opulence', but regarded the effective utilization of a societal division of labour as a necessity for the increase of the wealth of a nation. There were no fundamental differences between members of different groups in society and the economy, he argued; the different professions of different individuals 'is upon many occasions not so much the cause as the effect of the division of labour' (Smith, 1776, p 120). Smith therefore saw what Marx would later call classes, but valued the economic relations between these groups differently, and his classic text is concerned largely with how to arrange economic relations between these groups rationally so as to maximize national wealth creation. Writing during the age of British imperial expansion, Smith noted that a key motive to increase the wealth of a nation in general, and of England in particular, was the need to maintain military strength. That is, to become a strong nation capable of expanding its territory and defending itself, a nation needed resources to finance a military capacity commensurate with the national project, and the only way to secure these resources with any continuity, Smith argued, was maximizing the profits from the division of labour under adequate market-friendly state regulations.

The class structure that Smith and Marx wrote about does not look the same today, and as a result of globalization new ways to categorize and understand people's relation to global production abound. As already mentioned in Chapter 1, Guy Standing (2014) notes that the emergence of new flexible forms of employment means that those who do most work in the global economy have an essentially precarious relation to global industry, with traditional unionized employment security disappearing and global production organized in flexible networks. Other terms, such as 'flexibilization' and 'informalization' (Peterson, 2003), or 'anywheres versus somewheres' (Goodhart, 2017), are being coined to illustrate what is happening to people in the restructuring of everyday life under globalization. For our analytical purposes in this book, the most interesting thing is not to scrutinize the value of each of the new taxonomies of class. The vital distinction is that between three groups: the group that owns and controls the productive resources of the world; the second group, which has sufficient economic and other resources to have control over its own work; and the third and largest group, which has no such control. In everyday life, the differences between these groups do not play out in only economic ways. To understand class we also have to understand its social and cultural nature.

People's class origins can usually be deduced from how they talk, dress and move. In an equal world, such differences would not matter, but as Loïc Wacquant (2007) argues, the dialects and behaviours of groups are integral to the processes of class formation. The middle class in particular, positioned between the upper controlling class and the disempowered working class, retains its position in society by adhering to and embracing certain norms and behaviours, which on the one hand distinguish it from the working class and on the other allow it to interact socially and intellectually with the upper class. The concept of 'social capital' has often been used to designate these norms and behaviours, and to describe how power comes not only from access to economic resources, but also from social networks, where you can manoeuvre more aptly if you master the social codes and norms and understand how to benefit from this manoeuvring. French sociologist Pierre Bourdieu (1985) describes these processes as 'social fields', in which you can move more or less constructively depending on how much social, cultural and economic capital you control. According to Bourdieu, one form of capital can substitute for another, to different degrees, with the result that you do not necessarily need to have access to a lot of monetary capital (although you will need some) if you have enough social and cultural capital to do well within the social fields of, say, academia or business. On the one hand, the idea of social and cultural capital loosens up the structural predestination of class understood strictly as economic and professional position. On the other hand, as long as the norms and habits of the middle and upper classes are deemed normal, admirable and respectable (Skeggs, 2005), those living according to working-class or other norms and habits will continue to be exposed to exploitation, social exclusion and denigration, and this will appear 'normal' as long as a neoliberal discourse prevails.

Intersectionality

Kimberlé Crenshaw, the researcher who coined the term 'intersectionality' in 1989, has shown that it helps to uncover blind spots in oppressive structures. She showed that even though there were federal laws in the US against discrimination of women and laws against discrimination based on race, a firm could discriminate against black women and get away with it by pointing to the black men and the white women they had on their payroll. Gender, race and class are hierarchical systems and social structures that benefit some and oppress others. It is important to understand these systems in themselves, but also to be aware of how they intersect discursively, institutionally and socially when gender, race and class influence how the global political economy weaves itself into everyday life. Our positions in each of these structures deeply affect how our lives are formed socially and economically, which opportunities we get and how much agency we enjoy. Upper-class white men have a completely different relation to, and opportunity structure in, the global economy than precariat women of colour. But the three dimensions are not only added to one another; they also tend to overlap and intersect, so that oppressive norms and mechanisms in one dimension serve to normalize oppression in the other dimensions.

Patriarchal gender norms are most prevalent in informing and normalizing race and class hierarchies. Traditional patriarchy depicts masculinity as characterized by rationality and strength, and promotes male superiority with reference to these qualities. The opposites of rationality and strength are consequently deemed feminine characteristics, and we interpret upper-class opulence as a sign that the wealthy person has been rational and strong when accumulating personal resources. From this follows that those who have not managed to acquire as much must be less rational and strong, or in other words more feminine, not as much 'a man' as the richer person. This intersection is not something that people arrive at in a conscious analytical operation, but a contagion between gender and class structures that makes class divides and unfair distribution appear more normal and legitimate if the people at the bottom are feminized. This contagion may seem a bit far-fetched the first time you read about it, but if you look at how popular culture depicts working-class people, you will see how they are usually portrayed as more emotional (that is, less rational) and as victims of bad decisions made by themselves or others (therefore weak). Dramaturgically this works, because as an audience we are expected to buy this depiction thanks to the prevailing hierarchy of masculine and feminine values. Colonization was also discursively normalized by reference to the same gender dichotomy: people of colour and those from 'the Orient' were portrayed as having distinctly feminine or childish qualities, with imperialism thus framed as a natural and necessary political and commercial project, a kind of international 'fatherhood' over other peoples. This stance is most ardently romanticized in Rudyard Kipling's poem 'The White Man's Burden', which he wrote after the US invasion of the Philippines in 1899.[1]

Love

If the global economy gets its shape from capitalists and market actors utilizing the possibilities for exploitation that these oppressive structures opens up, why do women, people of colour and the working class not rebel (more often) and overthrow these structures? The left has grappled with this question for a long time, and Antonio Gramsci provided a preliminary answer in the concept of **hegemony** (Cox, 1983). Hegemony exists when the ruling elite controls the state and runs a country in a way that allows most people to create meaningful lives for themselves, and the creation of these lives at the same time supports and furthers the interests and norms of the ruling elite. If the ruling elite are unable to make people's everyday interaction support their rule without violence and oppression, then we do not have hegemony but dominance. Robert Cox (1983) has applied Gramsci's conceptualization to the global political economy, to understand how the US and the Bretton Woods institutions (more on these in the next chapter) became successful as a Western global economic order. Member states of this order, Cox argues, pursued economic policies that allowed the electorate to create meaningful lives in a way that supported and furthered the interests and norms of the ruling global elite.

But what fosters this sense of a meaningful life that Gramsci and Cox refer to? I suggest it is love, in the broad sense meant by bell hooks (2000). Central to hooks' conception of love is that it is a practice, a verb rather than a noun. Love as a practice is of course performed in romantic relationships, realizing what in ancient Greek was called 'eros' – the theme of many thousands of films, books and songs. This romantic love, however, is just one version of the love practice. More important and prevalent is the practice of reciprocity, friendship, solidarity and understanding, where we practice love socially with others. The bonds we create in this way result in communion and networks that become strong and vital as we nurture the bonds. This is the love practice that Aristotle called 'philia', which makes individuals and collectives flourish and develop in (more or less reciprocal) social interaction. Although less exhilarating than 'eros', this love practice has deep societal and personal consequences when it is made possible. bell hooks points out that exploitative and oppressive structures, such as neoliberal capitalism and patriarchy, diminish the room for both these love practices; both romantic and social love – 'eros' as well as 'philia' – get perverted or destroyed by oppression. Religious conceptions add another layer to love as a vital force in the global political economy in the form of what Aristotle called 'agape', which views the human condition itself as a call to love humanity and God as God loves humanity. This is the love practice that leads the Bible to tell us to love our enemies. A more secular version is bell hooks' 'love ethic', which points towards societal and institutional change that might counteract violent, exploitative and oppressive structures and processes.

As the global political economy weaves into everyday life, it provides the material setting – and a large part of the means – for our love practices. This fundamental human need and practice can make us endure quite severe oppression and hardship, as long as we can maintain an everyday life in which we can love and be loved. In Marxist terms, we are not completely alienated from our true selves as long as we can practice some form of love. Or, as Judith Butler phrases it, piggybacking on Sigmund Freud: 'Subjection exploits the desire for existence, where existence is always conferred from elsewhere; it marks our primary vulnerability to the Other in order to be' (Butler, 1997, p 21). So while the intersectional dimensions might subject us to specific colonial, patriarchal or capitalist discourses and structures, it is also within these discourses and structures that we have to find our identities and selves (Foucault, 1971). We are social creatures who need to love and be loved, and in order to make this real we participate in the global economy, so as to exercise our subjectivity and create a material setting conducive to this practical existence. Young men do not work in the mines of South Africa because they are keen on back-breaking work and health damage; they go there to work because it offers money they need to support their families, and/or that they need to save to be able to marry. Seamstresses do not labour 16 hours a day in Bangladeshi or Indonesian sweatshops because they belong to a textiles guild, but because they too are supporting their families and children, or sometimes saving to start a life of their own. Business CEOs typically try to legitimize their exorbitant salaries with reference to the financial security of their families and their children's university tuition fees. As Arlie Russell Hochschild (2000) has shown, the capacity to love, or the love practice, has become commodified in the global 'nanny chain', where Third World mothers are employed, often informally, to perform the love practice to children of rich parents in the rich world. Almost every job in the global economy, be it in the reproductive, productive or virtual economy, is done by someone who will start talking about love in one or another form when pressed on why they are doing what they are doing.

Reconstructing everyday life

When you are working to understand and plan changes to everyday life in the global economy, the first step is to determine where in the intersectional matrix your referent everyday life is lived. There is always the positionality of the people concerned to consider. We all have a 'subject position' that influences our opportunities and life chances, and also who we become as human subjects. This was forcefully argued by feminists from the South during the 1980s, when feminists in the North appealed to the idea of global sisterhood as a means of doing away with patriarchal oppression. The feminists of the South did not dispute that patriarchy was a problem, but argued that the call for universal sisterhood neglected the very different circumstances and degrees of precarity that women in the South faced when challenging gender oppression. The risks associated with protesting patriarchy were different and greater for women workers in the South than for those in the North (Mohanty and Alexander, 1997; Benería et al, 2016). To identify an actual subject position in the intersectional matrix, you need to determine whether the problem you are working with is a problem of the class, gender or racist structure. Some issues clearly overlap (as with Crenshaw's black women), while other issues are formed and driven primarily by oppressive dynamics in one of these structures. The intersectional perspective equips the researcher to see if and how oppressive structures influence each other, but analytically we do not always need to work with all these structures. If you have identified a subject position in this matrix that is primarily determined by, say, racist oppression, your analysis will be strengthened if you can focus on this and produce a clear result. If this result has the potential to help end this oppression, you might bring the intersectional matrix back in when designing appropriate policy, so as to avoid aggravating class or gender oppression by undertaking antiracist measures. In other words, the need to change many oppressive structures does not always call for the analyst to work with all those oppressive structures at the same time in every analysis.

The second analytical issue, or question to ask, is that of power. Which forms of power are at play in this specific everyday situation? Are we dealing with a discursive power that produces unfair and unsustainable life situations for people, based on a combination of oppression that legitimizes knowledge and an institutional order constructed in accordance with this knowledge, or 'truth'? If this is the situation, our analysis would need to address the knowledge system as well as the institutional structure. Think of the apartheid history of South Africa as an example. The apartheid regime defended the system based on a discourse that stated: 'All South Africans have equal value but its peoples are different, and the best way to preserve the value of everyone is to keep South African peoples apart'. This discourse then led to the establishment of homelands for black South Africans, characterized by bad infrastructure, low-quality education and poverty, while settlement control and passport laws effectively prevented black citizens from participating in society on equal footing with white citizens. If our analysis of this situation engages only with the discourse, while neglecting its consequences in everyday life, the problem-solving or critical strength of the analysis will be weak. If we address only the formal institutional manifestation of this situation, on the other hand, the discourse will continue to manifest itself in social interaction, and it will materialize an everyday life still partitioned along racial lines. This brings us to the issue of structural power.

As described in Chapter 1 and in the section on class in this chapter, differential access to economic resources creates differences between people as regards their relation to economic structures. Abundant personal resources give you the ability to use those structures for your own purposes, and if you are rich enough you can even change them single-handedly. On the other hand, having scarce resources, or none at all, gives you very little power to use the structures for your own purposes, and no ability to influence them. Iris Marion Young (2006) states that all participants in a social structure are either supporting and furthering the structure, and its exploitation and oppression, or acting against the logic of the structure in order to change or topple it. Here she introduces the distinction between **guilt** and **responsibility**, which is relevant if we want to change existing structures. An analysis of guilt alone – for instance, an examination of whose actions were most decisive in creating unsustainable production structures – creates a historical record of who is to blame for sweatshop work and environmental degradation. This record of guilt, however, is of limited use when we want to change how production happens and what kind of working conditions are socially and ecologically sustainable. We might find the worst culprits, but how much would really change if we put them in jail? In order to make structures change, to end or ease their oppression and exploitation, Young proposes instead an analysis of responsibility, because all participants in a structure are responsible for its maintenance or its transformation. This responsibility falls more heavily on those who, in their everyday life, possess more powerful instruments that can be used to change the structure. A CEO of a global textiles corporation has a greater responsibility for the nature of global textiles production than both the Bangladeshi seamstress and the British shopper, but all have some degree of responsibility. When we analyze structural power, Young's call to focus on responsibility rather than guilt is well worth listening to. Who holds which structural positions that would allow them to change the structured process in a sustainable direction, and consequently what level of responsibility can different participants shoulder? Which political measures can we take to make the relevant actors shoulder their proportional responsibility in their everyday life?

A measure often highlighted as an answer to this question is changing the **formal institutional order** – that is, rewriting laws and regulations to change behaviour and interaction. It is important to think of everyday life as the place where such changes become productive, not just in themselves, but also by producing long-term consequences. Institutional changes have social and material effects when they make people interact and behave differently. We mentioned this in the previous chapter, as regards how different laws around commercialized sex services produce different outcomes in different countries. If we want to change oppressive structures related to gender, race and class, laws have proved to be an effective instrument. If you make the beating of spouses illegal, domestic violence will decrease and those (mostly women) who are beaten and molested will get a legal instrument they can use to hold the violator responsible in court. If you make it illegal to refuse to serve people of colour in restaurants, racial discrimination will decrease in this commercial sphere. Laws like these are written either because the norms of society change and the electorate and social movements demand new laws, or because politicians want to change everyday interaction so that it materializes a different social situation. In both cases the materialization of the new societal situation depends on the **institutional capacity** to hold those breaking the law accountable. There needs to be a police and judicial system able and willing to uphold the new laws and regulations, and to hold those who break the law accountable and distribute punishment accordingly. In terms of power, a discursive change that leads to institutional changes needs effective direct power mechanisms to have material social effects. Making people interact and behave differently in their everyday life, in all three of Peterson's economies, is fundamental if we want to reconstruct the global political economy. Analytically, we need to think this through in a more overarching sense, on top of specific laws and institutions, to determine which general norms and principles should guide everyday interaction after institutional changes have been put in place and made effective.

The first general principle to consider is the extension of **market logic** in everyday life. Should the change we are planning depend on expanding or contracting the reach of the price mechanism, and which forms of social interaction should have monetized market exchange as an integral part? In discussions on the value of women's work in the reproductive economy, for instance, some feminists have argued for assigning economic, monetary value to presently non-monetized female work. This, they argue, would make this work visible in the economic sense, and therefore raise the status of traditional female work. Critics of this line of reasoning argue that it would subject reproductive work to the market logic and economistic reasoning unsuitable for regulating and structuring this activity. From this other perspective, what is needed is rather an expansion of the reciprocity principle, or a **decommodification** of everyday life. This would mean that less social interaction would involve money as an integral part, and more interaction would be motivated by social and human needs and emotions. A trend during the globalization era was the extension of the neoliberal market logic to new areas such as energy production, schooling and healthcare. The reconstruction of everyday life will involve a rethinking of this marketization trend. The extension of the market logic in everyday life is a political decision, but also a popular enactment and establishment of both market and non-market forms of interaction.

The second general principle is that of **ownership**, or who should have the final say on how assets in society are used and distributed. Part of economic globalization has consisted in the privatization of previously public or collective assets. This is a process that politics can steer in any direction, and some researchers argue that privatization and subsequent market distribution of assets is the very kernel of globalization (Woods, 2006). This change is not something that just happened thanks to market mechanisms or conspiring capitalists. Privatization and market expansion took place as a consequence of political decision-making. In the rich world the decisions were taken by elected governments as part of the neoliberal adjustment to a global political economy. In the Third World the debt crisis of the 1980s provided the lever the Bretton Woods institutions were able to use to force governments to privatize assets and expand the market logic in everyday life. Globalization, therefore, has meant a global shift in ownership, and privatization has put the control of assets in the hands of individual market actors instead of governments and (traditional) collective guardianship or ownership. Proponents of this shift argued that there would be an increase in efficiency, because the profit motive of individuals would make the use of society's assets more effective. Critics of this process have pointed out that commercial efficiency is not necessarily what is most needed socially, and that the theoretical basis of the efficiency argument is often contradicted by real-world examples of privatization. The ownership of medical knowledge in the form of patents is motivated by the corporate profitability necessary to finance research into new medicines. Critics, meanwhile, stress the public university origins of much of this knowledge, and the immorality of withholding vital medication from sick people – and their hospitals – if they cannot afford it. Private ownership of (concessions to extract) fossil fuels is motivated by the energy needs of society, and the need for private conglomerates to provide the real and financial capital necessary for complicated extraction operations. This makes society dependent on private energy firms and their profitability for its very functioning. In many oil-producing countries, governments have decided to submit petroleum extraction to public ownership instead, either because only the state can provide enough resources, or with the intention of keeping this vital resource under public control, or both. These are examples of how important the general principle of ownership is in the global economy, and the examples show how ownership gets its historical form from political decision-making and the resulting institutional order.

Lifestyles and sustainability

Since everyday life is where the global political economy comes to fruition, this is also where humans construct their individual relation to nature, as well as society's overall provisioning. In our present capitalist society humankind is rapidly destroying the biosphere, endangering human and biological existence as we know it. A changed global political economy would therefore require us to construct a sustainable relation to nature, or what Haberl and his colleagues term 'a new socio-metabolic regime', which 'encompasses the entire flow of materials and energy that are required to sustain all human economic activities' (Haberl et al, 2011).

Civilization processes have meant that humans have placed themselves above nature – intellectually, technically and socially. It is hard to argue against all these achievements in themselves, since they have made everyday life (for some of us) so much easier as regards physical comfort and life opportunities. The downside is that the planet is being destroyed, since the biosphere does not have the capacity to biologically process and absorb all the pollution that the modern industrial mode of production generates. As we reconstruct the global political economy, we need to take this into account so that this reconstruction establishes an ecologically sustainable mode of production. While thinking in terms of everyday life, there are some concepts and principles that might be of help.

Ecological footprint

Different lifestyles affect the biosphere to different degrees. An upper- or middle-class lifestyle weighs heavy on the biosphere, with private cars, air travel, high levels of consumption, and the heating or cooling and maintenance of large homes. A popular, but blunt, measure of the ecological impact of a lifestyle is the '**ecological footprint**'. What this metaphorically describes is the amount of farmland it takes to meet the needs of a given person or national population, including how much is needed to absorb and decompose the waste, pollution and vehicle exhaust of the person or population in question. From this follows that some countries have a footprint larger than their natural resources can sustain, while other countries have smaller footprints than their natural territories would allow them to have. Countries with large footprints over time accumulate an ecological deficit, while poorer countries run a surplus. This is partly a question of territories, but mostly one of how everyday life is lived in different places and within different classes or social groups. In all countries the personal ecological footprint shrinks as you move down the income ladder. My students often admit to feeling guilty about their ecological footprint, and I usually argue that this is misguided, because with their limited resources they cannot cause more damage to the biosphere than what is sustainable, but should rather be proud of their second-hand clothes and lentil soup. Their professors, with their conference trips, cars and summer houses, should be much more troubled. The ecological footprint of humanity as a whole became larger than the planet could handle somewhere in the 1970s, but by and large this happened because of the lifestyle of the global upper class. If we could get the richest tenth on the global income ladder to adopt a university student lifestyle, this would largely erase the global ecological debt. Such a change can hardly be expected to be driven purely by the personal morality and decisions of the affluent, but will require political struggles and institutional and structural changes.

A sustainable everyday life of the global upper class will require substantial technological development. This is often heralded as a promising aspect of sustainability because of all the demand this will create for new gadgets that global industry can produce and sell. While new, less ecologically damaging technology will be needed, it is also important to do a **life-cycle analysis** of these new products. The ecological footprint of an item is not just about what pollution comes out of the final product, but also about how the production and disposal of each item affects the biosphere. If the production of an item, such as a solar panel, requires a lot of energy-intensive materials, and this energy is produced by fossil fuels, the environmental benefit from the use of the panel might be outweighed by the environmental damage caused by its production. If the item contains components and materials that require a lot of energy and work to handle at the end of the item's life, this will also factor in to the ecological effect of the technology. Analyzing the effects of a broad social implementation of new technologies, therefore, calls for life-cycle analyses of this sort to identify which technologies and usages are sustainable and which are not. For instance, changing to a new Tesla electric sports car every two years may be better than swapping your conventional sports car with the same frequency, but the production of these cars will contribute tremendously to your ecological footprint regardless of which type of energy propels them on the motorway.

Energy return on energy invested

At the dawn of the petroleum era, the pressure in oil wells in the southern US made oil spurt out of the ground, and to refine and get it out to gasoline stations required energy equal to just 1 per cent of the energy in the tank of a car. Today petroleum has to be pumped up from sea beds and holes drilled in deserts far away from the final consumer, so today on average, production and distribution of conventional gasoline requires energy equal to 10 per cent of the final energy in the tank. With fracking and deep-sea drilling, this figure is constantly rising. This means that the **energy return on energy invested** (EROEI) is falling, and the fossil industry has to put increasing amounts of energy into extraction and distribution to produce the same amount of energy as before. So while combustion engines in automobiles and other machines have become more energy efficient, an increasing amount of the pollution from this industry is emitted before the gasoline or diesel reaches the final consumer. Under the term 'biofuels' we find such combustibles as ethanol and methane gas, which have both been introduced over the last few decades. While these fuels do not add to greenhouse gas emissions when consumed (they are made from organic materials already present in the biosphere), their sustainability has been a matter of debate. This is because of their often very low EROEI, and the farmland required for their production. To produce one litre of ethanol from North American corn requires the equivalent of up to half a litre of petroleum diesel. Since conventional diesel has a higher energy content than ethanol, the end result is that running a car on this kind of ethanol emits almost as much diesel exhaust as running it on diesel. Ethanol produced from Brazilian sugar canes has a better EROEI, but still not as high as that of conventional petroleum products. And we have not even started to look at the broad opportunity costs of using farmland for energy instead of food production. What we are beginning to see is that the present industrialized everyday life, with its high consumption of affordable energy, will be hard to maintain if we are to realize the Paris agenda and make everyday life more sustainable. The ecological sustainability of a reconstructed global political economy, therefore, will require everyday life to be lived in a less energy-intensive way.

A common debate concerns whether individuals in everyday life can really take on enough responsibility for ecological challenges to make a difference. As regards the ecological footprint of an individual household, individuals certainly do make a difference, and coordinated consumer behaviour can influence producers' behaviour to some degree. Everyday life, however, is a very complex economic phenomenon, and establishing ecological sustainability will require significant changes. Moreover, it is not in the private household sphere that the decisions leading to ecological sustainability will be made. The responsibility for these decisions falls primarily on powerful political and corporate actors, whose decisions have more powerful and wide-ranging social and economic effects.

Social justice

Changes in everyday life, which will be required if we are to take these issues seriously, evoke questions of fairness and justice, which cannot be dealt with politically without addressing the people concerned. Those out to save the world have too often appointed themselves guardians of those affected by the rescue operations (Li, 2007). But carrying out the analysis, identifying the problem and designing the plan does not make the analyst a legitimate arbiter of the everyday lives of the people affected. Legitimacy is given to a plan when those responsible for realizing it perceive it as meaningful and fair. Ideally the analysis, problem description and plan are made by the people themselves, but in most cases that is not what happens. What happens more often is that changes are brought about by more or less democratic regimes, and people have to live with the changes as best they can. So if a reconstruction is likely to change everyday life significantly for the many, it is vital to take the following two perspectives on social justice into account.

One perspective on social justice concerns **rules**, and the equality of everyone who has to follow them. This perspective stems from the civil and liberal principle that like cases should be treated in a like way. If we accept that all humans are equal, then all humans should also be governed by the same rules, be granted the same rights, and have an institutional system that upholds these rules and secures these rights for everyone equally. The Universal Declaration of Human Rights, which the United Nations agreed on in 1948, is based on this perspective. The document consists of one section covering civil and political rights, and another section on economic, social and cultural rights (Freeman, 2017). Most states today have signed covenants based on these two sections, as well as many other adjacent covenants on the rights of the child, against the discrimination of women and others. The human rights system, as well as other justice institutions based on this rules perspective, often gives rise to a range of questions. Are the rules really the same for everyone? Does everyone have the same ability and opportunity to follow the rules? Do rich white people get more rights than poor people of colour in real life, even if they are theoretically equal before the law? And what about 'universal' – does it mean that the same rights and rules apply equally and uniformly in culturally or religiously diverse societies? It is tempting to give these questions a sweeping negative answer, and to try to shift society to another perspective on justice. But if we are thinking about how a transformation of everyday life can be made to work, we need to determine which rules would be deemed fair and meaningful to follow. If people cannot accept and follow rules so that social interaction produces a sustainable and fair everyday political economy, it will not happen. And if it does not happen in local everyday life, it will not happen on a global level either. So we need to take rules-based justice seriously, and try to find answers to questions such as these.

Another perspective on justice is **distributive justice**, which concerns the way resources, opportunities and burdens are distributed. This perspective is concerned with the structural and systemic conditions of social interaction, and how these conditions produce results that systematically benefit some groups over others. So instead of analyzing the rules at the start of social interaction, this perspective begins the analysis by looking at interaction as it happens and its distributive result. Analyses of the intersectional dimensions outlined earlier in this chapter are most often driven by a normative commitment to distributive justice, and a desire to realize this through a transformation of oppressive structures. The long struggle for a New International Economic Order (NIEO) by a group of 77 developing countries (the G77), started during the 1960s and repeatedly brought to the UN General Assembly, is an example of a global call for justice based on this perspective (White, 1975). The common experience of these 77 countries was that the international political economy was structured in a way that left developing commodity exporters with deteriorating terms of trade. This meant that these countries had to export increasing quantities of commodities to be able to import the same quantity of industrial goods (O'Brien and Williams, 2016), which was (and still is) a structural disadvantage in the struggle of these countries to improve the everyday life of their citizens. Such conditions, whether on a global scale or in everyday life, provoke feelings of anger and resentment when identified. When reconstructing the global political economy, in all likelihood with the aim of improving justice, we need to ask the proponents of this perspective critical questions too, such as: how much of the distributive injustice that exists today is a result of oppressive and exploitative structures, and which inequalities are the results of other factors? Is all inequality distributive injustice, or can we live with some inequality? If the latter, what degree of inequality would be legitimate? What institutional order do we need to keep inequality at legitimate levels? If we are working to increase distributive justice, it is important to prepare answers to these questions.

Fighting racism and gender oppression

To achieve social sustainability and justice, racism and misogyny must be countered and ended. There are a variety of strategies for bringing this about, and here we will discuss three major types. Strategy number one can be called the **similarity–equality** strategy. Within feminism, the leading advocate for this strategy is Simone de Beauvoir, who wrote *The Second Sex* in 1949. The key message of de Beauvoir's text is that 'one is not born, but rather becomes, a woman' by living under oppressive structures, norms and institutions that force women to take on a feminine role. As social creatures we are all a blank slate at birth, capable of anything. Frantz Fanon can, roughly speaking be said to have made a similar argument against racism, in his analysis of how the violence of colonial powers mentally damages colonized peoples and countries (Fanon, 1961). This violence not only conditions the colonized to obey, and stay away from, the colonizer, but over time also establishes mental, social and material divides between the colonizer and colonized that are upheld and legitimized violently. These divides need to be eradicated for true decolonization to happen and racist oppression to end.[2] When today we are told we must be 'colour-blind', those urging this are usually disregarding the social and material divides in their similarity-equality strategy, and thinking primarily of the mental one. Structuralists do not necessarily disagree with being colour-blind, but prefer to emphasize the economic, material and cultural divides and structures maintaining and aggravating unjust inequalities along racist lines.

Strategy number two is the **difference–equality** strategy for social sustainability. Within antiracist movements, important proponents of this strategy were Aimé Césaire (literary critic and writer) and Léopold Senghor (poet and president of Senegal). The Negritude project that they started in the 1930s aimed to empower African and black peoples and their culture, and assert the value of that culture independently of the cultures of imperial states. The project tried to bring about a change of discourse among Africans, and African descendants everywhere, encouraging them to become strong and stand on their own terms. The black pride movement of the 1960s – with roots in the US civil rights movement and the Black Panther Party – owes a great deal to this strategy. The common element across these different organizations was their rejection of racist norms that placed whites and white culture above blacks and black culture. This rejection allowed black people to take pride in themselves and their culture, without relating to colonial and oppressive systems and norms. A similar shift happened within feminism in the 1970s and 1980s, when feminists started to revalue and uphold feminine qualities and norms, taking pride in adhering to these irrespective of men and masculine norms. **Difference feminism** was liberating in the sense that it gave the feminist struggle the chance to let go of the oppressive discourse, relax its focus on men, and cherish and develop women's own norms, culture, qualities and so on. Both the Negritude movement and difference feminists have been criticized for 'essentialism' – the idea that there are inherent qualities in all black people and women, and that they are physically or culturally constructed on the basis of these essences. While there may be both black pride and feminist essentialists, difference-equality is not essentialist as such; it is a two-pronged strategy based on revaluing previously denigrated qualities and features of oppressed groups, while refusing to accept oppression or exclusion on the basis of these qualities and features.

Strategy number three can be called **poststructural justice**, or perhaps **intersectional justice**. On the one hand, this strategy is a continuation of gender theory moving into **queer theory**, seeking to free everyone from oppressive positions within the heterosexual matrix. This is because it is not just women and feminized persons who are oppressed and prevented from reaching their full potential as persons in these positions. The lives and agency of men, and others in high-status positions in this heterosexual matrix, are also constrained by patriarchal norms and traditions. This strategy takes aim at all structures working in this way, with the goal of changing or eradicating them so that their oppressive mechanisms disappear. Antiracist efforts following this strategy take aim at the production of racist normative meaning, exposing how, for example, specific meanings of whiteness are a product of racist structures. Which socioeconomic and cultural structures and mechanisms give whiteness and blackness different meanings and values? How do these relate to masculinity and femininity? And how are these associated with working-class versus upper-class norms and culture? Analytically, this strategy quickly puts several issues of structural oppression on the agenda. But this complexity is not in itself the point of intersectional justice; the point is to address head-on the socioeconomic and cultural structures and mechanisms that produce and uphold racist, patriarchal and exploitative relations between different groups and persons. As Peterson (2003), Crenshaw (1989), Davis (1981) and many others have shown, these oppressive and exploitative structures intersect, which gives this strategy for justice and social sustainability its name. It is true that not all justice and equality problems are about patriarchy, or about racism, or about class, but we cannot be sure which structures and intersections to focus on analytically until we have asked the intersectional question.

Conclusion

Everyday life in the global political economy is the most theoretically complex site to work with. A farmer in Africa or Sweden has to deal with power structures and make decisions as complicated and multidimensional as those facing any business CEO. At the same time, everyday life is so familiar and close to home that we tend to lose sight of the richness of our own lives, and the complexity of the lives of others. I will therefore end this chapter with two words of caution. The first is from Tanya Murray Li (2007), who warns us that however analytically skilful we are in designing ways to change the lives of others, if we think of these changes as technical fixes and disregard the everyday meaning they will have for those involved, the changes will be worth less (perhaps even worthless) to the people concerned. The experts on everyday life in the global political economy are those living it. Analysts are spectators. This should not stop us from engaging analytically with gender, race and class oppression, or lifestyles with large ecological footprints, or injustice. And analytical results can be of great help to people in their complex, everyday decision-making. But as many failed development projects also show, technical fixes for complex life situations by outsiders can be of no help at all, or worse.

My second word of caution concerns love, and Butler's (1997) axiom that 'subjection exploits the desire for existence', which means that we do not put up with exploitation, exclusion and oppression in everyday life because we find it legitimate. We put up with these things because they allow us to exist in interdependence with others, which is the first condition for the love practice. I believe we need to acknowledge this as a primary motor force in everyday life, and understand what people are willing to do to create and defend the material, social and economic setting for their love practice.[3] A reconstructed global political economy will also realize itself in everyday life, and social sustainability components such as justice and equality are necessary goals if we hope to reduce this exploitation of our desire for existence.

Further reading

International or Global Political Economy has often concerned itself with everyday life in one form or another. In particular, gender theorists within GPE have long engaged with the linkages between and mutual interdependence of everyday life and globalized production. Well worth a read in this respect is Peterson's book *A Critical Rewriting of the Global Political Economy* (2003), which can also be used for understanding the intersectional justice strategy, but from a post-structural perspective as opposed to Butler's queer perspective. The book by Judith Butler that I refer to in this chapter is *The Psychic Life of Power* (1997). A 2016 book contributing to this discussion is *Gender, Development, and Globalization* by Lourdes Benería et al, which combines a Southern feminist analysis with constructive suggestions for how to influence and change the way that the global political economy hits along gender lines. In 2007–8 a group of scholars led by Leonard Seabrooke published a series of articles in *New Political Economy*[4] on IPE and everyday life, establishing the everyday perspective in a more general disciplinary and theoretical sense. These texts are well worth reading for a disciplinary position on the connection between everyday life and the global political economy. A good part of the academic discussion on gender and GPE takes place in the academic journal *Feminist Economics*, which has many articles discussing how global economic dynamics are gendered when they play out in everyday life. Within the United Nations there are several organizations focusing on gender. UN WOMEN (www.unwomen.org) is the one with a specific mandate to work for gender equality, but the UNDP (www.undp.org) also has a great deal of research and statistics on gender and gender equality. Both organizations produce yearly reports with global and national data on gender, economics and equality. Since gender equality was mainstreamed in the 1990s, most international organizations have data on the gender situation and equality progress in their respective fields.

Many critical writers have long engaged with racism and colonialism and their interdependent development. Frantz Fanon wrote two classics on the issue – *Black Skin White Masks* (1967) and *The Wretched of the Earth* (1961) – which keep resurfacing in the debate. The writings of Angela Davies are helpful antiracist academic works, moving from radical difference-equality analysis in the 1970s towards intersectional justice research in later years. Paul Gilroy also had a great influence on the discussion with his book *The Black Atlantic* (1993). A group of scholars gathered in 2015 for the project 'Raced Markets', with the aim of analyzing how neoliberal markets depend and feed on racist norms and mechanisms. Under the editorship of Lisa Tilley and Robbie Shilliam they produced a special issue of *New Political Economy* in 2018, where they presented their work on the connections between racism and globalized capitalism. An academic journal that publishes a considerable amount of research on racism is *Ethnic and Racial Studies*. Since the signing of the Universal Declaration of Human Rights in 1948, there has been no systematic data compiled on human 'races', since dividing humanity up in this way is considered a violation of human rights. The Office of the UN High Commissioner on Human Rights (www.ohchr.org) hosts a 'Network on Racial Discrimination and Protection of Minorities' consisting of over 20 UN departments that seek to eradicate racism within their spheres of influence.

Further readings on class can be found in two ways. On the one hand, structuralists such as Colin Crouch or David Harvey have published several books analyzing global capitalism from a class perspective, as have feminists like Spike Peterson and Beverly Skeggs. The International Labour Organization (ILO) (www.ilo.org) provides research and support to strengthen workers' rights and improve working conditions around the world. The ILO presents itself as an organization protecting human rights for employees, rather than working-class interests. If you want to study inequality without a structuralist class perspective, a lot of international statistics are produced by the OECD (www.oecd.org), the World Bank (www.worldbank.org), the UNDP and other organizations. In their international research and statistics you will find information on income and wealth distribution and unemployment – without explicit class analysis, but with high relevance for economic equality and social and economic sustainability. As regards ecological sustainability and economic change, Timothy Jackson's report *Prosperity Without Growth* (2009) is a good starting point for understanding how ecological sustainability relates to the global political economy of everyday life.

When it comes to justice, my general recommendation is to engage with the original writings of important theorists. Liberals and conservatives may benefit from reading Adam Smith, Thomas Hobbes, Immanuel Kant, Robert Nozick and John Rawls, while those with interests to the left of these ideologies may find useful thought in the works of Karl Marx, Antonio Gramsci, Frantz Fanon, Iris Marion Young or Nancy Fraser. Close examination of the original writings of important theorists is the shortest route to understanding their theories, and acquaintance with these will be of great help in finding a direction for your reconstructive analysis.

Markets Are What We Make Them

In this chapter I will describe the present global economic order, its evolution and the rationality behind its political and institutional organization. The descriptive part of the chapter will end with an account of the institutional effects of the 2008 crisis, and of how these effects open up new and perhaps plural economic rationalities. The analytical second section of the chapter will begin with a discussion on how our global economic institutions can be influenced and changed. It will then present some theories and concepts that may be of help in analyzing and designing this change. To end the chapter I will return to its title, and discuss concepts around market exchange that may help us to think about forms of economic rationality other than the version globally institutionalized at the moment. As Karl Polanyi (1944) taught us, there is no such thing as a 'free' market. All markets are political constructions; global ones too. Global reconstruction of the economy, therefore, means the political redesign of its institutional order.

The state as we know it

Every little European village has at least one monument to those who have died in the various wars of the last hundred years. Every family has lost someone in war, or has stories of relatives who came home from war, never to be themselves again. Every war has an end, marked by a peace treaty between the warring parties. One such ending was the Peace of Westphalia in 1648, which ended the Thirty Years' War. This treaty established that from that point onwards, the parties involved should interact as political entities in the form of nation states, according to a certain diplomatic and political protocol. This protocol defined a nation state as an institution with territorially defined borders within which it has control over the territory and its inhabitants. It would possess the military capacity to defend those borders from attack, and would control its internal territory with various instruments of power, such as a head of state, police and military forces, a fiscal organization and so on. A political entity displaying these features would be internationally considered a nation state if and when other states granted it this status by establishing formal diplomatic relations. Ordinary people typically had very little say in this process, but were regarded as part of the territory under a state's jurisdiction, to be controlled by whatever means necessary. Since Europe was, and still is, a continent of different tribes, with diverse modes of living, producing, talking and believing, what followed the Peace of Westphalia were centuries of violent nation state construction based on ethno-territorial principles (Hettne, 2009), according to which a state should be a culturally uniform social sphere ruled by a monarch through a state apparatus. This meant ethnic cleansing, religious oppression, construction and implementation of national languages, and enacting formal national laws for social interaction, including economic interaction. An important part of constructing a nation state, therefore, was the construction and maintenance of national markets.

A nation state has to be continuously upheld and reconstructed, not least in its economic provisioning of itself and its citizens. A parliament that no one votes for is nothing but a building. Taxes that are not paid are but scribbles on paper. Flags no one waves are just meaningless scraps of textile. Thanks to their monopoly on violence, states can make citizens do many things, but they cannot constantly force their citizens to act against their own will. They must provide a meaningful setting for the lives of the majority of their populations. For a state to exist, its citizens need to act in accordance with its cultural symbols and laws, use the national currency, send their children to its schools and pay their taxes. It is through this regulated interaction that citizens maintain and strengthen the institutional entities we call 'states'. Throughout the history of the state system, an integral part of state power has been the institutional regulation of economic interaction, including the maintenance, extension and taxation of market activity. With imperial expansion, technological breakthroughs and fossil fuels, capitalism and market interaction have been powerful determinants of nation state projects.

The industrial revolution, with its imperialist internationalization and huge socioeconomic changes, meant a shift away from the mercantilist seclusion of national markets towards more international trade, and a need for re-regulation of national institutions in order to spur industrial development and capitalist profits. But expansive capitalism and profit-driven markets were at odds with many religious and cultural norms. This conflict between economy and religion found its solution with the help of Adam Smith and his classic book *Wealth of Nations* (1776). To understand why this text became such a bestseller, we need to acknowledge that Britain and Europe were deeply religious societies. The Bible has many passages that are scornful and condemning of merchants and rich people generally: Jesus threw the merchants and money changers out of the temple; it is explicitly forbidden to charge interest on loans; it is harder for a rich man to get into heaven than for a camel to get through a needle's eye, and so on. In the 18th century the merchants, industrialists and banks were the ones driving national development. What Adam Smith gave the modern industrial world was absolution for these behaviours, by stating that individual gain obtained in a free market leads to increased wealth for the whole country in the long run. The role of the state was therefore to construct laws for and around such free markets, where entrepreneurs could act for private gain. Even though Smith had no respect for the egoism and the foolish luxury consumption that characterized extreme wealth, he nonetheless advocated letting the rich enrich themselves because this would, 'as by an invisible hand', spread resources among everyone involved in the resulting industrial and commercial activity. If old and inefficient industry and craftsmanship got outcompeted in the process, this would only lead to an overall productivity boost in the country, as those made redundant joined other professions where their skills could be employed in more efficient ways within more modern industrial processes. The British 'Reform Parliament' of 1832 was the first political body to embark on the institutional process of constructing a market based on this discourse (Polanyi, 1944) – a process that also led to a change in British customs policy in the 1840s, and hence the international application of this form of market-driven development thinking in the running of the British Empire. The 19th century saw an explosive development in capitalist production, operating in symbiosis with several European colonial projects. These projects expanded with economic, military and political force across the globe, only to come to a violent end in the high-tech, tribal European First and Second World Wars. The devastation, barbarism and cruelty of these civilizational cataclysms made obvious the need for some kind of international system of economic governance.

The multilateral institutional system

To establish workable relations among states, the UN system started in 1945. Its founding treaty was the Charter of the United Nations, where the norms that member states must adhere to are written. The first norm is the norm of peace. All member states must respect the borders of other countries, and no one, including the UN as an organization, is allowed to interfere in the domestic business of another state. This is called the non-intervention principle. However, in order to remedy the weakness of its interwar predecessor (the League of Nations), the UN was set up with two main decision-making bodies. The first of these is the General Assembly, in which all member countries are represented. This body cannot make decisions that are binding for all members, except as regards the running of the UN itself. Debate and communication in the General Assembly is considered conducive to international peace. The basic assumption behind this is the liberal peace axiom that as long as states communicate, we can avoid the misunderstandings and irrationality that lead to war. As the interwar years made evident, however, this is not a foolproof strategy, and the UN therefore also has another body, the Security Council, which can make decisions binding for all members if international peace is threatened. Five nuclear powers are permanent members of the Security Council and have individual veto power, to ensure that the Council does not start a global war against a military superpower, which would threaten planetary survival. The other ten members are elected for two-year periods, and have ordinary voting power. The Council can, by voting, decide to force warring parties to negotiate ceasefires and the like. It can also decide to interfere with peace-enforcing troops in a violent conflict. It has no military capacity of its own, but relies on UN member states to supply military capacity as needed. Both the General Assembly and the Security Council meet in New York, where the Secretariat of the UN is also stationed. This Secretariat overlooks and coordinates multiple other UN specialized bodies related to specific tasks and issues, such as development (UNDP), the environment (UNEP), global health (WHO), human rights (UNHCHR) and many more. Since its inception in 1945 the UN has grown into a complex international organization, working to uphold and realize the norms of its charter and a plethora of conventions and covenants. It is, however, only as strong as its member states allow it to be and become. Member states can choose whether to conduct foreign and security policy through the UN system, or to sidestep the UN and conduct these policies on their own. So it is an *inter*national organization, working between states, not above them. Only the Security Council has some sort of supranational direct power and can make states do what they would otherwise not have done, and since five permanent members have veto power in the Council, it seldom makes decisions that override the sovereignty of a nation state.[1] UN member states can change how the organization operates and which powers are granted to its different bodies, on which terms.

The example of the UN is vital for understanding how the multilateral institutional system is owned by and made up of member nation states. When a state becomes a member of a multilateral organization, it agrees to adapt its national laws and policies to the rules and routines of this organization, pay any membership costs there may be, supply a required quota of personnel and other resources to make the organization function, heed the organization's calls to help out with specific tasks and global challenges it might be dealing with, and participate in the development of the organization itself. So the multilateral institutional system operates through nation states, and it is by states following or breaking the rules and norms of its organizations that the system is strengthened or weakened.

Multilateral economic institutions

The institutional system for the global political economy is a product of the Second World War. The system started with a conference in Bretton Woods, a small ski resort in New Hampshire, in the summer of 1944. Over three summer weeks all 44 countries from the winning side in the war, designed the international economic order to be realized once they had defeated Nazi

Germany and its allies. The diplomats and economists gathered there had the problems of the 1930s fresh in their memory, and the design of the system is marked by their desire to solve these problems in a liberal economistic way.

The first problem was the financial and currency instability of the interwar years. German hyperinflation and its resulting wealth redistribution and poverty effects during the early 1920s created social tensions that the Nazi Party was able to exploit to get elected. The crisis of the 1930s, following a stock market crash in 1929, also meant that the international exchange rate situation became chaotic when states individually tried to support their domestic industries with unpredictable exchange rate devaluations. The risks associated with international trade and investment, in such an unpredictable international situation, increased considerably. This led many entrepreneurs to withdraw from international business, which aggravated the crisis. On top of this, states started to change their import tariffs and trade regulations at unpredictable intervals and levels, to protect national industries from foreign competition. This increased risk on international markets, at the same time as it slowed down business internationally, further deepening the crisis.

What was agreed in Bretton Woods in the summer of 1944 was a series of organizations meant to stabilize the international system of payments and finance post-war reconstruction, with the end purpose of reviving international trade and creating international conditions conducive to growth and continued capitalist modernization.

The International Monetary Fund

To prevent a repeat of the exchange rate chaos and financial instability of the 1930s, the Conference agreed to found the IMF, with the overarching purpose of stabilizing the international system of payments. The IMF is a member organization; to become a member, you must show that you have a functioning state and central bank, which can conduct fiscal and monetary policy in an orderly and transparent way. When joining as a member, you pay a membership fee proportional to your country's international economic size in GDP terms. This size and fee determine how much voting power your country gets on the board of the organization, since voting power is also proportional. As a member country you agree to participate in the activities of the Fund and to follow its 'Articles of Agreement', the charter that regulates the IMF's activities and specifies its goals.

The first activity of the IMF, which all members have agreed to participate in, is the surveillance of member countries' economic policies. As regards fiscal policy, members must make their government budgets, official payments and debt situations transparent. Regarding monetary policy, the IMF scrutinizes central banks' monetary policies and financial market developments. The books regarding both these policies must be made accessible and auditable to IMF staff on a continuous basis. The aim of an IMF staff audit is to identify and report on situations and policies that might endanger the financial stability of the country at an early stage, so that problems can be avoided.

The second activity of the IMF is giving advice to member states on how to fix existing or impending problems with their fiscal and monetary policies. Membership rules stipulate that a country must meet with IMF staff on a yearly basis to have 'Article IV consultations'. In these consultations auditors present their evaluation of the country's policy, highlighting which aspects they consider commendable or problematic, and give advice on remedying existing or potential problems. The IMF is not allowed order a member state to pursue specific policies; these consultations follow the principle of non-intervention. Ideally, members who follow IMF advice will not run into exchange rate problems, international payment difficulties, or fiscal or financial problems, since IMF staff are meant to be the best economists recruited from the best universities in the world.

The third activity of the IMF is supplying loans. International developments beyond a country's power to influence may cause international payment difficulties, regardless of whether it has followed IMF advice or not. If there is an international fall in commodity prices, for instance, because of a recession in industrial countries, a commodity-exporting country may get into payment difficulties when export earnings coming into the country are lower than what is needed to pay for imports. If this continues (without other compensating flows of foreign money), the country will eventually be out of money for international payments. When this happens few international banks or entrepreneurs will dare to do business with the country, since they will be unable to trust that they will get paid in international cash. This situation is a national economic crisis, and IMF loans are meant to help a country through such crises so that it does not lose too much international business on the way. An IMF loan is not a large shipment of cash, but an account that the IMF opens for the country, on which the country can draw when or if it runs out of internationally convertible currencies. Ideally the opening of this account will create confidence within the international business community, so that its actors continue to do business with the crisis country, assured that they will get paid in good money. With time, and by following IMF advice, the country will hopefully get through the crisis less harmed, without losing its creditworthiness and with smaller international reverberations than if the IMF had not supplied the money. These loans are also a power instrument for the IMF and member countries with strong voting power, because a country that needs substantial support (more than what it has paid as a membership fee, or 'quota') must follow the advice of IMF staff, or else no loan will come. This means that rich, industrialized countries are seldom forced to follow IMF advice, since they can obtain money elsewhere if needed, whereas poor countries in crisis often have no alternative to IMF loans, and therefore have to follow the conditions attached to these loans.

In summary, the IMF is meant to stabilize the international system of payments by advising member countries so that they maintain long-term solvency, and by supplying short-term liquidity support to help them through international payment difficulties. Stability is not achieved by operations on an international macro level, but by working to maintain the creditworthiness and trustworthiness of member states that issue currency into the international system of payments. The idea is that if all IMF members are solvent in the long term, and are helped with conditional liquidity support in times of crisis, the international system of payments will remain stable.

The World Bank

What today is called the 'World Bank Group' also has its origins in the Bretton Woods Conference, where the first components of the World Bank was agreed upon. The first organization, still the most important today, is the International Bank for Reconstruction and Development (IBRD). The name spells out fairly clearly what this bank does. It provides loans to war-torn countries so that they can rebuild their economies, and also to non-industrialized countries to help them adjust their economic structures in order to industrialize better and trade with the world in a modern way. To negotiate and get these loans, a country has to be a member of the IMF, to assure the IBRD that it has a well-functioning market economy in a state with its vital economic parts working properly. The IBRD operates as a normal bank, and its loans are made out under normal commercial conditions, if ordinary private banks are not willing to give the state a loan. So the IBRD is meant to step in when normal banks are not willing to lend to states, and the loans are granted on normal commercial terms since the founders of the organization saw competition with private banks financed by international public resources as market-disturbing. The public financing of the IBRD is, however, rather limited, and the bulk of the resources needed for its lending operations is raised on ordinary financial markets through the issuing of bonds. This dependence on financial market actors for their financing limits the kind of projects the IBRD can support, since bond investors want to know that the activities of the bank are such that their money remains secure, and the projects therefore need to deliver a profit of a kind that bond investors recognize.

To complement the IBRD's lending to states and other public bodies investing in things such as electricity grids and harbours, the International Finance Corporation (IFC) began operations in the mid-1950s. The purpose of the IFC is to lend money to private businesses wanting to invest in developing and industrializing countries. These private businesses can be domestic or international or a mix of the two, and the investments are evaluated and supported by the IFC based on their contribution to the development of the market economy of the country in question. The IFC's lending is done on a similar basis to that of the

IBRD: money is raised on the private financial market and loans are made out on normal commercial terms.

The International Development Association (IDA) started in the early 1960s as a section of the World Bank that could make out loans for 'softer' societal sectors, such as primary schools and healthcare. The softness of these societal activities stems from the fact that you cannot calculate the profitability of individual investments. Even though the developmental effect of increased literacy is striking – resulting in higher productivity, more advanced organizational possibilities, stronger civil society and so on – the profitability of an individual village school is hard to calculate. Since education is an inalienable human right, ethical problems also arise if you treat the supply of education to children as the supply of any profit-motivated consumer good. The IDA was set up in order to address investment needs like these. The loans it makes out are on non-commercial terms, meaning that they typically have longer repayment periods and lower interest rates, and are easier to renegotiate when a state has fiscal problems. As a consequence of these non-commercial terms, the IDA does not finance its lending on financial markets, but is instead financed using the official development assistance (ODA) budgets of rich World Bank members, who channel parts of their development aid through IDA loans.

The key to understanding the power of the World Bank is the fourth clause of the first article in the IBRD articles of agreement ('Purposes'), which reads: 'To arrange the loans made or guaranteed by it in relation to international loans through other channels so that the more useful and urgent projects, large and small alike, will be dealt with first'. The political effect of this clause is that in all development projects in which it participates, the World Bank gets the power to determine what is done. If it is not given this power by governments and other participants in the project, it has the right to withdraw its funding and participation. Any member country seeking World Bank assistance has agreed, through its signing of the articles of agreement, to grant this power to the organization.

Apart from lending money for reconstruction and development, the World Bank also pursues a range of other activities. The first of these, very important politically, is its Development Economics research. This results in a number of national, regional and global reports that are highly influential in setting the agenda for development policies, identifying which issues are most pressing at the moment and how they should be understood and remedied. The most influential publication is the annual *World Development Report*, which has a specific theme each year highlighting issues such as gender, inequality or technology in order to push them to the forefront of the global debate and deliver the World Bank's academic framing of the discussion. This gives the World Bank strong discursive power, on top of its direct power over the projects in which it participates. Yet another division of the organization, the Multilateral Investment Guarantee Agency (MIGA), serves as an insurance company for investments that cannot be insured on the regular market. When conflicts arise between investors and states hosting their investments, a specialist body – the International Centre for Settlement of Investment Disputes (ICSID) – handles the disputes. The World Bank supplies the disputing parties with legal guidance and arbitration, which may not always exist in the states hosting the investing corporation.

In summary, the World Bank Group is not in fact a bank for the world, but an organization working with specific projects in individual countries and with individual investors, with the overall aim of developing and adjusting the economic structures of its member countries. As in the IMF, the board of the organization has a weighted voting system, which gives the rich world a majority of the voting power here as well.

Free trade and growth

The Bretton Woods institutions were not designed with only a stable payment system and general economic development as motives. Another broad purpose of the organizations and their activities was to support and further international free trade. This purpose rested on two important ideas or beliefs, which are still at the very heart of the global economic discourse.

The first is the belief in **interdependence** as a mechanism for peace. The idea here is that if you have two countries, and you make these two countries increasingly dependent on each other economically, you will reach a point where war becomes an irrational political instrument. With this degree of interdependence, going to war would mean such a substantial destruction of the attacking country's own economy that a war would hurt it as much as the country it attacks. This idea is central to the theory of liberal peace, and also to the global economic institutional order. It has been hard to prove empirically, but its existence as a political and discursive fact is indisputable.

The second is the belief in free trade as incrementally beneficial for growth and general prosperity. The idea behind this stems from David Ricardo and his concept of 'comparative advantage in production'. Ricardo's theory states that countries always benefit from specializing in the area of production in which they have a comparative advantage, and then trade with each other. In Ricardo's iconic two-country model, both England and Portugal are able to produce both cloth and wine, but if one of them is comparatively better at producing wine, and the other is better at producing cloth, both countries will be better off if they specialize and use their limited resources to produce the item with which they have an advantage. If, after specialization, they trade with each other, then both will have more of both items than if they had produced cloth and wine themselves. What you theoretically achieve with specialization and free trade, therefore, is more goods produced with the same amount of productive resources. And since goods are good for welfare, the extra goods bring a 'welfare effect' to both countries involved.

The General Agreement on Tariffs and Trade

When you read reports and memoirs from the Bretton Woods Conference, as well as the articles of agreement of the resulting organizations, it is obvious that all parties involved had an international trade organization in mind, and were expecting this to be operating in the near future. The regulating institution for international trade became the General Agreement on Tariffs and Trade (GATT), a diplomatic product that became operational in 1947. This agreement must also be understood in the light of the interwar years, with its economic crises and international political and economic disorder. The purpose of the GATT was to provide states and private entrepreneurs with a multilateral, transparent, predictable, rule-based order for their international business. In line with the Ricardian theory of free-trade growth, the GATT also was – and still is – explicitly intended to make trade not only free, but freer. Since 1947 more agreements have been added to the GATT, which was primarily about tariffs and other trade regulations for industrial products. The most notable of these additions are the General Agreement on Trade in Services (GATS), the Agreement on Trade-Related Aspects of Intellectual Property Rights (TRIPS), the Agreement on Trade-Related Investment Measures (TRIMs) among several others.

The development of this complex of international trade agreements has taken place over negotiation rounds, each spanning several years of diplomatic efforts. The last negotiation round to finish was the Uruguay Round, which ended in 1994 and resulted in the establishment of the WTO. The current round, which started in 2001 in Doha, has not resulted in a final deal. To make the rules-based system predictable and all-encompassing, an overarching principle of these negotiations is the 'single undertaking', which means that all signing countries must agree on the entirety of all negotiated agreements. This is to ensure that the system remains a predictable 'level playing field' for countries and their entrepreneurs. If one or more countries were allowed to participate without accepting the full agreement, these countries would be able to trade on different terms than other WTO members, and the playing field could tilt in favour of the non-signatories. This is why 'nothing is agreed until everything is agreed', and why the Doha Round has not been concluded after two decades of negotiations.

Once a country has signed the final result of a trade negotiation round, or when it becomes a new member of the WTO, it is obliged to adjust its trade policies and laws so that they become compatible with the treaties overseen and arbitrated by the organization. The international free-trade system, therefore, exists because individual nation states adhere to it and adjust their national policies accordingly. International free trade is the very fundament of the global economic institutional order, and in Chapter 4 we will take a deeper look at global trade and its institutions and related negotiations. Before that, however, change in the global economic institutional order needs to be discussed, both as a historical fact and as a future necessity.

Change in the global economic order

The IMF, the World Bank and the GATT/WTO were instrumental in building the Western World after the Second World War. Countries that did not opt for the Soviet model of development and participation in the Comecon international economic collaboration instead entered the Bretton Woods institutions and traded with each other on capitalist and market terms. This international economic interaction was vital for the establishment of an international order under US leadership, within the security structure of the North Atlantic Treaty Organization (NATO). Upholding military hegemony while tying countries closer together economically through free trade and international institution-building came to be known as Pax Americana (Cox, 1981) – a reflection of the fact that security, societal stability and economic growth were overseen and handled by the US as the new hegemon. This hegemony changed over the years, and with these changes the political-economic project of the Bretton Woods institutions also changed. To finish the empirical part of this chapter, I will here give a quick summary of the changes the system has undergone, to show that there is substantial room for manoeuvre within this system, but also to show the contingent nature of it.

In the first decades of the Bretton Woods system, the role played by the IBRD in European reconstruction quickly became marginal, since its resources were too small and its lending conditions poorly suited to war-torn European countries. Europe and other US allies were instead rebuilt with US aid through the Marshall Plan, a scheme deemed necessary for tying European allies closer to the US economically at a time when post-war working-class suffering in Europe threatened to drive Western countries into the Soviet sphere. The rebuilding of Europe and Japan using Marshall aid recreated the material structure necessary for international business. As countries also became members of the IMF, the international system of payments became operational again, and by 1957 all European currencies had returned to convertibility. The exchange rate policies during the first decades of the system were regulated so that the price of the US dollar was tied to gold at US\$35 an ounce, and other member currencies were tied to the US dollar at fixed exchange rates. To keep exchange rates stable and predictable, financial flows between countries were regulated so that all major payments between actors in member countries had to be approved by their central banks, and only foreign payments related to trade or productive investment were allowed. This was to avoid financial speculation and arbitrage, which were understood as threats to the stability of the system (O'Brien and Williams, 2016).

The control of capital flows, in combination with the Keynesian Economics discourse of the time, created considerable freedom for Bretton Woods member countries to pursue economic development projects of their own choice. Thanks to this, the free-market ideology of the system became 'embedded', and did not materialize in full in everyday life in Western countries (Ruggie, 1998). Welfare states of different kinds could participate in the system, alongside more liberal market-based capitalist countries, and since all were members of the IMF this worked fairly well up until 1970. By then the US had printed so many US dollars – to finance the Vietnam War, a growing world economy and Lyndon B. Johnson's Great Society welfare programme – that the gold reserves intended to stabilize the US dollar exchange rate had become insufficient. This pegging of the US dollar to gold was the foundation of the Bretton Woods exchange rate system, and with an excess of dollars circulating in the world economy the situation became untenable. In 1971 President Nixon quite simply declared that the US would no longer guarantee the price of the dollar in gold. There was an attempt to resurrect another multilateral exchange rate system based on gold (the Smithsonian Agreement), which failed, and by January 1973 the era of this coordinated exchange rate system based on gold was definitely over. Since then we have been living with floating exchange rates that every country has to manage in its own way, unilaterally or in cooperation with other countries. The disappearance of the Bretton Woods exchange rate system meant that the power over exchange rates – the pricing of a country's currency – was handed over from politicians, diplomats and central bankers to actors on the international currency market, who continuously set exchange rates through the mechanism of supply and demand.

Member countries of the IMF, at a meeting in Jamaica in 1976, took the non-decision to preserve the organization with an unchanged mandate, even though the international exchange rate system that was its raison d'etre had crashed (Strange, 1988). The logic behind this non-decision was that in a world of floating exchange rates, there was still a need, perhaps a greater need, for an organization that could audit the fiscal and monetary policies of member countries, give advice on these policies and help countries through liquidity difficulties. And if this activity could give some stability to a system of floating exchange rates, so much the better.

The 1970s also saw a range of political-economic issues. The first of these was the oil crisis, which led to a quadrupling of oil prices from US$3 to US$12 per barrel by the Organization of the Petroleum Exporting Countries (OPEC). When these countries took control over the extraction of, trade in and pricing of oil, this sent a shock wave through the industrial world. Industrialized countries had up until this understood fossil energy as something cheap and abundant. But the OPEC cartel changed that perception, and rising energy costs slowed down global growth.

The second issue was that the internationalization of trade and production had reached a level where Keynesian macroeconomic programmes in the North no longer worked. Support for industry did not lead to more domestic jobs, but to automation and foreign investment. Support for consumer demand did not lead only to more consumption of domestic products, but also to increased consumption of imported goods, which deflated the effect of consumer support on domestic industry. Government support of these kinds did not create domestic jobs, investment and growth as before, but rather led to inflation, trade and budget deficits, and public debt. 'Stagflation' – meaning stagnating growth alongside inflation – became a fashionable term to describe this conundrum.

Debates over how to get out of this situation were lively and widespread. During the 1970s a new political-economic discourse was gaining traction in right-wing political circles, drawing legitimacy from Economics research at Chicago and other academic centres. The face of this movement was Milton Friedman, who in the early 1970s had written a 'Recipe for Chile' – a text in which the political-economic dimensions of what today is known as neoliberalism were spelled out clearly and instructively. The first of these principles is that the market should be understood as the primary historical force in economic development, and that the state should have a minimal role in this market. Politicians tend to want to maximize their vote share to stay in office, which is deemed inefficient in comparison with entrepreneurs, who seek to maximize profit. The market and its entrepreneurs should be 'freed' from state involvement and regulation. Since the market always trends towards equilibrium (in theory), it is better if resources in society can be allocated according to the principle of supply and demand than according to needs and rights principles. When a market reaches equilibrium, labour, resources and money are optimally distributed in the economic sense, whereas politicians and politics hinder the market in producing this optimal and efficient distribution, distorting prices and allocating resources inefficiently. A catchphrase of this new way of thinking was that 'we must get the prices right', meaning that prices should be set by market mechanisms and not by political 'intrusion' in the market from political or social motives. This was a drastic break with the Keynesian macroeconomic discourse that had dominated Economics as well as fiscal and monetary policies since the Second World War.

In the West politicians like Margaret Thatcher and Ronald Reagan embraced this new economic discourse in their respective political projects and campaigns, and since there was public support for trying something new, they got elected in 1979 and 1980, respectively. In 1980 the IMF and the World Bank, at a meeting in Cancun, also gave notice that they were changing the theoretical basis of their advice and lending to this new economic discourse. It had already been tested in Pinochet's Chile and in IMF conditions attached to its loan to Britain in 1976. From the Cancun meeting onwards it became the official doctrine of both organizations, a doctrine that all lenders had to relate and adhere to if they had need of resources from these institutions. This change in the economic thinking behind IMF and World Bank advice and conditionalities had a huge impact on national economic policies, especially after the debt crisis of 1982. This debt crisis broke out when many developing countries ran into payment difficulties caused by skyrocketing interest rates, the result of a new US anti-inflationary monetary policy. This policy, known as **monetarism**, was part of the neoliberal package, and stated that in order to stem inflation you should only work to diminish the money supply, which you do by raising interest rates to make investment and debt more expensive and saving more profitable. Instead of people using their money for consumption and investment, they would put it in a bank account, and the macroeconomic effect would be less investment, higher unemployment, which would keep wages down, and less consumption. This monetary policy was successful in the sense that it brought down inflation in the US. An unlucky side effect was that it created a global recession and a severe debt crisis in the developing world, from which many countries are still recovering. What happened was that all debts denominated in US dollars were affected by the raised interest rate, and since debts in Third World countries were in US dollars, the costs of servicing them went through the roof.

As a result of the 1982 debt crisis, the Bretton Woods institutions took centre stage in global development, and used developing countries in debt trouble as testing grounds for neoliberal market experiments. The policies these countries had to pursue to get Bretton Woods funding promoted private entrepreneurs and the market mechanism as the primary motive forces for economic and social development. However, private actors and markets did not behave as predicted in the econometric theory used in IMF and World Bank advice, and the neoliberal development experiments were huge failures on all counts almost everywhere. Since the Asian crisis of 1997, the harsh neoliberal conditions attached to Bretton Woods funding have gradually subsided. But most of the national institutional adaptations to neoliberal economic globalization that were part of the 'structural adjustment programmes' (SAPs) in this era have remained. Even though the advice today is different, and has social sustainability and poverty reduction as vital components, the actual development efforts are undertaken in countries that are now institutionally geared for global market participation and competition. Jan Aart Scholte (2008) has termed this new Bretton Woods discourse the 'global social market' approach, to highlight how the IMF and World Bank today are socially and culturally much more sensitive than in the 1980s. Now their general belief is that capitalist markets will produce socially beneficial results if regulated and tweaked in the right way.

Reconstructive lessons from the 1970s and 1980s

The first lesson from the 1970s oil crisis is that the world can handle quadrupled energy prices. It spurred a lot of adjustment of national energy policies, including the spread of nuclear power, led to politically subsidized changes in heating infrastructure and new transport patterns, stimulated hoarding behaviour and black markets in gasoline, and had many other consequences. But most importantly, it gave both industrialized and developing countries valuable experience in how to get through such a crisis, and how to adjust to a new energy environment. This macroeconomic and societal lesson is important for policies related to the 2015 Paris Agreement.

The second lesson is that significant global political changes are possible with little institutional change in underlying and regulating treaties. The changes within the Bretton Woods institutions of around 1980 came about because of changes in the economic discourse among those member countries with the greatest voting power in the organizations. The national market economies that the IMF and World Bank have worked to create and support through advice and conditional lending were Keynesian in their early years – but then advice and conditionalities transformed these economies into neoliberal capitalist market experiments in the 1980s. The Bretton Woods institutions became very influential after the 1970s recession and the 1980s debt crisis, and the institutional changes they pushed through brought about uniform political change on a national level in both Northern and Southern countries. The resulting combined institutional order is what regulates entrepreneurial and everyday economic interaction to this day, and still gives the global political economy its neoliberal character. Even though we can see some discursive change in the Bretton Woods institutions, and a general loss of faith in neoliberalism since the 2008 crisis, we are still not seeing any similar sweeping, unidirectional institutional changes on a national level as those we saw in the 1980s. It is only when nation states adjust their laws and policymaking to a new situation, according to a different discourse on the global political economy and its challenges, that a true reconstruction materializes.

Markets for a sustainable future

Reconstructing markets means remaking economic policies and institutional orders on a national and an international level, and this last section of the chapter will present suggestions for how such a remaking might be analytically designed. We must, however, start this section with a reminder about everyday life as discussed in the previous chapter – for what such a change ultimately boils down to is influencing the behaviour of economic actors, and how individual workers, consumers, nation states and transnational corporations (TNCs) bring new markets into being through their economic interaction and agency. The neoliberal turn in development and economic thinking was institutionalized and made into actual policy in only a decade, so we know that a shift of similar magnitude in another direction is possible to achieve in the coming decades.

This section first presents problem-solving concepts and theory on how to achieve sustainability within existing economic structures, and then moves into more critical theory, where sustainability is analytically grounded in new socioeconomic structures.

Solving problems

The first and most fundamental problem that must be addressed is the real threat of planetary ecological disaster. The second problem is growing inequality.

Collaborating ecologists and political scientists recently found, through the processing of large amounts of data, that it is the aggravation of these two problems in tandem that has been the most common cause of collapse for historical civilizations (Motesharrei, Rivas and Kalnay, 2014). This means that both these problems need to be solved in the remaking of markets. There are already a host of measures and programmes being undertaken, which could be used in more radical and far-reaching ways.

Cap and trade is a mechanism for handling and limiting emissions. It is the idea on which the Tokyo Protocol from 1997 is based, and also the principle of emissions trading within the EU. It works by the parties involved agreeing on the quantity of, say, greenhouse gases that can be emitted without creating too much environmental damage. This agreed figure is the 'cap'. The amount of emissions allowed under this cap is then distributed among the main polluters, typically big industries, through a trading system in which polluters can buy emission rights from other polluters to keep producing as they used to do – or they can fix their polluting production, and if they do they will have excess emission rights to sell to others who need them to be able to continue polluting. A cap-and-trade system is meant to create profit incentives for polluters to adjust their production towards ecological sustainability. Existing cap-and-trade systems have so far dealt with end-of-pipe pollution, but theoretically a cap-and-trade system could also be designed for the whole production chain. As regards production of fossil fuels, for instance, there is nothing stopping us from creating a cap-and-trade system for extraction rights, which would mean that energy corporations would need to bid for limited rights to extract oil and gas. Other types of production with a heavy ecological footprint – such as meat, aluminium, electronics and so on – could also be subjected to cap-and-trade limitations, to minimize the ecological damage at the start of production chains rather than at the end. There are several questions worth considering when designing such systems. First, how many rights can be issued without overstretching the ecological system's capacity to take care of the resulting pollution? Second, how should the rights be priced for optimal allocation among emitters/producers? Through an auctioning system of some sort? Or through a needs-based system, with fixed prices for producers selected according to societal importance? Third, how should the market for these rights be organized? Should a second-hand market be allowed, or should the first buyer be the final owner? Should the market be national or international, and if the latter, what area should the market cover? Fourth, how should the proceeds from this market be distributed? Should they simply go into official budgets? Or should they stay inside the system and be used to construct sustainability for the production concerned? These issues are vital to think through when designing a cap-and-trade system, in order to make it as efficient as possible while making it legitimate both among the wider public and for the affected industry.

Taxes are an instrument that has been used to guide market behaviour as long as there have been fiscal policies. Apart from raising public resources, taxes also change how people behave: cigarette taxes are meant to make people smoke less; alcohol taxes are meant to make people drink less; exempting books and journals from value-added tax (VAT) – which some countries do – is meant to make people read more; and so on. Taxes, therefore, are useful for many things politically. If we focus strictly on ecological sustainability, there are a couple of tax measures that would make a big difference. The first measure is making income taxes more progressive, so as to stem the consumption and investment of the upper classes. A progressive tax scale means that the tax rate for the first €10,000 – or whichever currency – you earn is fairly low, and then the rate increases so that you get to keep a smaller part of what you earn for each additional €1,000. The level of tax that you pay on the last €1,000 you earn is called the marginal tax rate, and this rate was something around 60 per cent on average in rich countries in the 1970s, while today, after neoliberal institutional adaptation, it is around 40 per cent on average. Just resurrecting the progressive tax scales of the 1970s would mean that the upper classes would cause less ecological damage, and at the same time contribute considerably more to public budgets. But taxes can also be levied on specific, ecologically damaging forms of production and consumption to reduce those. There are a number of things worth considering when working with taxes. First, what is it you want to achieve with the tax? If you want to guide market behaviour, it might be most productive to levy the tax on the specific interaction you want to influence. A good example is the carbon tax levied on car fuels in many countries. If, on the other hand, you want to use taxes to fund public budgets, a more general tax, such as income tax or VAT, might be more viable since it affects market interaction more evenly, so that all market participants make a comparable contribution to the public budget in absolute terms. Second, what are the likely effects of the tax on economic behaviour? Market actors will adjust their behaviour with variable ease, depending on how everyday life functions. The carbon tax on car fuel, for instance, has not affected commuting behaviour very much due to the way modern cities function, with people tending to live in the same area for quite a long time. If fuel taxes were raised to levels prohibitive of private motorized commuting, we would see resettlement processes in every city, and the social, economic and ecological effects of these would need to be taken into account in our analysis. If we want corporations to keep more of their revenues for sustainability investment instead of doling it out as profits to shareholders, we might raise corporate and capital tax levels to stimulate this. Third, the legitimacy of specific taxes, as well as of taxes generally, needs to be considered. On the one hand, taxes become legitimate by the existence of a well-functioning and accessible public sector, supplying people with law and order, education, healthcare, efficient infrastructure and everything else people expect from the public sector. On the other hand, legitimacy is produced by the tax burden being distributed so that people pay in proportion to their income and wealth. If you finance the public sector mainly through a VAT on consumption, poor people who consume most of their income will bear a disproportionately large burden. If you finance the public sector through corporate taxes, you will place a heavy burden on firms, who might get disinclined to invest and build businesses, and will probably perceive their contribution to be disproportionately large. In utilitarian terms, the legitimacy of taxes can be understood as something that is produced in a zone where the tax burdens create a collective socioeconomic 'pain' smaller than the collective benefits and 'pleasures' that the public sector delivers. Fourth (and finally), how can taxes be collected? In many countries the state has a low institutional capacity, and there is therefore a lack of personnel and institutional mechanisms by means of which tax bases can be reached and taxes collected. If money flows are very thin, which they typically are in rural areas in a developing country, the opportunity cost of employing educated public servants to collect taxes can be high (as compared to employing them elsewhere in the public sector). Another thing to consider is the measurability of what is taxed. It would be nice to be able to tax a heavy ecological footprint heavily, but since 'ecological footprint' is a theoretical construction, we would need to tax the concrete products and activities that produce the footprint. In sum, taxes influence behaviour; they finance the public sector; they need to be legitimate and are collected at a cost; and they are an important instrument in the reconstruction of markets.

Laws and regulations are also effective instruments in the reconstruction of markets. Laws can make certain sorts of economic interaction disappear, or they can give it another form. You might allow one form of economic interaction, but only to be conducted under certain circumstances by specific actors in certain settings. For example, the production and selling of sausages is legal around the world, but to safeguard public health, production must follow certain regulations to meet hygiene standards, and if the sausages are not preserved by preservatives, smoking, drying or vacuum packaging, they must be refrigerated until the final consumer takes them home. In some countries pork might be prohibited as sausage content, while in other countries ingredients from genetically modified animals and plants are illegal. The concept of the 'sausage' is probably universal today, but the realization of actual sausages follows the traditions, laws and regulations of the specific countries and markets where the sausages are sold and consumed. This distinction – between **universalism** and **particularism** – is important as regards laws and regulations for markets. When nation states adapted institutionally for economic globalization, the logical end point for free-trade adjustment was that market laws and regulations should be universal and uniform, meaning that a sausage produced anywhere in the world should also be allowed to be sold everywhere. The world has come a long way towards this goal, but a number of critics across the ideological spectrum have pointed out how this universalization of laws and regulations, and the free trade it makes possible, is creating more problems than benefits. Dani Rodrik (2011) terms this 'hyperglobalization', and calls for more varied and particularistic laws and regulations for national markets, to make market interaction realize situations more conducive to specific societal needs and objectives in each country. A team writing on behalf of the UNDP in 2003 arrived at the same recommendations (Malhotra et al, 2003). When working with laws and regulations in market reconstruction, it is worth asking yourself a couple of questions. Which ideas, values, needs and objectives are important for this particular market, and how can we design laws and regulations to realize these while upholding universal values? Which forms do people give universal ideas and values, such as fairness, security and love, in this particular market? Changing markets is an exercise of power, and as we discussed in Chapter 1, power is generally more efficient when those subjected to it perceive it as legitimate and meaningful.

Democracy means that all political power originates from the people. It can be either direct, where all decisions are made by the people directly, or (as is more common today) representative, which means that people elect representatives who exercise political power on their behalf, within constitutional limits. Markets today are said to be democratic when they are guided, circumscribed and formed by laws and regulations decided on and designed by democratic institutions – such as parliaments, governments and ministerial departments – that are staffed by persons elected through the principles of representative democracy. As long as people in market economies act within the bounds of laws and regulations, they are free to do as they please with their resources. According to the neoliberal discourse of the globalization decades, there is also a democratic quality to this market-based freedom: when people are free to do what they want with their resources, they will over time also develop a taste for democratic interaction as regards rational political decision-making and debate. The examples of China and several other countries are beginning to contradict this belief: in these states, market freedom is not in itself furthering political, civic and intellectual freedom and democracy. Critics of this discourse go even further and state that free-market interaction is undemocratic, in the sense that actors with the most money and resources tend to get their way. Inequality of financial and other resources, therefore, brings about a situation which may go against the general will of the people concerned (Amin, 2004). According to this criticism, it is not enough that democratic laws and regulations circumscribe market interaction – this interaction in itself should be guided by democratic principles, so that important market decisions are taken by all the parties concerned and affected.

Markets should not be conflated with capitalism. The market is a system for the allocation of things using some sort of price mechanism. Capitalism is a special form of ownership of the means of production, especially land and financial and real capital (Gilpin, 1987). Real-world examples of economic democracy are sparse and often small-scale, such as the occupied factories and independent municipalities that emerged in Argentina following the 2001 crisis, or coffee cooperatives in Rwanda after the genocide.

A concept helpful in designing a democratization of markets, or a 're-embedding' of market interaction, is the ancient idea of **just prices**. This concept predates the marginalist model of supply and demand, that defines market price as the point where curves of supply and demand intersect, and where this point moves towards equilibrium over time. A just price is not an equilibrium between two different social mechanisms in a theoretical model, but a price settled in mutual recognition of the needs and value of two or more parties. The money in a just-price transaction becomes an expression of this recognition of an economic social subject, who is important to the buyer. Large sections of today's market interaction already follow this principle in a social sense, but the institutional changes of globalization have led to laws and regulations written to promote the supply and demand principle from Microeconomics in order to 'get the prices right'. A remaking of markets might equally well aim to 'get the prices just', through institutional changes based on the ethics of reciprocity.

Transformation of market structures

Market reconstructions of a more critical character are not solutions to problems in markets, as Economics teaches us, but alternative forms of economic interaction based on other discourses and principles. There have been many other forms of economic interaction throughout history, and a many different visions of how to organize the societal metabolism. There is not room to present all of these here[2] – instead, I present some of their underlying concepts that may be helpful for analytical thinking.

Central planning was the principle underpinning the economic system of the Soviet Union. The idea was that the state department for planning charted what needs there were in society, and then organized the economy, from industrial investment and operation to retail stores and collective agriculture, so that these needs would be fulfilled. For some decades after the Second World War, this system was successful, growing as fast as the Western system and providing for its people fairly well. From around 1970 the system began to show problems, such as inefficiency, swollen bureaucracy, substandard products, shortages of necessary consumer items in shops, a loss of creativity in economic interaction, and so on (Aganbegyan, 1988; Nove, 1989). Many of these problems can be attributed to the dictatorship of the Communist Party. Central planning is also an option in democratic countries, and when done within democratic institutions many of the Soviet problems can be avoided or pre-empted. If we are going to end today's gargantuan consumption, central planning in some form, of at least some items or sectors, will be a useful tool. Energy especially is a sector where central planning could replace the market principle of distribution, since reducing emissions from energy consumption is essential for stopping climate change. A vital question when thinking about central planning is: what will happen to the economic and social creativity that today finds its home and outlet in market interaction, and how can central planning foster such creativity?

Social re-embedding of economic interaction is another theoretical entry point for the reconstruction of markets (Polanyi, 1944). Globalization has often been described as a disembedding of economic interaction from the social fabric, resulting from the reconstruction of allocation so that is performed by private entrepreneurs according to the price mechanism, instead of through other social mechanisms such as reciprocity, tradition, political decisions and redistribution, religious belief, and so on. Another word for this is **marketization** – the macro-transformation of a polity into a **market society**. A possible analytical approach to the transformation of markets in this vein is what might be termed 're-embedding' or 'demarketization' (since it represents a reversal of what happened during the globalization decades). In principle, the degree of re-embedding has no end point. It could mean a complete eradication of the market principle of allocation, replacing it with reciprocity, needs-based allocation or some other principle. It could also mean that some economic sectors are reconstructed to work according to other principles, while the price mechanism continues to regulate allocation in the remaining sectors. As a starting point for analysis, you might think of what interaction takes place using money as a means of exchange in the form of a mediating ingredient, and work out how this interaction could be organized without money.

The last important point on the checklist stems from the contempt for manual work and commercial interaction that has been prevalent among intellectuals since at least ancient Athens. This last point is a call for self-reflection, a reminder for critical analysts to look seriously at the economic interaction being examined and ask: to what extent is this interaction already socially embedded as a market? If we find that it actually is socially embedded already and that the market aspect is generally legitimate, its injustices and unsustainabilities might not be best addressed with demarketization, but with some other measure.

Conclusion

Markets are what we make them. In our interaction in the market we can strengthen or weaken the discourses institutionalized in laws and regulations, as well as support or oppose (according to our means) the prevalent actors and structures in the market. We do this not only through price and consumption signals, but also by acting politically to change how our markets function and what effects market institutions are designed to have. Even if few of us can be held responsible for the markets we have today, the political trajectories and opportunities for market formation are open. From our everyday consumption, through national legislation and domestic and international policy, all the way to the WTO, the World Bank and the IMF, markets have been and will be politically reconstructed.

Further reading

The standard work to read on market formation and the disembedding of market mechanisms is Karl Polanyi's *The Great Transformation* (1944), which describes the political construction of markets, from Britain in the 19th century up until the Second World War. One of the arguments Polanyi builds in this description is that market mechanisms have been disembedded several times throughout history, because they serve capitalist interests, and each time the negative social effects have accumulated until popular reaction has forced political authorities to re-embed markets into the social fabric. He terms this dialectic the 'double movement'. John Gerard Ruggie is a GPE scholar who, inspired by Polanyi, wrote a couple of seminal articles about the Bretton Woods order, which can be found in his 1998 compilation *Constructing the World Polity*. The role that these institutions played in economic globalization is critically assessed in Ngaire Woods' *The Globalizers* (2006), and scathingly criticized in Naomi Klein's *The Shock Doctrine* (2007). For further critical assessment of the IMF and the World Bank, visiting the Bretton Woods Project (www.brettonwoodsproject.org) is well worthwhile.

To get a more sympathetic picture of these global economic institutions, the first places to visit are the home pages of the IMF (www.imf.org), the World Bank (www.worldbank.org) and the WTO (www.wto.org). Here you will find their regulating treaties, a lot of statistics and many a self-sympathetic description of what the institutions are doing. It is hard to find writers who unequivocally approve of the institutions and their global governance, but writers such as Jeffrey Sachs and Joseph Stiglitz are generally positive about the ideas they are built on, even if they are critical of the way they try to realize them.

4

Trade Constructs

There has always been trade between societies, groups and countries. Trade has always been politically regulated and part of international politics. The fact that we have a global economic institutional order promoting free trade can be attributed largely to the painful economic crisis and international disorder of the 1930s, and their traumatic culmination in the Second World War and Nazi genocide. After 1945 there was a genuine need for order in international trade, and the most prevalent discourse guiding the design of a new institutional order at the time was David Ricardo's theory on comparative advantages in production (see Chapter 3). The theoretical academic debate around the theory of comparative advantage is huge and research is ongoing. A problem with the theory is that no rich country has managed to industrialize while pursuing free trade to a degree commensurate with the theory (Chang, 2010; Rodrik, 2011). On the contrary, the most common trade strategy conducive to successful industrialization, from Britain to the US to China, has been to protect growing industries while they are vulnerable to international competition, and to lower tariffs only when industries are robust and efficient enough to compete internationally. The US, for instance, had high tariff walls to protect industrialization in its northern states, and these tariffs were even raised after the Civil War of 1860–6 (Bairoch, 1993). Countries trying to build industries while pursuing free trade according to Ricardo's theory have failed, because existing foreign industries typically outcompete such infant industries with cheaper and better exports. What stands out instead in the historical record is that free trade systematically benefits the more industrialized country in a bilateral free-trade relationship, while poor countries participate in free trade at considerable risk. Ricardo's theory on comparative advantage may be logically coherent, but it is not borne out by real-world development and national trade policies. This chapter will first tell the story of the political dynamics around the institutional construction of the global free-trade regime, before going on to discuss how a reformed or completely different global trade regime might be constructed on the basis of sustainability and justice.

The global free-trade regime

The GATT, signed in 1947, was a first step to creating a new order for international trade. As we saw in the previous chapter, the diplomats and economists designing and negotiating it worked to achieve a multilateral rules-based order for international trade. This order was intended to be transparent – so that entrepreneurs would know which rules and costs their trade would have to follow and cover – to give trade between countries and entrepreneurs predictability and stability. In addition, its rules and tariffs were designed to establish a level playing field for entrepreneurs from different member countries. To bring international trade closer to these ideals, the GATT and subsequent additional treaties were written and negotiated based on a number of principles, which came to regulate both the order itself and the political and institutional principles governing its development.

The first principle of the free-trade order is the **most-favoured-nation** (MFN) principle. The meaning of it is the opposite of what the acronym intuitively brings to mind. A country that is a member of the order, according to the MFN principle, cannot have different trade rules for merchants from different foreign countries, which would make it more expensive and/or difficult for merchants from one foreign country to export there than it would be for merchants from another foreign country. Instead, a member must apply the same tariffs and trade-related laws to all member countries as those it applies in its relations with the nation meeting the most favourable conditions for exporting to it. In other words, entrepreneurs from all member countries must face equal and uniform trade barriers when they trade with a member country.

The second principle is that of **non-tariff barriers** (NTBs), which should be kept to a minimum. Historically, many NTBs have been quotas, establishing the maximum quantity of imports that a country can handle without its domestic industry being endangered or outcompeted. A quota is constructed so that a specified quantity of a certain item can be imported with a fairly low tariff levied on it, but from the nth item imported onwards, a much higher or prohibitive tariff is levied. Quantitative quotas of this sort are regarded as very trade-disturbing, since the importing entrepreneurs cannot know which importer will end up importing the nth item and getting hit by the higher tariff. In order to safeguard against possible big losses, importers might abstain from importing more than the maximum 'safe' amount, or shy away from trade in that particular item completely. Much work within the GATT and WTO has gone into the eradication of quotas as NTBs. Other forms of NTB can be standard requirements, beyond what has been agreed upon, government regulations of different kinds and the like. A problem with deciding what constitutes an NTB is that very often two countries have very different views on specific issues. Countries with a comparative advantage in agricultural production might regard a particular hygiene standard in an industrial country as an NTB protecting farmers of that country, while the industrial country might say that it is a standard that must be upheld for consumer health and safety or national security reasons. This means that NTBs are a matter of continuous debate.

The third principle of the free-trade order is that of **national treatment**. This states that once an item has crossed a national border, it must be allowed to compete with domestically produced items on the same terms in the market. Member countries are not allowed to have separate regulations for things imported from other member countries. Imported goods and services must be offered to the customers on the same terms as those produced domestically. Ultimately the preferences of customers should steer demand, and not tariffs or other politically imposed regulations. This national treatment principle also means that members of the order must agree on such things as chemical standards for pharmaceuticals, sanitary and phytosanitary standards for agricultural products, safety standards for vehicles, and so on. These standards establish a lowest common denominator, or bottom floor, as regards the quality and nature of traded items that producers have to ensure. Since meeting these standards is a cost for producers, they are also a matter of debate, but as long as they are upheld imported products and services can compete in national markets on equal terms with domestically produced items.

A fourth principle is the **safeguards** principle, which allows member countries to maintain trade barriers, even raise them, if national security or development are threatened by imports. This might seem contradictory, but since the overall aim is to expand and deepen trade and interdependence, it is more important for the guardians of the order to keep countries on the path of increasing free trade than to constantly have to defend existing treaties against popular and economic interests in member countries. Industrializing countries in particular might in certain situations need to protect national industries they have invested heavily in. These industries often have substantial state ownership, and to guard against unfair competition the safeguards principle operates in tandem with the principle of 'commercial considerations', which means that even if an enterprise is state-owned, it is supposed to act as a private, profit-driven commercial actor or firm. So a state-owned enterprise cannot operate at a loss for political reasons, but should instead work to maximize profits. If subsidized or state-owned enterprises compete internationally with subsidized exports, it is considered unfair and trade-disturbing.

What is evident when you see these four principles is that the free-trade order, of which the GATT was the first agreement, has no end point when trade will be considered free enough. The institutional order resting on these principles – and on its various agreements – is constructed to make existing international trade freer, regardless of how high or low the trade barriers are. The order has the same driving force today, when the average applied tariff for industrial goods is 3.7 per cent, as it had when the GATT was signed in 1947, and the same trade-weighted applied tariff was around 22 per cent.[1] The order today concerns itself with many other issues apart from tariffs, such as NTBs, government procurement and subsidies, in order to make trade freer. This concern with multiple issues manifests itself most clearly in the negotiation rounds where the order is developed. These rounds are special political-economic processes, which are structured according to a number of principles of trade negotiation.

The most important negotiation principle overall is the single undertaking. As we saw in Chapter 3, 'single undertaking' means that all members have to be in consensus on the negotiation result before it is finished. 'Consensus' sounds nice and courteous, but there is nothing especially nice about these negotiations. They are characterized by mercantilist behaviour from the individual parties, who try to open up as many foreign markets as possible for their export industries, while allowing as few imports as possible to compete in their domestic markets. In this haggling process, rich industrial countries with large markets have a much stronger bargaining position than small non-industrialized countries with small domestic markets. For a long time this imbalance allowed the rich world to get its way in the negotiation rounds. Today this has changed a little, but the imbalance remains, and deeply qualifies the 'consensus' sometimes held up as evidence of the democratic quality of trade negotiations and the single undertaking principle.

The second principle in the negotiation rounds is that of **reciprocity**, which states that a concession – an agreement to lower trade barriers – should apply both ways between the negotiating parties. In the early days of the free-trade order, reciprocity related to just one type of goods in both directions, since treaties were negotiated and written item by item at different levels of processing. But since the Uruguay Round (1986–94), reciprocity has been negotiable 'across the board', so that a lowering of trade barriers for (say) car exports to a developing country can be reciprocated with a lowering of trade barriers for the export of (say) cotton and similar commodities to an industrialized country. This 'across the board' approach was adopted after protests from non-industrialized countries, which had little use for a lowering of trade barriers for the export of industrial goods to industrialized countries. While this made negotiations somewhat fairer, it did not make them less complicated.

The third principle is that the purpose of negotiations is to determine the highest allowed trade barrier. As regards tariffs, for instance, the negotiation result concerns 'bound' rates of tariffs – that is, the highest tariff allowed to be levied on a specific item. In actual trade the tariffs applied are often considerably lower, to free up trade between important trading partners and the like. Applied tariff levels might typically differ from 'bound' tariff levels, but this does not make bound levels irrelevant, since bound levels establish what policy space there is within the agreements for industrialization policies, agricultural policies and so on. A country might have policy space to protect infant industries, even within the realms of the free-trade order, but might abstain from doing this from fear of losing export markets when importing countries reciprocate and raise their applied tariffs. This use of bound and applied tariffs, which is perfectly consistent with the ethos of the order, also helps us understand the prevalence of customs unions and free-trade areas. These might seem like deviations from the global free-trade order, but they are not. Remember, the whole idea of the free-trade order is to make trade freer, and if a group of countries want to apply zero tariffs to trade among themselves, this is in keeping with the overall aim of the order.

A fourth principle of the negotiations is that only those countries that have the highest stake in the issue under discussion should be at the negotiating table, to make bargaining manageable. One group of bargaining parties allowed at the table is that of countries that have a certain percentage of global trade in the item, as either exports or imports. Another group is that of industrializing countries that get a substantial proportion of their export earnings from trade in the item. This principle has been vital for reaching many agreements at all, but it has also been fiercely criticized, since it tilts negotiations in the larger economies' favour. Small and poor countries might be very dependent on the negotiated item, either for strategic imports or for export earnings, but might not even be allowed into the negotiation room simply because of their small economic size in the global economy.

A fifth issue, which is not really a principle but a phenomenon, is that of the **green room deliberations**. These are discussions that take place when negotiations get stuck and the bargaining parties have reached a deadlock that prevents an agreement from being finalized. When such a stalemate occurs, leading officials of the free-trade order, such as the director-general of the WTO or the chairman of a specific council, call the negotiating parties into a closed room and try to break the deadlock and work out an agreement that all parties can live with, even if it deviates from the positions of one or more of them. This is a non-transparent and undemocratic routine, but it has been important for the furthering of negotiations on many occasions. Those defending the green room highlight the possibility of getting things done more easily when negotiators are out of sight of their home constituencies and out of the public spotlight. Those critical of the procedure point out that it makes it far easier to twist the arms of weaker countries to get a deal favouring the stronger parties, and emphasize the overall political problem of using the green room to further a politically contentious free-trade regime.

The WTO: a victim of its own success

The Uruguay Round took place during the crumbling of the Soviet Union, the deregulation of financial markets, the political-economic triumph of neoliberalism and a general rightwards shift of the political-economic mainstream. When a discursive shift is this successful, depoliticized issues are transferred to institutions and organizations, where they are handled by experts as technical problems rather than questions of politics or ideology (Mouffe, 2005). This is what happened to free trade. Previously a matter of political contestation, it was now reframed as a technical issue. This also affected the trade regime. In the Uruguay Round the negotiating parties agreed to set up the WTO, which was founded on 1 January 1995.

The job of the WTO is to oversee and to further the free-trade regime. To fulfil its purpose the organization facilitates and organizes negotiations over its trade treaties. It also oversees how member countries implement and abide by the treaties. If members get into a dispute over trade, it also has a trade dispute settlement body, in which trustworthy economists and diplomats can help the disputing members to solve their problems and continue trading with each other. Prior to 1995 the free-trade regime existed as a body of treaties, continuously overseen by diplomats from an office in Geneva, and regularly renegotiated in rounds, named after the places where they were launched. Now this body of treaties is assembled under the banner of the WTO.

The Battle of Seattle

In late November 1999 a new round of trade negotiations was meant to be launched by a WTO ministerial conference in Seattle. Such ministerial conferences have the institutional function of finalizing years of diplomatic work, and then launching a new series of diplomatic meetings and negotiations based on what the conference has decided. When ministers meet at such conferences, therefore, the bulk of the haggling and bargaining, the drawing up of agendas, the hashing out of preliminary agreements, and so on, has already been done by the diplomatic corps of the member countries. Ministers fly in to negotiate any outstanding issues, sign the agreement, get photographed in front of an impressive building and then fly home. The WTO had planned for this to take place in Seattle, to mark the start of a millennial negotiation round.

The 1990s, however, had also been a decade of globalization and economic restructuring, which had led to deindustrialization in OECD countries, accelerated environmental degradation and climate change, harsh social consequences in developing countries opening up for international trade, and slow economic development in countries that had been debt-burdened since the 1980s. These diverse and adverse consequences of globalization spurred reactions in civil society. Different organizations had mobilized around these and other globalization-related issues throughout the 1990s. Free trade, and especially the WTO, was a major cause of many of the issues these organizations mobilized against. This mobilization was speeded up and expanded tremendously with a new '90s phenomenon called 'the Internet'. As the ministerial conference approached, many organizations from this broad global justice movement teamed up to protest against capitalism and neoliberal globalization generally, and the WTO specifically, in Seattle.

As ministers flew in to the conference, NGOs and grassroots movements gathered in the city. In the days leading up to the conference various peaceful protest meetings, seminars and street parties took place. On 30 November several marches organized by labour unions, Third World solidarity organizations and environmental organizations started towards the conference hotel. At the same time, various radical groups started to block intersections in central Seattle to stop delegates from reaching the hotel. Radical anarchists, who had formed a 'black bloc', walked towards the centre while smashing windows of banks and retail stores. The peaceful demonstrations drew tens of thousands of participants, the more violent protest perhaps a couple of hundred. With the city besieged by protesters and police in head-on confrontation, the conference opening was cancelled around noon.

The protests stopped the symbolic conference routines, including the official opening and ministerial photo opportunities. The negotiations themselves were also in a state of upheaval, since the Third World was displaying a new resolve, demanding that the promises made to developing countries in previous rounds be delivered on before any new negotiation round was launched. In new alliances, and emboldened by media debate on the effects of globalization and protests against these effects on poor people all over the planet, Third World member countries of the WTO – and several rich countries as well – refused to start a new round of negotiations unless the demands from developing countries were explicitly put on the agenda.

The Doha Development Round

The first round of negotiations organized under the aegis of the WTO started in November 2001 in Doha in Qatar, and was consequently named the Doha Development Round (DDR). After much neglect of the needs of developing countries in previous rounds, the promise was made that this round would specifically cater to these needs, and would arrive at a single undertaking and result that met the demands of the Third World. Some 20 areas were opened up for negotiation, but Third World members soon discovered that OECD countries did not intend to deliver on their development promise. Instead many rich countries continued negotiating and haggling in the usual mercantilist way, disregarding the trade-related development problems that the round was allegedly trying to solve. Third World members, however, were not the same kind of trading partners as they had been in previous rounds. Now they were 'emerging markets' attracting foreign investment and outsourced production from rich countries. The resulting increases in GDP and international trade participation increased the negotiating clout of these industrializing countries tremendously. Diplomatic skills and negotiating competence among Third World countries had also increased a great deal by the new millennium, which made it impossible to bribe, lobby or threaten their negotiators in the DDR, as had often happened in previous rounds (Andersson, 2012). The round experienced two major breakdowns in 2003 and 2008, and has been declared dead many times since then, even though trade-related diplomatic interaction is still going on in Geneva. At the time of writing no one expects the DDR to reach a final single undertaking agreement. The breakdowns were accentuations of conflicts inherent in the global trade regime, and laid bare a new power distribution in the global political economy.

The Cancun breakdown (2003)

During the preparation phase for the WTO ministerial conference in Cancun in September 2003, it became clear that negotiations were going to be difficult. The conference was meant to be a meeting taking stock of what had been achieved so far in the DDR, and to prepare for the finalization of the round. But diplomats did not arrive at any comprehensive proposals beforehand to put on the table for ministers to negotiate and sign. Instead a number of contentious topics were brought to the conference, with the hope that ministers and their teams would be able to resolve tensions and find a way forward.

The disagreements concerned agriculture, and how a final deal over international trade in agricultural products would be reached. The US and the EU had drafted a proposal for how countries would lower tariffs and other barriers to trade in agricultural products, but this proposal failed to deal properly with the most pressing concern of many developing agricultural exporters. What was conspicuously absent from the proposal was a coherent idea about how to handle agricultural subsidies. For developing countries these subsidies could have two trade-disturbing effects. First, they could flood developing markets with cheap agricultural imports, which outcompeted local products by being priced below domestic production costs with the help of subsidies. In particular, export subsidies that helped the agricultural industry dump surplus products in the Third World sometimes hit Third World farming hard. But even more general subsidies, such as guaranteed minimum prices for (say) cereals, had the potential to cause overproduction in the rich world that would flood the world market and subsequently outcompete exports from the South with non-market, subsidized prices. Second, subsidies acted as a form of NTB against imports, lowering prices in protected domestic markets in rich countries to a level where it became impossible for imported, non-subsidized products to compete. From an agricultural exporter's perspective this was not a level playing field. Twenty developing countries dependent on agricultural exports formed a group to muster collective negotiating strength and demand a rewriting of the US/EU proposal. This group also had the support of richer agricultural export countries – the so-called Cairns Group – which also wanted to negotiate subsidies.

African cotton-exporting countries were particularly eager to negotiate subsidies, because US subsidies to American cotton farmers had a tendency to drive prices down on the world market for cotton. When US cotton farmers were supported with product subsidies, they produced more than the US market could absorb, and the industry would dump the surplus on the world market. The cotton subsidies in the US, therefore, could produce severe current account and macroeconomic problems for developing countries that depended on export earnings from cotton. The US, for its part, viewed these subsidies as an important means of support for its hard-pressed farming community, and argued that the subsidies were in line with the agreement reached in the Uruguay Round. The EU and the US both preferred to negotiate ways to increase market access for international agricultural trade, rather than national agricultural policies themselves.

Another thorny issue that hampered the negotiations were the so-called 'Singapore issues', named after the WTO ministerial conference in 1996 at which they were raised during negotiations – with a working group created for each issue. The issues concerned trade-related aspects of government procurement, investment, customs procedures and competition policy. Since such issues were integral to industrialization and national development policies in the South, many developing countries opposed having these issues open for negotiation at all. Government procurement, for instance, has throughout history and across the whole world been instrumental for economic development, and governments have regularly placed large orders with national industries to support them. A WTO agreement delimiting what governments would be able to support with their procurement was not in the interest of these developing countries. The idea of subjecting investment and competition policy to WTO regulation met with a similar response.

The diplomatic preparations prior to the Cancun conference had not had the opportunity to deal with this complex picture and settle on an agenda that all participants accepted. Once all delegations were present, the WTO coordinators of the conference did not manage to convince the different parties of this debate to agree on an agenda, or to get them to the negotiating table. The agricultural G20 had many big economies as members, including China, India and Mexico, which were already intertwined with the global economy to an extent that made them impossible to ignore or bully. Even when the EU and the US made (limited) modifications to their initial proposal, the positions proved irreconcilable, and the conference ended without having made any solid progress towards a final agreement.

The Cancun breakdown was a wake-up call for the global political economy of the new millennium. First, it signalled the arrival of powerful and self-assertive industrializing countries, ready to go their own political and economic way if the agendas up for negotiation did not relate meaningfully to their interests. Second, it was a clear indication of the limits of what could be achieved within the multilateral framework; some even point to the complexity of negotiations among the 146 (at the time) WTO member countries as the primary cause of the breakdown. Third, the continued expansion of global trade after the breakdown showed how successful the free-trade regime had been. Economic globalization had been achieved. The question now was if the WTO was up to the task of governing its trade.

Breakdown in Geneva (2008)

After the breakdown in Cancun, negotiations continued on a diplomatic level, and several interim meetings were held. By 2008 it seemed that the positions of all members were sufficiently clear and negotiated for a concluding ministerial conference to be held. Even though a final deal was now well overdue, leading the DDR to a single undertaking agreement looked possible. One might wonder why a new deal was necessary at all, given that most members (except Third World cotton exporters) were fairly happy trading according to the results of the Uruguay Round. But as stated earlier in this chapter, there is no end to the free-trade process; the regime is designed for constant deepening and expansion. One metaphor often used to describe the process of developing the free-trade regime is that of a bicycle: you have to continue pedalling or you will fall over. In other words, if the WTO could not lead the DDR negotiations to a final agreement, the process of continuously making trade freer would stop, and if it stopped the whole regime would be in danger. So stitching together a final agreement in Geneva in 2008 seemed necessary for maintaining functioning global governance.

In the run-up to the ministerial conference it was unclear how much members had to gain from a final deal. Calculations used to estimate the effect of a new trade agreement indicated that global trade would expand by some US$400 billion per year; the global welfare effect of this would be some US$50 billion, most of which would end up in rich countries (Gallagher 2008). Industrial countries met very low or no tariff walls or NTBs for their exports to their main trading partners; applied tariffs were down to about 3.7 per cent; and globalization had established a deep interdependence among the OECD countries. Opening up to increased agricultural and low-value exports from the South, therefore, would not be a problem for most of these rich countries. Many member countries from the South were well on their way to becoming middle-income industrialized countries, attracting investment and production relocated and outsourced from rich countries. But industrializing Southern countries were not eager to sign a final deal, since it would bring down trade barriers helpful for protecting their infant industries. China, for instance, did not show any willingness to renegotiate the deal it got as a developing accession country when it entered the WTO in 2001. The poorest, least developed countries would gain increased market access to OECD countries if a deal was made, but they were not major traders in most of the items under discussion, and were consequently not invited to many of the negotiations.

It was negotiations between the US and India that collapsed and made the whole Doha Round break down. India wanted to keep a special safeguard mechanism that would allow it to erect high tariff walls on cereals if world market prices dropped to a level where the survival of Indian farmers was threatened.

The US did not accept the height of this potential wall, but did in turn demand the right to protect its cotton farmers with subsidies and tariffs, should their survival be threatened by weather conditions or low world market prices for cotton. The two parties held stubbornly to their positions, and India had the support of China. When an agreement in this negotiation could not be reached, it meant that a single undertaking conclusion of the DDR was also out of reach.

It might seem odd that these big players allowed the Doha Round to collapse over what appear to be peripheral and minor trade issues, when most other negotiations were completed successfully. But we must remember that by 2008 global free trade had largely been achieved. A stark sign of this is that the business lobby, which had been very active in trying to influence the outcome in previous rounds, was almost absent in the Geneva 2008 negotiations. Apparently they had got what they needed in the Uruguay Round. Diplomats also expressed a sense of frustration and abandonment, complaining that no top-level politicians were present to put their weight behind the offers made and positions taken in their countries' negotiations (Andersson, 2012). The WTO had apparently become a place where countries went to uphold and negotiate the norms of the free-trade regime, and to defend their position within it. But given the continuous increase in global trade as a share of global GDP, alongside a long period of growth and high corporate profits, the value of the best alternative to a negotiated agreement (BATNA) (Albin, 2001) was sufficiently high for these countries to bring the round to collapse. Alarmist reporting in the media about the breakdown was soon calmed by economists and politicians pointing out the burgeoning global trade under the Uruguay Round agreement that was still in effect. Paul Krugman wrote on his *New York Times* blog (30 July 2008) that 'life, and trade, will go on'.

Prevailing free trade?

An indication of the strength of the free-trade regime came after the 2008 financial crisis. In a series of meetings, members of the G20 group agreed to abstain from all 'protectionism' – an agreement they honoured. Global trade recovered, and by 2010 trade volumes were back to pre-crisis levels, around a third of global GDP. This trade-to-GDP ratio has remained stable since then, indicating that globalization and trade dependence have reached a level that it is hard to advance beyond. Even so, countries continue to strive to expand their export markets in accordance with the free-trade discourse – though not necessarily under the WTO umbrella.

As new actors become economically and politically important, and new forms of trade such as trade in services expand, the existing WTO institutional order for free trade is 'drifting' (Stephen and Parizek, 2019). In other words, the global free-trade institutions and organizations are losing relevance in international trade as it exists today. In parallel to the Doha Round, WTO negotiations have begun to be replaced by bilateral and regional free-trade agreements such as the North

American Free Trade Area (NAFTA) and the Comprehensive and Progressive Agreement for Trans-Pacific Partnership (CPATPP). These are negotiated by two or more countries in a bid to make mutual market access easier by imposing fewer border restrictions and customs procedures, lower or no tariffs, and mutual recognition of each other's product standards. This will make entrepreneurs from those countries forming a free-trade area able to compete, collaborate and/or trade with each other at lower transaction costs and in a larger market than if they had traded with each other in accordance with the WTO agreements. When the Doha Round proved unable to move trade closer towards the theoretical ideal of free trade, nation states and regional organizations kept pushing free-trade policies on their own.

Free-trade areas (FTAs) or **regional trade agreements** (RTAs) can have their own problems, however. In NAFTA, for instance, Mexican maize farmers have been severely hit by imported maize from the US, with its more industrial agricultural sector. This new competition has changed the Mexican countryside as well as everyday Mexican culture, of which bread baked from maize flour is an integral part. Mexican industry has also been reshaped since NAFTA freed up trade flows with the US, which has had social effects that have put severe strain on some sectors but benefited others. In policy terms, Mexican governments have lost a lot of their policy space for development, and domestic policies have been circumscribed by NAFTA in a way that limits what the state can do to protect farmers, workers and domestic industries. This exemplifies how entering an FTA or RTA is done at a cost, and developing countries are becoming increasingly cautious about doing so, weighing the potential economic benefits and costs against the ways an RTA restricts what can be done within domestic economic policy. If an RTA under negotiation involves both industrial countries and poorer developing countries, caution is especially important, since if large corporations from the wealthier states decide to try to capture markets in the developing countries, the latter will have little policy space and insufficient economic resources to defend themselves. Such a market capture might lead to GDP growth and meet consumer demand, but at the cost of unemployment and deindustrialization in significant parts of those countries and their populations. Readers might object here that this is what free trade has always done, and this is correct, but if it happens within an RTA the affected country might have even less policy space (depending on how the RTA is written) than under WTO agreements. Developing countries who wanted the conclusion of the Doha Round highlighted this as one of their reasons: that a Doha agreement would establish a base level of sorts for the concessions developing countries would have to agree to in an RTA. Without a Doha agreement these countries were largely left to themselves to negotiate what trade deals they could get, and were therefore more susceptible to rich country power diplomacy in RTA negotiations.

If RTAs and FTAs are examples of how the free-trade discourse is furthered outside WTO negotiations, the late 2010s have also shown how this discourse has been met with a powerful political counter-discourse in some areas. In 2016 the UK held a referendum in which 52 per cent of the population voted to leave the EU – partly because of racism and nationalism, and partly because the Leave campaign promoted the idea that the industrial and economic restructuring driven by globalization and the EU's internal market could be dealt with better if Britain left. In the xenophobic rhetoric dominating the Leave (or 'Brexit') side in the referendum, these two processes often intermingled and provided the answer to the populist notion that 'all our industries are moving abroad while foreigners flood our country to take what jobs are left'. At the time of writing, Britain is negotiating its conditions for leaving the EU, and it is unclear whether – and to what degree – Brexit will lead to a reversal of the free-trade trend or a stricter migration policy. Meanwhile US President Donald Trump is attacking the free-trade discourse, NAFTA and the WTO from a similar nationalist and conservative standpoint. Trump has unilaterally left the negotiations on a free-trade agreement between the EU and the US, the Transatlantic Trade and Investment Partnership (TTIP), as well as the Trans-Pacific Partnership negotiations. He is raising tariff barriers for a host of Chinese imports, and has threatened to do the same against European imports. China has countered this with tariffs on imports typically produced in Trump-voting states in the US. In media reporting and debates, both Brexit and Trump's trade policies are causing considerable commotion. This is not only because of the potential economic effects of these processes, which will be substantial but manageable, but also (perhaps more) because they are clear and significant breaks with the free-trade discourse that is the foundation of the international institutional order of the WTO, the IMF, the World Bank, and many other global and regional institutions and organizations. Xi Jinping, general secretary of China's communist party, made a powerful impression by promoting global free trade at the 2017 World Economic Forum in Davos and negotiating free-trade deals with several African countries, but has also continued to protect the Chinese home market with tariffs and subsidies, as well as financial corporate support via a semi-private state-controlled banking system. It is too early to say whether these counter-processes will change global trade as we know it under the WTO. Suffice it to say that the free-trade regime is being challenged and sidestepped, and the agenda for future global trade is being rewritten. In terms of social and ecological sustainability, this may not be a bad thing.

Reconstructing trade

When analyzing and debating trade, we can easily fall into the trap of comparing the present free-trade regime to the idea of a world with no trade at all, or to the self-reliance policies of 1970s socialist development (more on these in the next chapter). International trade, however, has had many different shapes throughout history, and we need not confine our analysis to the concepts and theories inscribed into our present global institutions. In this last part of the chapter I will present a number of concepts helpful for rethinking how trade might be organized and pursued. I do not by any means pretend that this is an exhaustive list, nor is it a theory per se. It is just a list, covering both problem-solving and critical concepts.

Among the problem-solving concepts that might help us redesign the global economy within its present discursive and material order, I would first like to highlight two initiatives. The first is **aid for trade**, which is part of the Doha Round negotiations and has already led to some development cooperation. The aim of aid for trade is to assist developing countries to conduct international trade. This assistance can be in the form of infrastructure development, improvement of customs procedures, capacity-building as regards trade-related bureaucratic routines, support for producing export goods to certain standards and so on. The initiative is designed to give developing countries the opportunity to participate in international trade competition with industrial countries on more even terms. In terms of justice, it is an attempt to put poor countries in a better position to play a good trade game according to the rules of the international trade regime. The second initiative is the **Clean Development Mechanism** (CDM), a trade-related product of the 1997 Kyoto Protocol. Under the CDM, if a rich country assists a developing country to industrialize using more sustainable technology that makes the new industry emit less than a traditional industry would have done, the rich country can count the reduced emissions in the developing country as part of its own domestic emission reduction. Instead of buying emission rights for themselves, therefore, a rich country can create room to emit for its own polluting industries by helping poor countries build cleaner industries. In the long run this is meant to reduce or curb total global emissions. The Kyoto Protocol established a new international market for emission rights, with the CDM as an extra developmental quirk in this market, channelling part of the resources traded in it to sustainability projects in the South. Most of the projects getting CDM money concern electricity generation. While this mechanism has some good developmental and environmental consequences, the principle of deducting any reductions achieved from the emissions of rich countries smacks of colonial inequality, with poor countries supporting rich-world excesses. As an idea, however, the CDM is interesting in an institutional sense, exemplifying how international markets can be constructed to further sustainability.

A related problem-solving measure, complicated but in line with the prevailing economic discourse, would to price in **externalities** in global trade. The concept of externalities refers to the social and environmental effects caused by production and distribution that are not priced in or dealt with in ordinary market interaction. The Kyoto Protocol, for example, aims to put a price on the externality of greenhouse gas emissions, and if the cost of emission rights affects the consumer prices of products produced in Kyoto Protocol countries, the externality of emissions is priced in when the affected products are sold. Within the discipline of Environmental Economics this is a mainstay (Sterner and Coria, 2013). There are two major kinds of environmental externality: those that affect human and ecological well-being, and those that have negative impacts on the ecosystem. Both forms 'diminish the natural or environmental capital', in economistic terms. The difficulty in pricing in externalities is placing the right price on affected well-being and the right value on natural and environmental capital. What is a correct price for breathable air? What is the value of a river without dams? How much is biological diversity worth in monetary terms? If there is no conventional market for these entities, prices have to be set by political or technical decision-making. When these decisions are made, prices can – roughly speaking – be set in order to meet one of two opposed objectives. On the one hand, you can set prices low enough to minimize the effect on market interaction and growth; on the other hand, you can set prices high enough to minimize the harm to well-being and the reduction of environmental capital. The risk with the former is that you get no positive effects on sustainability at all (the Kyoto Protocol is often criticized for this), and the risk with the latter is that the market in the affected item dies altogether. As the present global economy is structured to maximize growth, we have so far got nowhere near killing, or even shrinking, markets by pricing in externalities. There is nothing stopping us from doing this, however. We could levy a water consumption fee on all cotton products. Many countries already have a carbon tax on fossil fuels, and such a tax could also be levied on international trade in fossil fuels. We could price the externalities of plastics so high that they become too valuable for bags and packaging, and thereby stop them from polluting the oceans. There is really no theoretical limit to what prices on externalities could achieve – the complicated part is deciding on and institutionalizing these prices. Another potential drawback of pricing in externalities is that it involves deferring to market activity to achieve a desired outcome. Market activities are creative and profit-driven, and you cannot tell exactly what they will do in advance – for instance, how they might handle higher prices on, or a new institutional framework for, trade in a specific group of items. If you levy a high environmental fee on coal, for instance, market actors may start burning plastic waste instead (if that is available at lower cost), and emissions may stay the same or even rise.

Some trade-related externalities are so destructive that an outright prohibition is called for. The Montreal Protocol of 1987 (effective from 1989) is the primary example of an international law that successfully banned the production of substances responsible for depleting the ozone layer in the atmosphere. The most important substance that the Montreal Protocol banned, and all countries subsequently phased out, was a range of chlorofluorocarbons (CFCs), which in gas form were used in refrigerators, air-conditioning appliances and aerosols. It took only 14 years from the scientific discovery of the destructiveness of CFCs for the international community to draw up and sign the Montreal Protocol. In global institutional terms, that is quick decision-making. Three reasons can be given to explain this unusual speed. First, a depleted ozone layer would have killed most of us, so something needed to be done. Second, in most cases there were technological substitutes readily available to replace CFCs. Third, most of the manufacturing costs for technological adjustment could be passed on to consumers. In comparison, the planetary greenhouse effect from burning fossil fuels has been known for about a hundred years, but the same imminent danger to humanity has only recently become clear. Nor have there been substitutes readily available to use after similarly quick and cheap technological adjustments. If, on the other hand, we arrived at an international consensus that global warming was a threat of a similar magnitude, there would be nothing to stop countries agreeing on a similar global treaty to phase out fossil fuels. Some countries have already decided to do so in the coming decades, but the pace of global restructuring is so slow that overall fossil emissions are likely to continue to rise ominously for several decades. Trade might seem only remotely connected to greenhouse gases and global warming, but the connection is only as loose as we allow it to become, and if we want to reconstruct the global political economy, the Montreal Protocol is an example of how coordinated changes in laws and institutions can be used to reach sustainability.

A social sustainability issue related to trade is that of labour standards and workers' rights. Much of what we buy today is produced in countries with low wages and then shipped to rich countries to be consumed. Price competition and bulimic consumption in the rich world therefore depend on international trade with industrializing countries with low wages. Naomi Klein's book *No Logo* (2000) is a critical analysis of working conditions in sweatshops around the world, where clothes by major global brands are sewn. This book raised the issue of labour rights higher up on the trade agenda. Nonetheless, developing states were reluctant to discuss this issue within the WTO framework, since they perceived it as a threat to their international competitiveness. Cheap labour is a production factor they want to use to stay competitive as exporters. At the same time, workers in the rich world can be paid less if they dress in clothes from Asia, use Asian cell phones and shoes, and the like, so protecting workers in the South would also mean that profits from working-class consumers in the North would shrink, as they would be able to consume less. There is nothing stopping us from including labour protection in trade agreements, and many regional free-trade agreements already contain such clauses (Polaski, 2004). These clauses are drawn up mostly because of state ambitions to create a level playing field for entrepreneurs in the FTA, with social justice and sustainability concerns a distant second. Applying the same logic on a global scale is entirely possible.

A concept helpful for determining the justice and equality of a trade relationship between two or more countries is **terms of trade** (ToT). In commodity terms, this is a measure for how many items of a typical export product the country must sell in order to finance the buying of a typical import item. How many cars must Sweden export to be able to import a box of oranges? How many tonnes of bauxite ore must Jamaica export to be able to import an X-ray machine? This is a price relation between products on the world market, and by studying this relation you can get a fairly good idea about how international trade relations are positioning different countries in the global trade order. A classic development problem for many countries has been deteriorating ToT, meaning that import prices, typically of industrial goods, have been rising while commodity prices have fallen, stagnated or fluctuated. To import the same quantity of, say, antibiotics or pumps, a country has had to export increasing quantities of sisal or copper. Prices for industrial goods can be influenced by the producer through changes in technology or quality or the like, while the prices of commodities are largely dependent on how industrial demand in the North changes with the business cycle and technological development. Developing countries are **price-takers**, having to accept what they can get for their exports, while capital- and knowledge-intensive industries can influence prices for their products to a much larger extent. This observation underpinned the critique of the dependency school theorists, and also lay behind the NIEO proposal put forward by the G77 in the UN General Assembly during the 1960s and 1970s (see Chapter 2). This new order would be characterized by features like fixed price relations between industrial goods and raw materials, international buffer storage of commodities to keep world market prices stable above certain thresholds and price controls on commodities to guarantee developing countries a minimal export income from their production (White, 1975). As IR students know, the UN General Assembly cannot make decisions binding for all members (only the Security Council can do that), and this meant that although there was a majority vote for the NIEO, it did not materialize because the OECD countries did not want it. They were doing well within the colonial structures of the global economy. The only thing to come out of this debate was the establishment of the United Nations Conference on Trade and Development (UNCTAD), set up to research global trade and investment on behalf of the developing world. When reforming and/or reconstructing global trade, reopening the NIEO debate would be one way to restart the work for a more just global order.

Another, more critical, analysis could connect to the discourse of **degrowth** or **post-growth**. This analytical approach starts from the premise that we have enough money and stuff in the world today, and that a furthering of free trade in order to maximize the Ricardian welfare effect is both misguided and ecologically disastrous (Jackson, 2009). In order to allow for a heavier ecological footprint from poor countries, whose people are in desperate need of more energy, food, textiles and the like, the rich world needs to scale down its consumption of most things and start on a trajectory towards stable or falling GDP figures, while working to restructure its economies for environmental and social sustainability. Integral to this project is a decrease in international trade, and a new global trade order that maximizes sustainability rather than the Ricardian welfare effect. Such an order might be built around global sustainability standards for all traded items, stipulating how and with which materials traded items should be produced.

The EU, for instance, already refuses to import anything that does not live up to the standards of the REACH (Registration, Evaluation, Authorisation and Restriction of Chemicals) directive. In a post-growth trading order, such standards could be set (globally or nationally) with much more radical criteria as regards social and ecological sustainability. This would not only stop unsustainable products from entering certain markets, but would also influence production aiming for export to these markets.

During the 1960s and 1970s several developing countries embarked on a self-reliance or **delinking** development strategy. Under socialist or communist ideologies these countries aimed to break out of the capitalist global economic structure, and build a national industry planned and designed to produce for their own specific development needs. In terms of social development, such as health and education, these countries often did rather well. But in terms of economic sustainability the new industries often faired pretty badly in international comparison, producing below average international quality at prices above the international average. The trade balance of these countries subsequently deteriorated, and developed into trade deficits and macroeconomic problems of various sorts. While this was a problem in the era of competition between capitalism and socialism, the technology of the 2010s in combination with the sustainability needs of the planet might make the delinking strategy attractive again. At present it is mostly clothed in xenophobic nationalist rhetoric in India, the US, Europe and elsewhere, but the trading strategy could equally well be formulated in terms of sustainability, and the need for a country or region to delink from the global economy and trade regime in order to shrink its ecological footprint and develop sustainable production behind trade barriers. The possibility of delinking from colonial and capitalist trade, while maintaining international bonds in terms of solidarity, migration, development and culture, is a valuable lesson that can be learned from developing countries of the self-reliance era. A delinking today, following the logic and discourse of sustainability and with today's technology, would produce a different result than what the Southern import-substituting industries experienced in the 1970s.

A special and selective type of delinking has been at the centre of the recent debate about **food sovereignty**. This comes from a critical perspective on the free-trade regime generally, but focuses specifically on the food production and rural development of nations. The logic behind this critical concept is both social and ecological. The social dimension takes note of the fact that farming is still the most common profession in the world, and since a majority of the world's farmers run very small businesses and use much of their produce for individual family subsistence, it is unfair and insecure to expose these farmers to competition from the industrial agriculture of the rich world. The ecological sustainability dimension of food sovereignty rests on the judgement that the international baseline standards for agriculture are insufficient to protect ecological diversity and sustainability (Bello, 2002). Instead of allowing industrial (and other) farmers to maximize their yields by using fertilizers and pesticides with unclear or destructive consequences, each nation and region should protect its environment and agriculture according to its specific biotopes, as well as its farming needs and traditions. In order to achieve food sovereignty, a country must be allowed to use tariffs, quotas, subsidies and NTBs as it sees fit, but under the current WTO agreements this is not possible, which leads proponents of food sovereignty to argue that the WTO is endangering both the environment and the subsistence of a majority of the world's farmers.

Yet another critical concept as regards global trade is that of the **commons**. This term used to refer to land, fishing waters and other resources that were collectively owned and managed by those using them and depending on them. As many of the raw materials and natural resources of the world are needed by all of humanity and not just commercial businesses, there is a push from sustainability quarters to regard more resources as commons. This would mean that things like oil reserves, mineral ores, drinking water and the like would no longer be treated as tradable goods belonging to certain countries or corporations. Instead these resources would be handled as commons, able to be utilized sustainably by deserving interests according to some form of commons regime. Elinor Ostrom has shown how commons are managed by **collective action**, which historically has been very successful in balancing preservation of the resource with optimization of production and outtake (Ostrom, 1990). We are already seeing this develop globally (but slowly) as regards management of the oceans and regulating fish stocks. Under similar global trusteeships, a great many other resources could be turned into commons. This would require institutional changes in which individual nation states would lose their sovereign control over natural resources on, beneath and above their territories. Politically this is sensitive, but nation states are already giving up control over things like mineral ores by selling mining rights to global corporations. Similar concessions would be possible to sell, give or let (or similar) to a global trusteeship overseeing the use of and dependence on new commons.

Conclusion

In the globalization era we often hear the saying that 'global problems demand global solutions'. This is not correct. Global problems can be handled and solved on any political level. Positive as the Montreal Protocol was for our survival, it has also led to the perception that all global issues can and should be decided on by a global assembly of heads of state, and handled by a global organization. As regards trade, the existence of the WTO has led many to expect similar solutions to many problems pertaining to trade from this organization. But as Dani Rodrik (2011) has forcefully argued, there are many different solutions to trade-related issues, and it is only if we want to save the global free-trade regime that we are in need of a single global solution. We are already witnessing the development of differing trade policies among the world's major economic powers. There is an increase in the number of countries deviating from the WTO's Ricardian orthodoxy, and the universal and uniform adherence to the freer-trade trajectory of the organization is disappearing. What will come instead is not yet entirely clear, but most likely there will be a historically significant opportunity for countries to try different recipes for sustainable economic development. These recipes will all have different roles for trade. Whether these roles are compatible with institutions such as the WTO is an open question. The only thing history tells us is that international trade will live on. If carefully analyzed, managed and institutionalized, it could be made fair and sustainable after a reconstruction of the global political economy, even if we end up with many different national and regional trade regimes.

Further reading

For understanding the global free-trade regime, and the discourse on which the WTO is founded, the WTO's own website (www.wto.org) is very informative. The website offers an educational and thorough justification both for the expansion of free trade and for the organization itself. As always, it is also both interesting and inspiring to read the original text that helped found the discourse. David Ricardo's *On the Principles of Political Economy and Taxation* (1817) contains much of his influential thought, and can be read freely on the website of the Library of Economics and Liberty (www.econlib.org). In 2010 Soo Yeon Kim published a critical political study on the effects of the GATT and WTO systems, and laid bare how this institutional construction has benefited OECD countries much more than developing countries. The name of her book is *Power and the Governance of Global Trade*. Cecilia Albin examined WTO negotiations in her 2001 book *Justice and Fairness in International Negotiation*. In 2012 a research group under her leadership published a special issue of *International Negotiation* based on the project 'Improving the Effectiveness of Multilateral Negotiations'. Trade data in figures can be found on the WTO website, while research on this data is conducted both by the WTO and under the umbrella of UNCTAD, and can be found at www.unctad.org.

An economist critical of the 'hyperglobalization' caused by the WTO free-trade order is Dani Rodrik, who recently brought out a volume titled *Straight Talk on Trade*, and frequently publishes research on his home page on Harvard University's website. Another prominent critic of the WTO and free trade from a Southern perspective is Martin Khor, executive director of the South Centre. A great deal of trade-related critical research by Khor and others is published at www.southcentre.org. Walden Bello's work often addresses unjust patterns and practices of the global trade regime, and his book *Deglobalization* (2002) had considerable impact. The same year, Ha-Joon Chang published *Kicking Away the Ladder*, in which he shows that no country has ever industrialized under a laissez-faire free-trade policy.

What Development?

Since at least the birth of the nation–state system with the Peace of Westphalia in 1648, the question of how to develop society has occupied modern rulers and politicians (Hettne, 2009). Social life, the economy, science and politics – and the security provision for all of these – are developed by means of political interventions. History may evolve according to certain dynamics, such as Smith's human propensity for market interaction or Marx's exploitation in capitalist structures, but knowledge-based, intentional political (and other) measures are seen as able to change the course of events so that society develops in a desired direction.[1] The role model and ultimate goal for this idea of development has throughout its history been the richest and most powerful industrial nation, where people live in a society and situation characterized by what Rostow (1990) termed 'high mass consumption'. A logical corollary to the idea of modernization as development and development as modernization is that some countries are more developed and modern than others. While we have a couple of role model nations in the world, the rest of the world is on its way to becoming like those countries but is at the moment not there yet; and the countries far back on this trajectory to high mass consumption are called 'underdeveloped' or 'developing'.

European colonial powers drew on this 'civilizational' idea, in combination with racist conceptions of the colonized peoples, to legitimize their exploitation and oppression of the colonies. The colonized were said to be subject to developmental and civilizational interventions by benevolent imperial powers (such as Kipling's 'white man's burden' that we discussed in Chapter 2). In case these interventions were received unwillingly, the colonial subjects had to be forced, punished or rewarded to obey, to improve their own and everyone's situation. For most colonial subjects and agents this was mere superficial window-dressing, badly covering the looting, enslavement and oppression of colonized countries and people.

With the incumbent dissolution of political empires after the Second World War, US president Harry S. Truman, in his 1949 inauguration speech, outlined the new Western hegemon's view of development and the global political economy. In his view the world had been divided into three parts. The first part consisted of the Western industrialized countries allied to the US economically and/or militarily. The second part was the Soviet Union and its allies, who were enemies of the first. The third part consisted of non-industrialized countries with widespread poverty. In this speech President Truman presented three arguments for why the Western world should assist developing countries economically and politically with ODA. The first argument rested on altruistic premises, stating simply that it was an obligation of the haves to support the have nots so that the latter could develop. The second argument was based on economic self-interest, with Truman stating, 'Experience shows that our commerce with other countries expands as they progress industrially and economically' (Truman, 1949).[2] The third argument was more complicated, but decisive for the formation of the global political economy generally and development assistance policy specifically. Truman stated, 'More than half the people of the world are living in conditions approaching misery. Their food is inadequate. They are victims of disease. Their economic life is primitive and stagnant. Their poverty is a handicap and a threat both to them and to more prosperous areas' (Truman, 1949). The last sentence here is key, as it presented foreign poverty as a threat. The subtext was that if the US did not help those in poverty, it ran the risk that they would either resort to communist development and become allies of the enemy, or strike violently at 'more prosperous areas' like the US. In this speech, the altruistic logic, the self-interested interdependence logic and the geopolitical logic for starting ODA in collaboration with international allies was spelled out clearly. The combination of these logics was termed 'the geopolitics of poverty', and came to frame the modern project, US hegemony and development thinking in the early post-war era (Hettne, 2009).

As colonized countries reached independence after the Second World War, they strove to develop economically and politically by pursuing policies similar to those that had enabled European countries to industrialize and develop. This was during the Keynesian era, and the strategy involved a strong state participating in the running and development of newly independent market economies. The state was supposed to play a vital part in the economy, and build and run production of what the country needed, if private entrepreneurs did not or were not sufficiently capable. The state should also actively steer the economy, support it in business downturns and cool it down in boom periods. Vital in this modernizing development strategy was international trade, expected to bring export earnings to countries that could be used to finance necessary imports. The relation between states and markets during this first independence era can be described as **corporatist**, meaning that the public and private interests were understood to collaborate and support each other to make national economies grow and modernize. The experience of Europe and America in the 1930s, where the building of welfare states coloured the writing of their development history, indicated that this could be a successful strategy, and for some countries it was, for a little while. But then it changed.

What became increasingly apparent during the 1960s and 1970s was that the former colonies were locked into a global economic structure that gave them a role as commodities producers for the industry of rich countries. This role was something that the new hegemon had envisioned and planned for. But it was not primarily the will of the hegemon that exploited these countries and kept them in an economically subordinate position, but the global economic structure itself. In Chapter 4 we discussed ToT as a central analytical category helpful in examining the effects of international trade, and what the newly independent nations discovered was that they had to export increasing amounts of their traditional export goods from the colonial era in order to even maintain stable levels of necessary imports. In other words, they had deteriorating ToT. Attempts to finance the modernization of their economies with export earnings appeared increasingly futile, since there was no chance that these revenues would cover the imports of machinery, chemicals, knowledge and technology necessary for substantial developmental undertakings. Dependency school theorists such as Andre Gunder Frank (1966) described the former colonies as locked into 'underdevelopment', where they had to stick to their old low-tech commodity production to finance necessary imports just to survive while getting increasingly exploited in global capitalist structures, and therefore had no chance to develop economically or technically to break out of this position.

Another problem, aggravating the economic difficulties, was that many countries had institutional problems. Before independence, laws, regulations, the bureaucracy and its routines were all designed for colonial control and to the benefit of the imperial state. After independence, the new states had to rewrite their laws, redesign regulations and populate related bureaucratic positions with local people. Since many bureaucrats who had run the institutional structure disappeared when the imperial state withdrew, new bureaucrats had to be trained and installed to make the young states function. The states were constructed as blueprint copies of European states set up to govern countries with large territories and populations, many languages and cultures, and often in parallel with traditional institutional and religious institutions and traditions expected to co-exist in compatibility with the new states. The institutional structures, therefore, had to be reinvented and redesigned at the same time as they were meant to start to function for the new states striving to create economic and social development. That institutional efficiency, stability and predictability were not prevalent during this era is no surprise, and that this slowed down private commercial activity is also clear (de Soto, 2001).

In the 1960s and 1970s several newly independent countries chose a development path inspired by the dependency school and post–Marxist analysis. In economic terms this meant that they started building production capacity to break the dependence on imports from OECD countries, which also meant that they aimed to break out of the colonial economic structures for which their export goods were produced. This strategy included the building of industry for local needs and purposes, inspired by the delinking trade strategy (see Chapter 4). This economic development strategy was termed **import substitution industrialization** (ISI) and aimed for a higher degree of self-reliance and local production, which would make decolonized development possible. This alternative development path had a stronger focus on social development and sustainability, and industrialization was combined with campaigns for literacy, immunization, public health care, free higher education and the like. In terms of education and health this strategy often produced good results quite fast, such as regards Tanzanian literacy or the Cuban health sector. In terms of macroeconomic development the picture was less rosy, for three reasons. First, the new industry could not compete well with similar foreign production. Since it was typically state-owned, its ability to produce what was needed was regarded as more important than doing so efficiently and profitably. Productivity – the amount of time, labour and resources reserved for the production of each item – came second to needs fulfilment, which over time made ISI industry occupy disproportionate amounts of a country's resources (as compared to if productivity had been prioritized). Second, in the Cold War logic of the era, countries that embarked on this development path were often driven into the arms of the Soviet Union, as collaborations with Western commercial actors and countries were cancelled. But the Soviet Union had less efficient technology to offer and an institutional economic structure that did not promote increased productivity or technological development to the same degree as capitalist development. Third, the institutional and general societal adaptation deemed necessary for this development strategy was often so large that everyday life became disorganized during the transitions, which also affected the economic development of these countries negatively.

During the Cold War era, the two superpowers applied a geostrategic logic to development cooperation, which led them to military and strategic collaborations with countries pursuing development policies that were to their liking. This often involved propping up or installing (by supporting or instigating military coups d'état) political dictators of varying brutality and corruptibility. Mobuto Sese Seko in Zaire (today's Democratic Republic of the Congo) and Pinochet in Chile are examples of US-supported dictators, while Siad Barre in Somalia and Fidel Castro in Cuba were supported by the Soviet Union. I will not discuss here whose dictatorship was the worst or most illegitimate; suffice it to say that the two competing hegemons typically did not make development policy any easier with their ideological and military struggle over the Third World.

Overdevelopment in the North

Meanwhile in the rich world, industrial development began to display serious problems with environmental sustainability. The first signal that something was seriously wrong was the inability for birds of prey to hatch. Various poisonous substances accumulated in these top predators, which made the shells of their eggs so thin the birds often crushed them in the nests. Rachel Carson's book *Silent Spring* (1962) was a wake-up call, warning that if nothing was done, we would no longer be able to hear the birds sing in springtime. Since then, emissions of poisonous substances and the like have been reduced in the rich world, while the process of reduction has been much slower in industrializing countries, which often promote lax environmental policies as a boon when trying to attract industrial investment from abroad.

Another inherent problem with the modern project in rich countries was pointed out by the Club of Rome, an environmental sustainability think tank, in 1973. Based on statistical analysis they argued that if we continued on the 1970s paths of industrialization, production, population growth and consumption, the world would run into huge shortages of food and raw materials in a couple of decades, and there would be such environmental damage that the biosphere would be destroyed. The solution they proposed was a cleaning-up of industrial technology and a curbing of population growth. Industrial technology has since developed, and some of the worst fears that the Club of Rome evoked have not materialized. The issue of 'overpopulation' has also been taken off the political agenda, since it is morally impossible in the era of Human Rights to talk about the existence of human beings as unwanted or destructive. Who should be considered part of the surplus population, exactly? And who should have the power to decide that? For some countries rapid population growth can cause problems, if there is a lack of resources, that is correct. But this is a problem of resources and their allocation, not one concerning the existence of actual persons. Many areas in Europe are as densely populated as India or Rwanda, and the ecological footprint of each of these Europeans is many times larger than that of the average Indian or Rwandan. So the problem description of the Club of Rome has changed, and even though we are still on our way for the same ecological disaster, the problem today is described as a problem of lifestyles, consumption and technology, and the (non-)existence of human beings are not part of the equation for how to solve it. The world produces enough food to feed 11 billion people, but a third of all food produced goes to waste. This means that even with the present production and consumption patterns overpopulation is not an issue in terms of nutrition.

The debt trap

During both the modernization era and that of import substitution, many countries borrowed substantially from abroad in order to finance their development projects. After OPEC raised oil prices in 1973, this borrowing increased among oil importing Third World countries, both to buy oil and also to compensate for decreasing export earnings when OECD growth slowed down as spiralling energy costs claimed a larger chunk of their GDP. This increase in Third World borrowing was furthered by the interest of commercial banks in finding investment opportunities for the 'petrodollars' that flowed from oil exporting countries to banks in Europe and the US. These banks could not just sit on sacks of US dollars and pay out interest to oil exporters; there was need for them to find borrowers if they were not to make huge losses from petrodollar deposits. Logical candidates for this lending were the US, whose treasury bonds absorbed some of this liquidity, and Third World countries. Since the banks were flooded with petrodollars, they offered extremely attractive conditions for countries willing to borrow. With inflation at the time running almost as high as the nominal interest rates on these loans, the real interest rate[3] was near zero. For a finance minister in a country with developmental investment and import bills to finance, these loans appeared very attractive and safe. Especially in all the cases where the banks had the assistance of IMF staff in designing the lending agreements. This IMF participation was meant to help borrowers and lenders arrive at loan deals beneficial to both parties. For most of the 1970s this was also the case, but in 1979 something happened which made the debt trap close.

In 1979 a new chairman to the Federal Reserve, Paul Volcker, was appointed with the explicit purpose and task to bring down inflation in the US. The Keynesian Economics paradigm for fine tuning the economy, with government spending in business downturns and tightening budgets in boom times, did not work as planned. After the oil shock Western economies had tried to speed up growth by increasing government spending, but this extra money did not generate investment and employment opportunities. When national economies did not grow as planned the extra money sloshing around in the system only produced inflation, and the job of Paul Volcker was to stop it in the US. He did so by using a new (at the time) theory on monetary policy called 'monetarism', which basically said that you can control the inflation rate by controlling the money supply: if there is too much money circulating in the economy, make people put more money into the banks; if there is too little money circulating you should aim to get more money circulating in the economy. The instrument for regulating the money supply is the interest rate of the central banks. When they raise the interest rate that private banks have to pay them, private banks have to raise interest rates to their customers, both depositors and borrowers. So, in order to stem inflation in the US economy Paul Volcker and the US Federal Reserve raised the interest rate, US citizens put more money in the banks, investment and debt-financed consumption slowed down, increased unemployment put a downward pressure on wages, and US inflation went down. From a domestic US perspective, Volcker was successful with his task. Other central banks had to follow and raise their interest rate, so that financial capital should not flow out of their countries seeking higher returns in the US. Interest rates all over the Western world went up, slowing down growth and investment while increasing unemployment.

An unfortunate side effect, not generally considered at the time, was that the higher interest rate did not just affect lending in the US and the West, but all lending in the world. Consequently the calculations done for the loans that developing states had taken in petrodollars were completely trashed. When interest rates went up and inflation down, the real interest rates on these loans were suddenly not around zero, but rather 10 or 15 per cent per year. To add to the misery, the business downturn in the West made demand for commodities and industrial inputs go down, which led to decreasing export earnings in the South. Since the loans had to be repaid in dollars, decreasing export earnings were the least wanted thing when debt service costs skyrocketed. In the summer of 1982 Mexico was the first country to announce that they would not be able to pay back to its creditor banks as scheduled in the autumn. Many other countries in Latin America, Africa and Asia followed in Mexico's footsteps, declaring their debt burden too heavy. A general rule in banking is that a loan given to someone becomes an asset and a future money stream on the books of the lender. After the petrodollar lending spree a large portion of Western banks' assets consisted of claims on Third World states. The debt crisis, therefore, was a threat not only to the countries overwhelmed by the costs of debt, but also to the banks that had made out these loans. If indebted countries defaulted completely on repayments, several big banks – today they would probably have been termed 'systemically important' – would cease to be creditworthy. The international financial system, as well as the international system of payments, was in danger and the IMF moved centre stage in the global political economy.

The debt crisis made the IMF ascend to the role of first global arbiter of development policy in the 1980s. This role was not a shift in the organization's mandate, but a consequence of the widespread need for IMF money to handle the debt crisis, and a country in need of IMF money must follow IMF advice. As described in Chapter 3, the job of the IMF is to stabilize the international system of payments by assuring that all member states are creditworthy. Assuring creditworthiness was done by what is called 'financial stabilization': a process in which a country was first handed a list of measures that had to be undertaken if any IMF money was to be made accessible, and was subsequently given access to this money in proportion to how well they undertook the measures on the list. In the 1980s these lists were densely ideological documents, specifying how the debt-ridden countries should adjust their economies according to neoliberal economic thinking. The swing from Keynesian to neoliberal Macroeconomics was part of the general rightward shift on the ideological scale around 1980. What could not be done in the rich world in terms of neoliberal adjustment (because of the political cost and popular unrest it would produce), could be done with Southern indebted countries and populations as real-world Economics laboratories. The lab assistants of this new thinking were IMF staff, and their primary instrument was the list with measures, called 'conditionalities', the undertaking of which were conditional for getting access to IMF money.

The lists of conditionalities pertaining to IMF and World Bank lending during the 1980s displayed a remarkable uniformity in different countries. The term 'Washington Consensus' was coined to capture the nature of this uniformity (Williamson, 1990), referring to a common discourse among IMF, the World Bank and the US State Department, which are all based in Washington. Central tenets in this discourse were a strong belief in the constructive capacity of market forces, and a disbelief in the state and politics to produce economic development or to constructively engage in it. Strengthening and disembedding market forces was therefore a primary objective of the SAPs of the Washington Consensus. As more and more countries became dependent on IMF and World Bank money, SAP reconstruction swept over the South. Such a thorough societal and economic reconstruction, based on a uniform discourse and with a strong ideological motive force, rarely happens in the world. It is instructive to describe a typical list of SAP conditionalities in closer detail, and the consequences these would have, since this description indicates the sheer magnitude of what is possible. For even though the SAPs were disastrous, they teach us important things about global economic reconstruction.

SAP reconstruction

The SAPs were pursued with the IMF and the World Bank working in tandem, not always peacefully, but at the same time in the same countries. The SAP lists were a mix of measures – from both these Bretton Woods siblings – aimed at financial stabilization, alongside the adjustment of economic structures meant to help countries grow economically and participate in the world economy efficiently. None of the organizations has any mandate to intervene politically in domestic affairs of member states (as explained in Chapter 3), but are supposed to act technically and scientifically according to the best Economics knowledge to stabilize the international system of payments (the IMF) and develop the productive resources of their members (the World Bank). The neoliberal nature of the dominating Economics discourse in the 1980s, and the promotion of this discourse by strong states like Reagan's US and Thatcher's Britain, nonetheless made the SAPs into strong political interventions in indebted states. As we describe the main points on the list of conditionalities, the political nature of these interventions will become clear.

The first and central item on the list was **budget balance**. From an IMF perspective this is crucial: in order to stabilize the international system of payments, states that issue money in this system must be creditworthy, and if official budgets are not in or moving towards balance the decreasing creditworthiness of the state in question is endangered, which means that the whole payment system becomes weaker. The overarching and most important measure, in the eyes of the IMF, was to restore the budget balance quickly after the debt crisis hit. SAPs therefore meant drastic cuts in government spending, cutting down on everything from military spending to health care and education. This also meant that citizens had to pay part of the costs for public services leading to school fees and hospital fees. These quick and drastic cuts materialized in society as serious and often detrimental cuts in general welfare provisions resulting in reduced health and education standards, alongside increased unemployment as public jobs disappeared. The effects of budget cuts were typically played out according to local gendered priorities, so that male needs were seen to first. If the army and the schools needed money for wages, the army was paid first. If a family could afford only one school fee, the son went to school. One cut in public spending that tended to breed extra public protest was the cut in subsidies. On the one hand, these cuts, often complete scrapping, were meant to ease government budgets. On the other hand, they were part of a drive to 'get the prices right', meaning that market mechanisms should determine retail prices. Subsidies were seen as disturbing and thwarting 'true' market prices, leading to inefficiency and backwardness. In everyday life, the cutting or scrapping of subsidies meant drastic increases in the cost of food, fuels and other staple items.

The other side of balancing state budgets was tax reforms. Before the SAPs, many states had financed themselves with high corporate taxes, wealth taxes and customs fees, and to a lesser extent with income taxes and VATs. Since the SAPs generally were striving to promote corporate activity and exports, to raise hard currency so foreign debts could be repaid, the tax reforms shifted the collection to tax bases that did not affect entrepreneurship and exports in (what economists at the time regarded as) negative ways. Corporate and wealth taxes were therefore cut to stimulate business, and instead VAT was typically introduced. The logic was that corporations move production if taxes are high, and rich people dodge taxes and take their savings elsewhere if you have high wealth taxes, but consumption in a country cannot move. Everyone's daily consumption is an immobile tax base, so a VAT is a tax that will be easier to collect and will not flee the country. Such tax reforms were supposed to stabilize and raise government revenue, and when put in place they sometimes did. The distributional effect, however, was politically contentious as it shifted a large part of state financing from profits of corporations and rich people's savings to everyone's daily consumption; and since poor people tend to spend most of their incomes on the consumer items on which a VAT is levied, the tax as a proportion of the individual tax payers' incomes falls more heavily on the poor. A new five per cent VAT on the retail price of staple foods means quite little if you can save large parts of your income; if you can save nothing it means you have to reduce how much staple food you consume. The purpose of this 'broadening of the tax base' (as the reform was called) was to stimulate entrepreneurship and stabilize government finances. The public protests often spurred by an SAP the IMF termed 'political costs', thus covering the political intervention in a veil of economic scienticity while passing on the responsibility for the resulting 'IMF riots' to the indebted governments.

The public spending still possible after budget balancing should go to activities benefiting the poorest. The logic for this was that it is money spent on the poorest that has the highest developmental effects. This meant, for instance, that universities and higher education should be scaled down, as part of government budgets, and the money saved there should go to primary schools instead. The literacy of 20 children has a higher value added for a country in terms of national productivity than, say, one new BA in Development Economics, but the cost for the respective teaching is comparable. Under SAP conditionality a country had to choose the reading capacity of 20 children, and university students had to handle much more of the cost of their education themselves. While literacy is of course good, the university students who had to handle raised tuition fees and classes with hundreds of additional fellow students had a harder time seeing the benefit. Governments having to prioritize between developmental efforts in this way faced many impossible choices.

One monetary conditionality on the SAP list was that a country had to achieve a 'competitive exchange rate'. Typically this meant devaluation of a fixed exchange rate, thus making the country's currency cheaper for foreigners to buy. When a country's currency becomes cheaper for foreigners, everything produced within that country also becomes cheaper for foreigners (if the producers' wages and bills are paid in the local currency). The devaluations under SAP were meant to stimulate international demand for the exports of indebted countries, in order for these states to get incomes in hard currencies that they could use to finance their debt service. The other side of the devaluation coin is that all imports become more expensive for locals to buy. Theoretically this will stimulate entrepreneurs to produce for the local market, as competition from imports will ease. But if local entrepreneurs do not respond to increasing import prices with local production, imports just become more expensive and will claim a larger portion of a household's disposable income. For many things, such as petroleum or high-tech products, entrepreneurs in many instances did not have a realistic option to produce for the local market. When this was the case, devaluations just translated into increased retail prices of everyday products such as kerosene and pain killers, without stimulating local production and with a substantial poverty effect.

To further stimulate exports, liberalizing the policy for international trade was added to the list of conditionalities. This meant a lowering of import tariffs, with the hope that trading partners would do the same and open up to one's own exports. Eradication of export tariffs (introduced for the sake of government revenue and/or to steer products to the domestic market) would also have to be taken away. These tariffs were deemed extra detrimental for entrepreneurs since they added to a country's export prices. Theoretically, this liberalization will stimulate local industry in two ways: first the extra demand for exports will increase entrepreneurs' revenue from abroad and stimulate investment; second it will open up the economy to foreign competition which will force industry to raise productivity and keep a check on costs. The IMF and the World Bank also advised the countries to specialize in the Ricardian way to export whatever they were able to produce at a comparative advantage. This trade policy reform is logical on paper. In real life, however, industrial entrepreneurs in countries opening up in this way often found them self in a landslide of imports priced below their local production costs. Since many countries were advised to specialize in the same export production at the same time, the world market for typical export products, such as coffee, were flooded, which drove down prices to levels far below what individual coffee producing countries had planned for in their specialization policy. So domestic industries were not primarily stimulated but crushed, and export earnings became sluggish and lower than planned and needed.

To stimulate the building of a financial system, needed for market economic and capitalist development, the policies for interest rates and lending were deregulated. Banks had previously often had a ceiling for interest rates, and lending had often been politically steered to projects deemed especially valuable for national development. Apart from engendering corruption, these policies were also considered market disturbing, and instead the private initiative would be allowed to 'get the prices right' also for bank lending. Deregulation of interest rates and lending meant that banks and other financial institutions could demand whatever interest rate they deemed appropriate for a specific loan. What usually happened after deregulation was that commercial interest rates shot up, which is quite natural if you consider the level of risk creditors had to be compensated for in developing countries undergoing major restructuring. What also happened was that ordinary loans became impossible to finance for ordinary small- and medium-sized businesses, which slowed down ordinary private and entrepreneurial investment considerably.

In order to attract foreign direct investment (FDI) – that is, in order to encourage TNCs to set up subsidiaries in indebted countries – another conditionality on the lists was building an 'investment-friendly climate'. In political terms this is the same thing as changing the laws and regulations of a country. But IMF and the World Bank are not to interfere in a member's internal politics, you might object. And yes, that is correct, but allegedly the staff of these institutions was still working according to the best economic theory available at the time, and the neoliberalization of the laws of indebted states was presented as a scientific process, not politics. What the Economics of the time stipulated was that FDI would bring real and financial capital, technological development, knowledge and skills, network connections to the global market and that all these things would spread from the TNC subsidiaries out into the country and contribute to economic development. To what extent this actually happened is a matter of debate, and the jury is still out on the issue. Typical changes made were: tax holidays for a period of five to ten years; free repatriation of profits, so that the subsidiary could send home what money it made to its foreign owners; rewriting labour laws to make it easier to sack and hire employees; restraining the power of labour unions; rewriting and commercializing the laws of land ownership and the land rights of indigenous peoples; and rewriting the more specific laws and regulations pertaining to these overarching changes. The cost for creating this investment-friendly climate in many instances was higher than the returns, especially when FDI did not happen to any substantial degree.

One part of this investment-friendly climate, meant to benefit also domestic entrepreneurs, was an overhaul of the bureaucracy. In the general institutional reorganization since independence, and during the ISI era, regulations and specific laws had been added and bureaucratic routines established, so that commercial activities were hampered and slowed down by many specific and sometimes haphazard and opaque rules, each one requiring its own form and official stamp to be cleared. A nickname for such bureaucratic friction is 'red tape', and friction in commercial activity was to be minimized during SAPs. The Bretton Woods institutions often had a strong case for this conditionality. But in the overhaul of public administrations, and given the big cuts in public budgets, what happened was often that bureaucrats were sacked, some regulations changed or scrapped, and all the remaining paperwork ended up on the desks of a small cadre of remaining public officials. As piles of applications and complaints grew on their desks, the opportunity for corruption grew with them. A Mexican cab driver once told me that it costs the equivalent of four month's revenue to get a taxi license approved, if you don't pay your application will rest at the bottom of the pile for God knows how long, and you have no business as long as it rests there. While such corruption can't be blamed on the SAPs alone, the overhaul of bureaucracies and shrinking of administrations did not help to diminish it.

A central conditionality, rooted deeply in the neoclassical Economics and neoliberalism of the SAP era, was privatization. The neoliberal discourse had one master signifier: politicians are always maximizing votes while entrepreneurs are always maximizing profits, and consequently private entrepreneurship will always deliver result more efficiently than politicians or public work will. Privatizing state-owned enterprises, infrastructure, health care and the like could be constructed as private businesses, and therefore became conditional for accessing IMF and World Bank resources. The one off proceeds from these privatizations was to be used in financial stabilization (primarily debt repayment), and once the private entrepreneurs had started working the expectation was that they would speed up productivity and modernize operations to the benefit of national development. SAPs meant fire sales of national and public resources in the South. The private owners, however, did not necessarily modernize and speed up productivity in the factories and infrastructure they had acquired. Sometimes larger and quicker profits could be made by, say, tearing up a railroad and selling it as metal scrap, instead of renovating it and starting transport operations. A story told to me by Ibrahim Shao from Dar es Salaam about a Tanzanian juice factory is perhaps emblematic. During the ISI era, Tanzania built a factory for canned fruit juices; it had a system for factory inputs picking up fruit harvests from farmers in the area securing a steady market income for those, it delivered the fruits to the factory where it was pressed and canned, and after this the factory distributed it through its own network connected to retail stores around the country. When this operation was privatized, the new owners did their calculations with the result that fruit deliveries to the factory were cancelled because that operation was too inefficient. The factory was deemed inefficient and too costly to rebuild, so it was closed. The one thing the new owners kept was the distribution network to retail stores, which they used to distribute canned fruit juices imported from India. In the business sense, this meant that the privatized firm became efficient and delivered a profit, but at the cost of a ruined fruit market for local farmers and lost jobs for the factory workers. How farmers and workers coped with this I do not know.

Each item on this list of conditionalities, in reality containing hundreds of specific measures the undertaking of which were conditional for access to IMF and World Bank lending, may seem logical and called for in specific instances in the global economy of the 1980s. What made the SAPs so destructive was the ideological radicalism in the neoliberal Economics design of them, and the forceful pushing through of the programmes giving countries perhaps two or three years to prove they had made policy of the whole list. The poverty effects of VAT introductions and devaluations, the unemployment created by budget cuts and privatizations, the children who were not sent to school because of school fees, the economic and social disorder created by the institutional restructuring, all this slowed down and pushed back social and economic development at a great human cost in lives and lost opportunities. In Africa, Russia, Latin America and the other places where the Bretton Woods institutions pushed through SAPs and exposed economies and populations to their 'shock therapy' the social effects were horrendous. After having tried the same recipe in Asian countries after the financial crash in 1997–8 the Bretton Woods rethought their conditionalities and adjusted somewhat. The IMF has also asked for forgiveness for its ideological exactions during the SAP era and 'the lost decade for development' during the debt crisis.

In the late 1990s the IMF renamed their Enhanced Structural Adjustment Facility into a 'Poverty Reduction and Growth Facility', to signal that they had changed. This change consisted in three major adjustments. First, the programmes conditional for lending should no longer be designed by visiting IMF and World Bank consultants, but instead be written by local politicians, academics, civil society representatives and the like, in consultation with Bretton Woods staff. This made the programmes less ideological and much better adjusted for the local circumstances in which they were to function. The most disastrous conditionalities were avoided by this new programme design procedure. Second, every programme should have a strong poverty reduction dimension, specifying how the poorest citizens and areas would benefit. If no such benefits were discernible as regards a certain measure or conditionality, it should not be in the programme. This insured against the worst social disasters of the 1980s. Third, while the same SAP list of conditionalities still should make up the other dimension of the Poverty Reduction Strategy, the ideological nature of the list was eased, and countries were given longer periods over which they would undertake each measure on the list, gradually adjusting their countries and economies to make the states creditworthy, solvent and economically well-structured in a longer run.

Lessons from the SAP era

If we are to try to find something positive in the SAP reconstruction, I would like to point at the degree of economic and political change actually achieved in a relatively short time. When we today are facing a coming climate crisis, and we know that a major overhaul of our socioeconomic metabolism requires us to reconstruct the global political economy, we can look at the SAP era and learn that, yes, changing national economies fundamentally is possible. What we also can learn is that this change, which globalized nation after nation in a uniform way (Woods, 2006), was done within the nation–state system. We may already have the institutional structure needed to adjust. It is true that states and populations of debt–ridden countries were held hostage by the Bretton Woods institutions, and that this speeded up the adjustment process, but it is a source of comfort that so many countries were able to adjust so profoundly in only a decade. We need change of at least similar magnitude today, but we also need a reconstruction that does not produce the same social and developmental disasters as the SAPs.

The second lesson is that markets do not just develop, they have to be constructed, institutionalized and run politically. The Russian shock therapy during the early 1990s bears the starkest proof of this. When this country shifted from central planning to capitalist ownership and market allocation of products, the economy crashed, people starved and oligarchs from within the old nomenclature schemed their way through this mess to build immense riches. If we want to understand why Vladimir Putin enjoys widespread popular support for his strongman politics, we must acknowledge that he was the one who cleaned the mess up and created some sort of order in the Russian economy after this shock therapy. So strong poverty effects in combination with social and economic disorder pave the way for plutocrats and oligarchs or worse if you do not (re-) construct economies carefully.

The third lesson is that one size does not fit all. SAPs as well as Poverty Reduction Strategy Papers (PRSPs) look the same from country to country, and this is because the discourse inscribed into the articles of agreement of the Bretton Woods institutions has to be heeded and abided by if you want any money to come. The change from SAP to PRSP meant substantial improvement in how financial stabilization and structural adjustment happens, but it is none the less one uniform programme that does not fit all. Even from a normal economist perspective, this uniformity makes adjustment inefficient in many countries. It also means that a lot of opportunities for alternative development paths, better suited for specific countries and situations are missed or stopped.

The Beijing Consensus

The Bretton Woods institutions are losing relevance for how development and the global political economy evolve. One reason is the commodities and food boom that raised export incomes of many developing countries around 2006–8. This boom led to export revenues large enough for many countries to pay back their debts to IMF and the World Bank, which at the same time gave them more policy space to design their own economic policies. The other major reason for the decreasing power of the Bretton Woods institutions is the People's Republic of China. During the spectacular growth and industrialization that this one-party capitalist state has achieved (Walter and Howie, 2011), it has also deepened ties with developing as well as industrial countries. When Chinese interests cooperate with developing countries, it does not interfere in domestic politics, but collaborates wherever business that benefits Chinese interests can be made. When China negotiates a collaboration it tries to achieve agreements that both parties can live with through the contracts, which means that they give host countries development assistance to deliver on their part of the contract. What that assistance consists of is not a major issue for China, which can collaborate with all countries pursuing different development models. This means that the term 'Beijing Consensus' (Ramo, 2004) is a bit misleading, since it does not refer to any consensus existing in Beijing, nor to any particular coherent development model opposed or comparable to the Washington Consensus. If it means anything, it could rather be described as a principle of pragmatic collaboration between self-interested parties respecting the sovereignty of each other. This respect, however, diminishes the closer a country is to the Chinese mainland, and neighbouring countries around the South China Sea are severely disturbed by the military claims and naval expansion of China in these waters. At the same time China hosts the Shanghai Cooperation Organization (SCO), consisting of eight major powers in its vicinity, four observer states and six 'dialogue partners'. The SCO describes itself as a forum for mutual consultation and understanding. All members agree to respect each other's sovereignty, but also to collaborate and hold joint military exercises in which they train together, and which therefore give them a brief look at each other's military capacity. With both India and Russia taking part in SCO meetings and exercises, this group is developing into a large military formation, but no clear motive or project for its existence has so far been declared.

China's development collaboration with Africa has drawn a lot of attention, and Chinese investment in the continent is substantial. Much of this investment is related to China's industrial needs for food, commodities, transport and oil. These needs have made government-backed Chinese firms sign deals for leasing plantations and land to produce foodstuffs, various mining concessions and contracts, and oil prospecting and drilling contracts on the continent. Chinese industry is also establishing subsidiaries on the African continent since labour is beginning to become comparatively expensive in China. In return, African countries get government loans, infrastructure projects and commercial investment. African government representatives have regular meetings with the leaders of China's communist party in Beijing, discussing and developing the relation between the continent and the second largest economy in the world. In 2018, at one such meeting, general secretary Xi Jinping granted Africa a new package worth US$60 billion. This package was made up of new loans, infrastructure investment, commercial investment and US$5 billion worth of debt cancellation of old non-performing loans. US$60 billion is a large sum, which can move a lot on the African continent and create a lot of development. In comparison the OECD members used US$146 billion for ODA globally in 2017 (OECD, 2018), while FDI to all developing countries in 2016 amounted to US$646 billion, of which US$60 billion went to sub-Saharan Africa (UNCTAD World Investment Report, 2017). China is, as you can see, a big player in development cooperation. It is still unclear what this will mean in terms of human development, social justice, environmental sustainability and policy space of its collaborating developing partners. At the moment it appears that China has no plans to shoulder the hegemonic role of US and the Bretton Woods institutions in the political sense, even though it is a contender in the economic sense. It has even led the establishment of an alternative development bank for Asian developing states, the Asian Infrastructure Investment Bank (AIIB). The AIIB aims to co-finance the Chinese Belt and Road Initiative creating a modern Silk Road type of infrastructural connection from China through Asia to Europe; at the same time the AIIB aims to support any country in the Pacific Region to modernize their infrastructure so as to connect more efficiently to the economies of one another. Its lending, however, since the start in 2016 only amounts to US$4 billion, and several of these projects are World Bank projects where the AIIB participates, as reported by Forbes in early 2018. The numbers and friends of the AIIB do not seem to indicate any substantial discursive or geopolitical shift in development policy design or lending.

Designing another modern project

When we look at the rich world today and its growing inequality, the opioid epidemic in the US, the spread of psychological ill health in combination with stress related sickness, and so on, it is clear that the traditional role model countries at the top end of the modernization trajectory are losing their lure. At the same time the poorest half of the global population have a legitimate and moral right to development, as agreed upon by all states in the Millennium Development Goals, and again stated with more detail and stronger emphasis in the Sustainable Development Goals (SDGs) of 2015. To create ecological space for this development, not least the increased climate gas emissions that the development of four billion people's everyday life will create, the rich world has to change and scale down on consumption. It is also becoming clear that private industry will not implement technological solutions adequate for making role model lifestyles in the OECD sustainable. The change will have to be politically designed, institutionalized and pushed through. As we have seen in this chapter, development is becoming more multifaceted and the Bretton Woods institutions are losing their discursive monopoly on development policy design. The many varieties of capitalism in the rich world will most probably make rich countries produce this change in multiple ways. We have learnt from the SAP era that one size does not fit all, but there are concepts and theoretical entry points that will be helpful when analyzing and designing a possible sustainable development trajectory, even though the actual policies will differ.

Poverties

The fact that hundreds of millions have left extreme poverty during the globalization era is often given as a central argument for the economic restructuring the world has undergone over the last decades. It is a spurious argument, since people were leaving poverty at similar paces before neoliberal reconstruction began to take momentum. This poverty alleviation will need to continue with increased speed, but in another form, after neoliberal globalization. At the same time we need to treat poverty as the multidimensional social phenomenon it is (Kothari, 1995; Sen, 1999), and deal with it as such. If we design poverty alleviation with only income figures as our focal point and material, this alleviation may create as many problems as it solves.

Income poverty of course needs to be addressed. In its acute form this is the extreme poverty in which an individual lives on less than US$1.90 PPP (purchasing power parity)[4] per day. Below this income level a person is understood to have problems with one's physical survival in terms of food, clothing and shelter, or in other words, below this level one cannot satisfy one's basic needs. The success story of globalization is based on the fact that a billion or so has been lifted above this line since 1990, mostly in China. If you live on US$2.00 or US$3.00 PPP a day, you will most probably also experience your everyday life as poor, even if you might not have acute problems with your physical survival. This means that social and political poverty problems do not disappear when people cross the lowest poverty line, but they change. As more countries qualify for middle- and high-income status, the numerical poverty measures for rich countries become relevant. These tend to differ from country to country (and this is in accordance with the SDG principles) but generally the income measure is that if you earn less than 50 or 60 per cent of the median income of a country, you qualify as poor by national standards of a rich country.

Inequality is an integral part of capitalism. From a perspective of social justice, inequality can be legitimate if it means that people have been and are rewarded in proportion to their efforts and societal contributions, and are not punished for being unable to contribute. Beyond a certain level, inequality becomes a macroeconomic problem. Adam Smith stated in 1776 that 'no society can surely be flourishing and happy, of which the far greater part of the members are poor and miserable. It is but equity, besides, that they who food, clothe and lodge the whole body of the people, should have such a share of the produce of their own labour as to be themselves tolerably fed, clothed, and lodged' (Smith, 1776, p 181). The exact level at which inequality becomes a developmental and macroeconomic problem is not agreed upon, and to a large extent it is an ideological question. The economistic convention for measuring inequality is the Gini coefficient, which is calculated as the deviation from the absolutely equal distribution of income, wealth, education or some other important societal resource. If this deviation is smaller than 0.3, a country is counted as relatively equal (as regards the distribution of the resource in question), and the greater the deviation is beyond 0.3, the more unequal a country is. Early in the post-war era, there was an active policy in many parts of the world to build equal societies, to avoid the social stress that inequality produces, and also to maintain legitimacy for the respective development paths on the two sides of the Cold War. During the SAP era, and the general neoliberalization of market economies, inequality was described and promoted as necessary to incentivize workers to accept the jobs available on the labour market. SAPs produced this incentivization by a hollowing out of welfare transfers, health and unemployment insurances as well as labour market reform, a reform package mirrored on the government budget side by a lowering of taxes for corporations, wealth and high incomes. While this project has been successful in producing inequality (IMF, 2017), it has also led to legitimacy problems for the neoliberal development path of globalization.

Relative deprivation is a concept designed to deal with qualitative dimensions of poverty not captured by the quantitative measures described in the previous section. This concept frames poverty as something that deprives you of something, or something that is rightfully yours is taken away (Sen, 1999). There are researchers who use this concept as almost interchangeable with inequality, but they miss the meaning with the first term 'relative' and what the deprivation relates to for those hit by it. To understand this concept, imagine yourself being a teenager leaving secondary school, looking forward towards a normal productive life. Your plans are to get some professional training, get a job, marry and have children, borrow money to start your own business, work and raise your children, and then retire and then die. This is a reasonable, productive plan for a life, or 'a reasonable aspiration curve'. If circumstances beyond your control stops you from realizing this, your plans are trashed and you have to live a life achieving less than what you could reasonably aspire to achieve, then you are subjected to poverty in the form of relative deprivation. What you are deprived of is the future you had legitimate reason to expect to be able to realize. You might, for instance, be a woman lawyer in Saudi Arabia, restricted by patriarchal and religious laws from working outside your home. You might be a black person in South Africa or the US facing racism that stops you from getting into a profession dominated by whites. You might be a British student unable to pay high tuition fees for university courses mandatory if you want a certain profession. You might have gone through the training to start a small business, but when you arrive at the bank the SAP deregulation of interest rates have made these so high that the business you would set up has no possibility to generate enough revenue to finance the loan. Relative deprivation poverty like these examples abounds in today's global political economy. Most of it escapes normal poverty statistics, because people like university students normally don't come from the poorest segments of society. This does not mean, however, that their experience of poverty and deprivation is less real, nor that this form of poverty has no social and economic repercussions. The IMF riots of the 1980s, as well as the demonstrations in Southern Europe after the debt and budget crises around 2010, were both to a large extent populated by students and middle-class people protesting how the austerity policies were depriving them of the futures they had planned for. If you stick strictly to the numerical definitions of poverty, you might argue that these protesters are comparatively well off as compared to the poorest, and therefore their experience of deprivation and poverty is less legitimate. But as seen from Argentina to Greece to Iceland, relative deprivation is socially frustrating and painful.

Addressing poverties

When addressing poverty it is important to keep all its forms in mind. Promoting growth with the sole purpose and focus of raising the GDP per capita figures, for instance, has been proved to affect other forms of poverty negatively. Especially when growth promoting reforms aim to diminish poverty 'in the long run', which indicates that there will be a period of adjustment and possibly aggravated poverties before welfare effects can be seen. There is a strong correlation between GDP growth and decreasing extreme income poverty, but what happens on the way to growth affects poverty in all its forms. It is well worth quoting John Maynard Keynes here: 'The long run is a poor guide to current affairs. In the long run we are all dead' (Keynes, 1923, p 80). This sardonic saying compels us to address all forms of poverty directly today without putting our faith in market mechanisms to solve the problem for us in the future. SDG 1 promises that all nations will aim to 'end poverty in all its forms everywhere', with the eradication of extreme poverty in 2030 as a first goal. What follows in this section is a list of concepts helpful for the designing of such a political task.

Redistribution is the conventional method to alleviate poverty. It is as old as humanity itself, and every civilization has had its way of doing it. There appears to be in us an almost biological instinct against letting people near you die from starvation, misery and squalor. Both the Koran and the Bible state that a certain portion of what you earn, if you earn anything, must be given to those who are poor enough to need help. Churches, mosques and other religious establishments were for a long time the major economic redistributors, often accumulating a handsome share for themselves while performing this task. With the birth of secular laws and the nation state came institutionalized forms of redistribution, securing the physical survival of citizens in one way or another. Often in the form of miniscule and humiliating life-supports, but none the less institutionalized forms of redistribution. In a functionally differentiated, industrial society where a majority of the citizens build their lives on wage labour, it becomes dysfunctional to let large sections of the population fall into utter misery between jobs or in business downturns. The Bretton Woods institutions, for instance, today want all countries writing a PRSP to include 'social protection' as one component of the package. Meanwhile in the rich world, neoliberalization of the economies and the neoconservative turn in many countries has hollowed out the redistributive systems established during the Keynesian era and reintroduced integrity intrusive support mechanisms, signalling the individual's own responsibility for their misfortune. The resulting holes in the social safety net are being patched together by civil society organizations such as trade unions and religious organizations, running food banks, garment recycling, soup kitchens, emergency social lodging and the like. When analyzing redistribution, this distinction between charity and official redistribution is important.

Charity redistribution is performed by organizations independent from the state and its institutions. They run on voluntary donations from individuals and organizations that find the causes of the organizations worthy of support. Often they also do social work for municipalities and regions on a subcontracting basis, for example so that instead of setting up official emergency social lodging, a town hires beds for the homeless in dormitories run by churches. These organizations save many lives and make a huge difference for those seeking their help. Respectable as this altruism is, there are debatable issues regarding charity redistribution. First, the dependence on donations from actors finding their cause worthy makes charity vulnerable to direct and indirect influence from donors. As the political and social climate changes, the will to donate to worthy causes also changes, and the organizations have to adjust accordingly to secure financing for their activities. Second, when these causes and organizations are based in certain religious beliefs or ideological projects, many people in need of help will be reluctant to seek help since they do not agree with these projects or beliefs. Third, to enjoy charity redistribution you must in most cases actively seek this kind of help; it is not something you have the right to enjoy, but something the charity has the right to give you, if it wants to. A charity therefore exercises power over those seeking its help, and by seeking its help you accept and subject yourself to this power, even if it is something you would not have accepted or voted for had you not been in need.

Institutionalized **official redistribution** is something you enjoy as part of citizenship, a right accruing to your person and personal features in accordance with the laws and constitution of a political entity, such as a municipality, a state or a country. In a broad sense, the modern state functions thanks to redistribution via the taxes and fees of fiscal policy. Primary schooling, roads, military protection and so on are supplied to the citizenry thanks to the tax payers, and the schoolchildren, drivers and soldiers depending on this redistribution are not the ones paying for the teachers, the roads or the guns. Things supplied by the state in this way are called **public goods**, and the benefits of those are distributed to all who need them, and those who need them would neither be willing nor able to pay the full price for them. The provision of public goods, therefore, has to be financed via redistribution from those who have money to those who need the public goods, or society would seize to function. **Poverty-alleviating redistribution**, specifically, can also be viewed as a public good, but are more often described as a right that comes with citizenship or domicile in a nation state. The modern welfare state extends many such rights to its citizens, and to others present on its territory. Vital health care, for instance, is generally regarded as something that should be provided to the sick by the nearest possible facility, regardless of a person's citizenship status. Redistribution in the form of cash transfers, such as unemployment insurance, social welfare or family allowance, more often takes place in accordance with specific situations and circumstances accruing to the individual person in the form specific for each country. If 'poverty in all its forms' is to be eradicated everywhere, as SDG 1 states, then monetary redistribution will be a central instrument. In the design of this instrument the following distinctions between its different forms will be helpful.

Cash transfers are generally the fastest and most effective way to alleviate poverty, as compared to transfer in kind. Cash can be distributed at lower cost than goods or services, and the recipients can use it to address and alleviate the most personally pressing poverty problem at the moment. The transfer can be needs-based, to cover vital expenses for those who cannot afford them. An example would be pensioners getting a needs based allowance to cover rent exceeding a certain limit. Transfers can also be universal, so that every individual with a certain characteristic gets the same cash transfer. Child benefit in welfare states is often universal, based on the norm that no matter what life choices and values your parents have, you as a child should be guaranteed a sum covering your basic survival. In recent years **universal basic income** (UBI) has been proposed in many quarters, extending this societal responsibility to all citizens regardless of age. Proponents of UBI say that it would eradicate extreme poverty; make citizens less exposed to the power of charities and the humiliation of displaying their personal needs and abilities to social workers and others; it would also put a pressure on employers to step up working conditions to attract labour, as well as freeing up the possibility for focus on their favourite spheres of creativity (Bregman, 2016). Those negative of UBI stress the high fiscal cost, the risk for a temporary effect on poverty that would subsequently be eradicated as employers adjust and lower wages in relation to the UBI; and the loss of the obligation of a citizen to contribute to society. In a macroeconomic perspective most industrial countries have enough money and public resources to finance a UBI.

The next issue with cash transfers concerns the **conditionalities** for receiving cash transfers. Traditionally the most prevalent conditionality was work, and many countries have different forms of activities or work that people must participate in to get cash transfers. A very successful conditionality in Brazil under Lula da Silva's Bolsa Familia programme, was a family allowance (to the level of a basic income for the poorest) conditional on the families sending their children to school and getting them immunized. This programme halved the absolute poverty prevalence in Brazil and brought down inequality considerably. It also had a great effect on school attendance rates and child health. One vital component explaining this success is that the money has been channelled via the mothers of the family, and what one can see generally is that cash transfers going to women have a much larger effect on development, schooling and family health than transfers going to males. The simple explanation behind this is that men are brought up to understand their own personal needs as the same as, or more important than, their family's needs. Keeping dad happy will make him work harder and that will make us all better off, or something like that, is the patriarchal logic behind this. Women, on the other hand, are brought up to care for children and men, so they use money in accordance with this caring logic. As long as this patriarchal logic lingers, it will be more effective to channel poverty alleviating cash transfers through women. Doing so, however, will undermine the traditional household role of men since it will give women money that they control, and men's role of primary bread winner will weaken. As gender systems change, which they do for many reasons, this 'woman coefficient' in cash transfer effects on poverty is likely to decrease. Until this happens, the gendered power order within households will affect how cash transfers are controlled and used, by whom and to what purpose. As we saw in Chapter 2, it is not only men who uphold and reiterate patriarchal gender roles, so just directing cash transfers out of the reach of men will not solve the issue, but being aware of how gender dynamics influence the result of cash transfers will be important for the foreseeable future. Summing up, cash transfers to individuals and households have been, and are, an important and effective instrument for poverty alleviation.

Redistribution with a specific poverty alleviation aim can also be pursued with interventions on the macroeconomic and market level. Taxes, and the collection of those from different tax bases, are useful for redistributing money and resources. The progressiveness of income tax scales is an important issue, and how the tax rate increases progressively as you move up the income ladder. Neoliberalization of the global economy has generally meant that this progressiveness has diminished or disappeared, but there is no law that it must be so. Taking from the rich to give to the poor, in an institutionalized and predictable fashion, was one of the central mechanisms in the construction of welfare states. A beneficial side effect already mentioned of progressive tax scales today in light of the SDGs is that the ecological destructiveness of the upper classes would be diminished. On the consumption side you can also work with differentiated VAT levels for different types of goods, and levy low VAT on items on which the poor depend for their survival, and high VAT on non-vital or ecologically damaging goods and services.

Subsidies are another redistributive instrument that can be used to ensure affordable access to staple goods for the poor. A subsidy is a publicly financed contribution to the production and/or distribution of a good or service deemed valuable to society. Different forms of agricultural and food subsidies have been a mainstay in most industrialization projects, ensuring affordable and predictable access to food for workers. Agricultural subsidies were also part of the welfare state projects in the OECD, helping to ensure comparable standards of living in the town and the countryside. The EU, the US and most other industrial countries still subsidize their agriculture to varying degrees. During the recession after 2008, subsidies where used to maintain demand for hybrid and energy efficient cars, solar panels and other stuff deemed more sustainable than the older varieties they replaced, and demand for those helped take these industries through the crisis. When constructing subsidies in market economies, one strategy is to direct the support to the production of the desired item, and support producers so that they can stay in business while producing their stuff at affordable prices in sustainable ways. Area subsidies in the EU is one such support, sending cash transfers to farmers to keep their farmland in shape, and the farmers can produce whatever is in demand on these fields. A previous strategy was to support farmers with a guaranteed lowest price for the produce, the aim of which was to guarantee the farmers an income they could support themselves on. The problem with this latter form was that farmers some years produced more cereals or milk than the market would absorb and consume, which led the industry to dump this surplus on the world market (sometimes helped further by export subsidies), which outcompeted foreign farmers with imported items priced below foreign production costs. A lesson to remember from this is that you should not construct a subsidy so that it aggravates poverty somewhere else in the national or global economy. Another subsidy construction strategy is to intervene on the retail side, and guarantee consumers affordable prices through government supports to wholesalers and/or retailers so they can keep low prices. Venezuela under Chavez even opened public retail stores with staple foods for the poor, and subsidized this unprofitable retail chain with proceeds from its oil industry. This was appreciated by poor Venezuelans, but became hard to maintain when the global oil price fell and fiscal resources became insufficient. As the Venezuelans learnt, if there is a shortage in a subsidized item there will be hoarding of it, which is subsequently likely to lead to an informal second market where this item circulates at much higher prices than intended. Cases like the EU's guaranteed agricultural prices and the Venezuelan public retail chain have given subsidies a bad name, and within neoliberal thinking they are generally seen as market distortions, but they are still in use in most countries and play an important role for alleviating poverty and supporting valuable production and distribution. In a future reconstruction they will most likely continue to be a vital instrument.

International redistribution in the form of ODA comes in many forms. One is **multilateral aid** distributed from rich countries to poor ones through multilateral agencies such as the UNDP or the United Nations Relief and Works Agency for Palestine Refugees in the Near East (UNRWA).[5] This aid is formed and constrained by the mandate of the specific multilateral organization, which also means that the power exercised over the recipients of the aid is formed and constrained in the same way. **Bilateral ODA** is aid from a rich country to a poor one, shaped by negotiations between the two countries. This relation is strongly informed by the inequality between the parties, and the rich country very often wants quite specific things to happen with the resources transferred. Resources normally come with strings attached and part of the resources will be used for check-ups and evaluations of projects and reforms to make sure that the receiving country uses the resources according to plan. A standard argument for these attached strings is that the tax payers in the rich country like to know that their money is used for good development projects; if they don't see good development happening as a result of their tax payment to the cause, their willingness to contribute to ODA will diminish. One way to entice the electorate to contribute has historically been **tied aid**, which means that aid money finances orders with the industry of the rich country to produce what the poor country needs. An example would be that the rich country reserves US$100 million in their government budget for a developing country, but sends it in the form of trucks and medicines produced in the donor country. The argument for this tying of aid is that it makes electorates in both countries happy, jobs in the rich one and trucks and medicine in the poor one. Common problems, however, is that it might be the wrong types of trucks and medicines, and if the country had had these US$100 million in cash instead, more and more appropriate trucks and medicines could have been purchased from some other country instead. If a country does not need trucks and medicines the most, but rather other things, but what the rich country wants to contribute is trucks and medicine, it might be hard to say no. If you represent a country in which most people live in different forms of poverty, a transfer of resources may be welcome even if it is not the most needed ones. Tied aid is very common, but it often produces suboptimal development results, and within multilateral institutions and academia, the general notion today is that **untied aid** results in more and better development. An increasing number of receiving countries today are turning ODA offers down and cancelling ODA relations, on the argument that it means an intrusion into their domestic affairs. As part of the reconstruction of the global economy, ODA will continue to be important, but the form it takes is changing.

Post-development is a concept coined to capture the discourses for poverty alleviation and societal development that are forming independently of the traditional modern project, without affluent role model countries as the final goal for development, and without identifying societies fundamentally different from these role models as 'underdeveloped'. Projects influenced by these discourses do not denigrate modern inventions and technology, nor romanticize a local or traditional past (well, some versions do this). Generally, post-development discourses stand on two pillars. The first pillar is a radical independence from the modernization project trajectory towards affluence in industrial societies. Instead, development is understood as securing a good life for all, in ways and forms specific for each project. The second pillar is an anticolonial stance, questioning the legitimacy of asymmetric ODA relations in which people from rich countries are supposed to develop (the lives of) people in poor countries. It is presupposed that poor people have a good grasp of what they need, and how they would use the lacking resources to better their lives if/when they got hold of them. The colonial white attitude that people of colour need help because of who they are has no validity whatsoever within post-development. Academics like Arturo Escobar and Wolfgang Sachs are central thinkers in this field. In terms of post-development ideology and actual politics in this vein, the Latin American movement Buen Vivir is perhaps the best known example. Emblematic for this movement is its many manifestations in different, often indigenous, forms, with the overarching purpose to establish Latin American style 'good living'. Common discursive elements are harmony among humans and in their relation to the ecosystem; collective interests rather than individual interests as those worthy to be met and realized; a rethinking of ownership so that land and nature cannot be private property but only put under human stewardship; a strong delimitation of the market and price mechanisms, re-embedding large parts of economic interaction in the social fabric; and production for local needs according to local preferences, rather than for the global market to satisfy corporate profit motives. The logic of Buen Vivir does not only sidestep the divide of developed versus underdeveloped, but also the capitalism versus socialism/communism divide. The movement is not one single movement, but a number of alternative, real life modern projects with a loose common discourse.

From a **socialist** perspective, poverty is a natural consequence of global capitalist structures maintained and made profitable by exploitation of the working class everywhere in the world. A thorough structural transformation of global capitalism, therefore, is necessary to eradicate poverty. Such a transformation is conceivable if understood as a gradual process, rather than a global uniform revolution. Walden Bello (2002) identifies the closing down of WTO, IMF and the World Bank as necessary first steps, in order to open up policy space for institutional changes on a national and local level. Through membership in these organizations nation states have accepted to adjust their national legislation and policies to support free capitalist trade, private ownership of the means of production, and the market mechanism as the primary allocative function in their economies. This institutional adjustment has secured a continuation of exploitation of the workers to the benefit of capitalists and of the South to the benefit of the North. Once this global institutional straightjacket is gone, there will be policy room to determine democratically how equal and sustainable economies can be built. As countries stop specializing along comparative advantage lines in an economy driven by TNCs and financial capital, global trade will reorient to support foreign countries to meet their needs, rather than to maximize corporate sales in rich countries. Bello has no uniform programme for how nations should deal with this transformed global economy locally, but points at local cultures and preferences and proposes that non-exploitative economies should be built democratically on the basis of these cultures (Bello, 2002).

Other critical projects focus on alternative money systems, on the claim that money is the primary social technology that makes the global economy function the way it does. Inventing alternative local currencies is a way to break local economic interaction out of global capitalist structures to establish local democratic economic systems. A widespread acronym for this is LETS (local exchange and trading systems), the currencies of which have been constructed and used locally in villages and neighbourhoods for several decades. The general principle is often that people agree locally what different goods and services are worth in relation to each other, and then a common system of tokens or coupons is launched, with an agreed upon exchange rate towards the national official currency. The tokens can then be used to purchase and trade locally (mostly) produced goods and services within the LETS community. There might be a certain hippie flavour to this idea, but it has also been used successfully by official institutions. In Argentina during the crisis in 2001, for instance, municipalities launched their own coupon system for exchange when the national currency dried up, to make purchases of everyday goods possible for their citizens. Tax offices and central banks are normally not happy if a LETS currency becomes big, since parallel currencies create monetary policy difficulties, and the tax office cannot collect taxes from trades that are not registered in the dominating national currency and its banking and payments systems. In poverty terms, a collectively controlled LETS can make possible economic interaction that would otherwise not had taken place. It can also be used to lock people into a local economy dominated by, say, a factory where the workers can use the coupons only in the company store, thus locking them into a very small economy dominated by one strong actor. So there is nothing inherently good about a local currency, but it is one of the instruments that can be used to construct alternative economic systems.

Degrowth and the upper-class problem

In the reconstruction of the global political economy, discontinuing the growth paradigm and the political focus on creating and maintaining growth at all costs is vital. Proponents of the present modern project have long argued that technological and societal development will 'decouple' growth from its harmful material and environmental consequences. As already discussed in Chapter 2, this is not happening nearly quickly enough to save us from climatic and ecological disaster. The EU seems to be decoupling its growth, but that is because so much of its dirty industry has moved to Asia. To halt the destruction of the planet, the rich world needs to degrow quite rapidly. Jason Hickel (2017) argues that in the absence of major technological breakthroughs in carbon capture and similar technologies, rich countries need to bring down production and consumption by 6 per cent per year to have a chance of keeping global warming below 2 degrees Celsius and making good on the Paris Agreement of 2015. The developing world also needs to curb its emissions of greenhouse gases and opt for another development trajectory than that based on fossil fuels, which has until now supplied the material basis for development and growth. After Hickel's radical downsizing of production and consumption, the political focus needs to free itself from its obsession with growth, and start on a post-growth development trajectory. This would mean that we would have to accept stable consumption levels in the rich world similar to those of the 1970s, with goods and services produced and supplied with the productivity and technology of the 2020s. For most people in the rich world this is not a scary or threatening idea. Most of us lived good lives in the 1970s; we were well fed and lodged; and had lots of fun. There is, however, one group in which this downsizing probably will evoke an acute sense of poverty: the upper class, which has benefited greatly during the neoliberal globalization era. The richest 0.1 per cent in particular have seen their wealth surge. The resulting lifestyle adaptations has been absolutely disastrous, with global flying habits, consumption patterns, food habits and continuous habitation adjustments, which together result in ecological footprints of a tremendous size and weight. The global upper class is responsible for most of the ecological damage today. At the same time, this group cannot be expected to silently accept having their lifestyles and plans for the future disrupted or trashed in global economic reconstruction. Their protests and resistance is also likely to be strong and potentially damaging, since they control vast resources and often have considerable influence on politics and the media. How to handle the upper-class problem during reconstruction is therefore vital.

From African and Latin American examples of reconstruction we learn that the countries that have treated their upper classes harshly during transition have run into major problems. Class structures were often radicalized by colonial rule, which used upper-class ethnic groups to run the colonies. With independence, revolutions and other types of reconstruction often came a political and social desire to avenge injustices and exploitation committed by the local as well as the colonial upper class during colonial rule. This vengeance dimension of reconstruction in many instances led to the expropriation of upper-class resources, politicized ethnic polarizations, and created new grievances among a group of people experiencing strong relative deprivation. If and when such a group sets out to recreate a future it feels has been taken away from it, the resulting disorder and wider societal consequences may be terrible. If there is a possibility of avoiding overly harsh relative deprivation for the upper class during the coming global economic reconstruction, it is likely to be much smoother politically and more effective in strengthening general sustainability. From this Southern experience we can draw a couple of conceptual conclusions.

Security concerns, along with the private industry that supplies security for the upper class, have grown during the globalization era. As Wilkinson and Pickett (2009) have shown, unequal societies are more insecure than equal ones, and as inequality has grown, the upper class has withdrawn from society into gated communities, private schools, tax havens and other segregated clusters. Within these clusters the upper class experiences a sense of security, and any indication of a change to this segregation – including a change in its underlying economic dynamics – is likely to be perceived as a threat. To minimize the risk that economic reconstruction is perceived as a threat, and that this leads to violent and/or populist reactions of – or on behalf of – the upper class, it is important to avoid vengeful and threatening language and measures. The economic changes during the globalization era have benefited the upper class tremendously, and it is only natural that it experiences changes to the benefit of economic, social and ecological sustainability as a threat to what it has hoarded. Certain aspects of this change, such as progressive tax scales and strong social security mechanisms, will affect the bank accounts of upper-class individuals in ways they will probably perceive as negative. But if sustainable upper-class lifestyles can be secured in ways perceived as largely legitimate, the likelihood that the upper class will resort to violent and/or damaging counteractions decreases.

Social status, as sociologists tell us, is often more important than wealth in absolute terms. With the same amount of money, or level of income, you might have economic working-class status in one country and upper-class status in another. In Pierre Bourdieu's terms, status can be compared to different forms of capital that are current in different social fields. So there are cultural, academic, social, economic and other forms of capital, and to a certain degree you can exchange one form of capital for another. But only to a degree; you will never achieve full status as, say, an artist with money alone, even if you invest heavily in art and socialize with artists all the time. You will have status in the artistic field as a buying participant, but will never be recognized as an artist until you have had your first professional gallery showing. In order to avoid upper-class exactions during reconstruction, it will be important to keep some social fields in which their culture, social capital and upper-class habitus have some purchase. If all social fields for the upper class are trashed in reconstruction, this will result in a dangerous sense of humiliation and resentment within this class.

One important aspect of keeping the upper class included and participating in the coming reconstruction is knowledge. Education, as we saw earlier in this chapter when discussing the Gini coefficient, is one of the things unevenly distributed, meaning that many of the most knowledgeable persons belong (at least in the economic sense) to the global upper class. Since the design and carrying through of reconstruction will require well-educated people, these will participate to a greater extent if their societal position and status are not damaged too greatly in the process.

You might ask, 'Why this focus on the global upper class?' To put it simply, if we are going to reconstruct the global political economy, so that it works according to different development logic from the growth-centred one, the global upper class will have to make the greatest changes in lifestyles. The middle and working classes do not have ecological footprints nearly as heavy, and even though they occasionally protest politically, they do not possess the means or the networks to stop or interfere with the reconstructive process. This process, if it comes anywhere close to the ideals of the SDGs, will mean the substantial betterment of the poorest part of the global working class, and small changes for the global middle class. Judging by the ideals at the fundament of the SDGs, the legitimacy problem for reconstruction is not as likely to arise here as it is with the global upper class. That is why a focus on the upper class is called for, and the lessons from Southern reconstructions are worth keeping in mind.

A class-based problem with post-growth development, however, is that most envisioning of it is done by middle-class academics (Timothy Jackson's report in 2009 has some telling examples, important as this report is). The pictures of a future post-growth society consequently appear very European and very middle class. It's all Sunday walks, poetry readings and violins, when we don't amuse ourselves in a part time job in some cooperative solar cell factory or such. What do we do in a post-growth society with workaholics like Steve Jobs? With drivers like Ayrton Senna? With Ian Dury and his 'Sex & Drugs & Rock & Roll'? The middle-class utopia so far dominating post-growth envisioning has few answers. But perhaps the answer to this question is not the most important one. Most likely we can trust democracy and the creativity of people to provide many answers during and after reconstruction. But the idea of a post-growth society is tainted by middle-class academics describing it as a middle-class dream village, which would be a nightmare to many.

Conclusion

Globalization has changed the world that Harry S. Truman outlined in his inauguration speech in 1949. We no longer have three worlds with two competing development projects; we simply have one development project that is losing both its sustainability and its traditional guardians. The role model countries at the upper end of the modernization trajectory are running into serious societal problems. Growth in China and other emerging markets is creating new middle and upper classes that are living modern role model lives. But global role model lives are increasingly being lived behind barbed wire and security cameras and a new social geopolitics of poverty is taking hold, with global security corporations providing security for those who can pay for protection. The economic and material provisioning of these role model lives is the very thing we need to change to save the planet.

As described earlier in this chapter, in our macroeconomic toolboxes we already have conventional as well as transformative instruments for eradicating poverty, and all over the world people have rational ideas about how their lives and futures could be transformed to secure good lives outside the modernization development and growth trajectory. This 'outside' orientation is not primarily an opting-out of modernity altogether, but a cultural, economic and social materialization of many projects unconstrained by the modernization discourse, which has been colonizing minds, lives and countries since the birth of the nation state. The modern project has produced many wonderful things, but it is heading towards an ecological and social dead end, and these achievements can and should now be used for a post-growth, sustainable modern project.

Further reading

Development research is a transdisciplinary field involving economists, sociologists, economic historians and many others. Björn Hettne, who started his career in Economic History, published *Development Theory and the Three Worlds* in 1990 and – after the various post-structuralist debates and ponderings – *Thinking About Development* in 2009. Books influential on the discussions that took place between these years include Frans Schuurman's edited volume *Beyond the Impasse* (1993), Ankie Hoogvelt's 2001 *Globalization and the Postcolonial World* (2001) and, from a social liberal perspective, Amartya Sen's *Development as Freedom* (1999). Critical postcolonial researchers such as Ania Loomba, Vandana Shiva, Mark Duffield, Wolfgang Sachs, Arturo Escobar, Fantu Cheru, Rajni Kothari and many others have since the 1990s contributed to a general freeing of Development Studies from its colonial discursive content.

Official development statistics and research develop around global nodes, such as www.worldbank.org, where data on countries and regions is assembled, and where you can also find the *World Development Reports*, which exemplify the current mainstream development discourse. The UNDP website (www.undp. org) publishes the less economistic annual *Human Development Report*, as well as many other reports with a broad developmental focus. On the UNCTAD website (www.unctad.org) you can find macroeconomic research focused on the

South, while the same kind of research focused on the North can be found on the OECD site (www.oecd.org).

Last but not least, global NGOs such as Oxfam in the UK, the South Centre in Singapore and the Bretton Woods Project present critical research and statistics from a perspective more or less critical of official development policy and research.

6

Financial Markets and the Future

Financial markets have become a decisive force in the global political economy during the globalization era. In 2014 Thomas Piketty showed how an increasing share of global yearly earnings ends up with private actors in the financial sector. The combination of financial growth, deregulation and agglomeration of wealth has made global financial markets an intrinsically destabilizing force in macroeconomic and development policies, as the recurring crises of the last few decades have shown. The growing importance of global financial flows and private financial decision-making in economic development is encapsulated in the concept of **financialization**, which today signifies two interrelated processes. The first process is the transfer of political-economic power from states and public institutions to private actors on financial markets (Helleiner, 1994). The second process is the increasing influence of neoliberal financial rationality and discourse on everyday life (Langley, 2008). Chapter 3 accounted for the institutional changes that paved the way for financialization. In this chapter, I will first describe the instruments and mechanisms through which the power and influence of financial markets flow. I will then discuss how these markets relate to everyday life and circumscribe the future, and how these relations create crises when they do not develop as planned. The analytical second section will present concepts and theories useful for designing a reconstruction of finance to make it commensurate with a just and sustainable future.

Financial instruments

An 'instrument' is something you use to do something, produce something or measure something. 'Financial instruments' as a term signals that the stuff that people buy and sell on financial markets are used for specific purposes. Most financial interaction today takes place simply because those involved want to get richer, and in that sense the things they use, logically enough, are instruments for self-enrichment. But there is a finer-grained logic to finance, according to which the instruments used symbolize different types of social relation: as

Peterson (2003) says, they are 'signs' that circulate in a 'virtual economy'. The relations they signify can be either between market and real-world actors, or between market actors. Understanding how this signification works is helpful for understanding the global financial market and its importance.

One of the most evasive and oft-debated things in modern economies and in financial markets is *money* – that thing that financial markets, economic growth, international trade and personal wealth are all about. We instinctively know what it is and have a feeling about it, but when asked to define it most of us run into problems. Conventional Economics bypasses the fundamental definition by pointing at three qualities essential for money: store of value, unit of account and means of exchange. If you can use something to accumulate value, count this value and make others accept it as payment for something, then it is money. Be it in the form of cowrie shells, gold, paper notes or clay tablets, if it is generally accepted as money, it is money. Later in this chapter I will be discussing the forex market, where money is treated as a commodity, and hence becomes a commodity like any other. Within national economies, in everyday life and in financial markets other than forex, money lives a much more multidimensional life within the intersectional matrix (Zelizer, 1994).

Distinct from the commodity definition of money is the **IOU** (for 'I owe you') definition and understanding of money, which stems from the historical origins of money in Mesopotamia. Here the state and the emperor started to keep accounts of what all citizens owed the king or what the king owed his citizens. This was in essence an early form of banking, and claims on the king soon began circulating as a means of payment (Graeber, 2011). Once claims on the king could be used as a means of payment, the custom arose of using other forms of claims certificates to settle debts and for payments. Money, in this perspective, is intimately connected to debt. The birth of silver and gold money did not come about until kings and emperors needed to hire foreign soldiers, who did not accept payment in the form of claims they would not be able to exercise outside the kingdom they were hired to fight for. Metal coins solved this problem, because gold and silver would be valuable in themselves across most of the world. Metal coins, especially gold and silver, were also vital for the growth of international trade from ancient times well into the age of European empires. When modern central banking started in the 17th century, the issuing of paper money was done with an IOU-like promise that all who presented the central bank with this paper money would get a fixed amount of precious metal in return. This was named the **gold standard**, and served to encourage people to trust paper money as a means of payment after centuries of monetary disorder resulting from wars and political power shifts. This connection between gold and paper money – effectively an IOU between central banks and economic subjects – did not end formally on an international scale until 1971, when the US unilaterally withdrew from the Bretton Woods system of exchange rates (as mentioned in Chapter 3). In this system the US dollar had a fixed value in gold, and all IMF member countries kept their exchange rates pegged against the US dollar. Since this exchange rate system came to an end, we have been living in a world with floating exchange rates, and central banks no longer owe the bearers of their money a specific amount of gold. Central banks instead operate on a promise that the bearer of their national currency will be able to use it as a means of payment within their jurisdiction, and also to exchange it for other currencies, at a predictable value. This promise from the central banks to economic subjects addresses society as whole, and central banks deliver on this promise to the degree that their currencies maintain their value, in terms of what they can buy nationally and in relation to other currencies.

The next financial instrument is **shares** (also called **equity** or **stock**), which are symbols of ownership. When you buy shares in a firm, you become the owner of a proportion of that firm based on how many shares you own. This does not mean that you become responsible for the firm's activities (at least not in the legal sense); the managers of the firm are the ones judicially responsible for its activities. The share ownership gives you the right to a proportional share of the yearly profits of the firm. In many countries you also get the right to come to the meetings of the owners and vote, in proportion to your ownership, on who sits on the board, who serves as the board's chairperson, and the like. The board represents the owners and appoints CEOs to run the firm. The CEOs answer for their deeds to the board, which also gives management long-term and strategic directives on where they should take the firm to meet the owners' expectations for profits and real-world results. Corporations issue their shares on stock exchanges in 'initial public offerings' (IPOs) in order to raise money, typically for investments of different kinds. This first sale of shares to the public is the only time when money flows from the stock market to the firm; trading done in the shares after the IPO is only the circulation of these symbols of ownership. You can buy a share because you want part of the yearly profits – called 'dividends' – or because you believe the price of the share will go up, or both. You sell a share when you think dividends are not high enough, when you believe the price of the share will fall, when you do not approve of the firm's activities, or simply because you need the money. Small investors and savers usually have very few obligations as a shareholder, but if you own a substantial proportion of the equity of a listed corporation, you are expected or compelled (depending on national legislation) to take a seat on the board of the firm and take part in the work of strategic planning and management of the CEOs and the firm itself.

This construction – ownership of firms without legal responsibility for what the firm does – is one of the most peculiar and influential institutional constructions of the modern project. It allows you to exercise power (in proportion to your resources) over what happens in society, without being accountable for what happens. You might lose money if the firm does not deliver profit, but that is all.

Debt, the substance of lending and borrowing, is what is traded on the **credit** or **capital market**. When lenders agree to lend a prospective borrower a sum of money, they first negotiate the terms of the loan. These terms may include the size of the loan, how long the lending period will be, the terms of repayment (pay back gradually or everything at the end of the specified period) and the interest rate. The interest rate is determined by the (opportunity and financing) costs of the lenders and compensation for the risk that the lenders expose their resources to when lending to a certain borrower. The opportunity cost is what the lenders would have gained if the money had been lent to someone else. Since lenders such as banks have borrowing costs (often from the state's central bank), there is a general floor for costs in the market, and lenders then try to get what they can in excess of that from a borrower. The level of risk is determined by the likelihood that a borrower of a certain type will default on the loan. A risk-free borrower, such as a trusted treasury of a state with a solid and balanced budget, is a low-risk borrower and pays a low interest rate. High-risk borrowers, such as unemployed people, Third World countries or students, pay high interest rates, since they are more likely to default on their loans. Different types of creditor specialize in certain types of borrower; payday loans, for instance, are offered to working-class people by one type of lender, while other lenders lend their money to states and corporations. Once a loan is made out, it becomes a claim on the borrower, a contract symbolizing a future stream of money from the borrower to the creditor, which is equivalent to an asset for the creditor. A special form of debt is the **bond**. A bond works like this: a corporation or a nation state needs to raise a couple of billion for something, and instead of negotiating many loans with many prospective lenders for parts of this large sum, the corporation or country constructs a bond, in essence a lending agreement with a set interest rate and set terms of repayment. The borrower then offers financial market participants the opportunity to invest in this bond for X number of years, with Z rate of interest to be paid back on Y terms. Investors who find this offer attractive lend their money to the borrowing corporation or state by investing in the bond. This claim – the bond – is equivalent to an asset for the investors, and can be used in various ways; perhaps as collateral for a loan for themselves, or as an asset they can sell on the second-hand market, or for some other financial purpose. The second-hand market for bonds is large, and bonds are a vital instrument when big actors are borrowing and investing. In addition, bonds are vital to central banks and their regulation of the money supply: when they wish to extract cash from the economy, they sell bonds (that is, borrow money on the markets to reduce 'liquidity' in them). When they want more cash to circulate in the economy and the financial markets, they buy bonds (in other words, buy the claims that market actors have on other market actors) so as to release more liquidity into the markets. Traditionally central banks operate with their own bonds or those of their state, but since the financial crisis many central banks have also bought bonds of various types from a variety of issuers, in order get more cash into the economy via the financial system. An important discursive power mechanism related to debt is the **credit rating**, which I will return to later in this chapter.

Derivatives are a special class of financial instrument used by market actors to distribute risk among each other. As the name indicates, these instruments are 'derived' from other financial instruments, and signify a special right or claim that an owner of the derivative has in relation to the underlying financial instrument. A simple form of derivatives are options, which can be either options to sell or options to buy ('put' or 'call' options, as the jargon has it). Options to sell were originally developed in the northern US as a way for farmers to ensure that they would get a minimum price for their harvest. To be assured of this minimum price, they bought an option to sell from a wholesaler, and if the price rose above this minimum, they simply tore up the option and sold at the higher price. But if the price of their produce fell below their minimum price, they presented the option and their harvest to the wholesaler, who was then obliged to buy their produce at the price agreed in the option contract. The option thus transferred the risk from the farmer to the wholesaler, who took this risk for a fee equivalent to a couple of percentage points of the value of the harvest. Stock options work in the same way. If you have €100 million's worth of shares in a listed corporation, and you plan to make an investment with these millions six months into the future, you can do three things. You can sell the shares today, put the money in the bank and wait six months. You can keep the shares and gamble that their price will rise and that you will make a profit from keeping them six more months. Or you can keep them and buy an option to sell that gives you the right to sell the shares to the options trader during a certain period six months ahead at a price agreed on today, in this case €100 million. Six months pass by, and now it is time to invest. If the share price has risen, you tear up the option, sell your shares at the higher price and go on with your life a little richer. The options trader has also made a profit, and is therefore also a little richer. If the price has fallen, however, you present your option to the options trader, who must then buy your shares at the agreed price. This trader would typically have done an 'off-setting' deal with someone else, so that s/he can sell the shares on to this someone, without making too big a loss. The important thing for you is that you have insured yourself against loss with your six-month 'position' on these €100 million's worth of shares: the trader who sold you the option carried your risk over this period, while you still had the chance to earn a few extra millions from your shares. You can construct options that give the right to the holder to do future trades in many types of financial instrument.

There are also other types of derivative. One of the biggest markets is in **swaps**, which are agreements between two parties to exchange assets and future money flows with each other for a certain period, for which they pay each other some kind of agreed remuneration (Hull, 2018). The logic behind swaps is that different financial actors have different needs for instruments depending on what they plan to do and where, and by swapping assets with each other, they can gain access to specific currencies or instruments at lower costs than if they had purchased the desired asset. Another derivatives instrument that is not really a swap, despite its name, is the **credit default swap** (CDS). This is a derivative you can use to insure yourself against the possibility that your debtors default on their loans. Its price is determined by an algorithm calculating the risk that a debtor will default; this calculation is performed a couple of times a year or such, and the buyer of the CDS pays a fee to the seller proportional to the risk that the seller bears on the buyer's behalf. You buy a CDS from someone to increase the quality of the asset that the insured loan represents because if you can make this asset risk-free for yourself, you will be able to borrow more money on it since it represents stronger collateral. If your borrowers do default on their loans, the body that sold you the CDS will have to pay you the missing money. In a normal market situation only a small proportion of CDSs are actually used for collecting money from sellers, due to the small number of debtors that actually default. In the debt crisis of 2008 large numbers of creditors sat on CDSs for defaulting loans, which created a crisis situation for CDS sellers such as American International Group (AIG), who quickly ran out of cash to pay all the CDS holders coming to their door.

Derivatives generally, apart from being an instrument for handling risk, are also used for speculation. Since a stock option only costs a trifle of the underlying share's value, you can make big profits from speculating with the help of options instead of the actual shares, because you can make larger bets with the resources you have. You can also make larger losses if you bet unwisely, and if you end up with a lot of risk-covering obligations you do not have the resources to cover, you will default.

Expanding derivatives markets have created a sort of market-endogenous **moral hazard**,[1] as investors no longer need to make their risk assessments of their investments as thorough as before. They can offload the risk to someone else, who will cover the loss if things go wrong. Speculation in derivatives can also put a lot of financial power in the hands of actors who are not capable of handling the consequences of their investments, such as when Nick Leeson made Barings Bank default after careless options trading in Asia in the 1990s.

Money, manifest as **currencies** on the foreign exchange market, has also become an important financial instrument thanks to globalization. To interact economically in a foreign country you need to exchange your own money for the currency of the foreign country. With the internationalization and globalization of the world economy that has taken place since the Second World War, and especially with the deregulation of financial markets since the 1980s, the financial operations of exchanging one currency for another has become a market of its own. On this **forex market** different currencies are handled as commodities, and are traded like any other commodity. On the one hand, this market is important for making international trade and production function (see Chapter 7). Transnational corporations, banks, funds, and many others use this market to raise money for their everyday global operations, and to insure themselves against unwanted exchange rate movements using derivatives. On the other hand, this market can be very profitable for speculators with access to large sums of money. If you exchange €1 billion into a foreign currency in the morning, this foreign currency appreciates by 1 per cent over the course of the day, and you exchange it all back into Euros in the evening, you are €10 million richer. If it depreciates by 1 per cent, you are €10 million poorer, but since you are smart you would not expose yourself to that risk, would you? As a forex trader you would have checked the likelihood of upward and downward movements in the exchange rate of the foreign currency, and would take only those positions with a good probability of moving your way, so that over time you would gain more than you lost, even if some days would mean losses.

Currency speculation can create big problems, such as when it makes exchange rates move in directions that affect the international trading conditions of a country. Even if trade figures might indicate that an exchange rate adjustment is called for, currency speculation on these figures can amplify this adjustment out of proportion. Currency flight from a country may happen at the whim of forex traders and create national crises, as in Asia in 1997.

This account of financial instruments is by no means exhaustive; the speed at which new instruments are invented for the financial markets is high. This account is meant to offer a picture of the main groups of instruments traded on financial markets. As we have seen, each instrument represents a relation to the real economy, or between financial actors. When we understand what circulates in these markets, the relations it represents and how it is valued, it is easier to understand the logic of the whole thing.

The logic of the whole thing

The first point to appreciate is that these markets are not about products in the traditional sense (even though some actors talk about these instruments and services as 'products'). Since these markets deal with symbols representing claims, risks and ownership, there is very little material real-world friction – such as mining, smelting, producing, assembling, shipping, wholesaling, retailing and the like – to slow down financial commerce. This means that the symbols on these markets can be sold and bought quickly, and consequently the turnover on these markets is very fast.

The second factor determining the logic of these markets is that prices are formed on the basis of the future: what actors in these markets extrapolate will happen in the future, and what this will mean for the values of, and profits from, their instruments and positions. A share, for instance, is highly valued if the corporation in question is expected to deliver large profits in the future, but worthless if it is about to close down operations. A lending deal is expensive – with a high rate of interest – if the borrower is more likely to default in the future, but has a low interest rate if the borrower is sure to repay the loan and its interest. The values circulating on the financial markets, therefore, are based on expectations about what will happen, and only a fraction of the value of all financial instruments represents material assets in existence today. As the future unfolds in the 'real economy' and market extrapolations are verified or falsified, expectations change and prices are adjusted accordingly.

Third, and finally, actors on these markets have to form and communicate their extrapolations in similar ways, to make continuous market interaction possible. People who do not understand each other cannot do more than one or two trades with each other. Since they do not interpret information in similar ways and do not form extrapolations on the same basis, one or both of the parties will feel cheated or insecure and withdraw. To make continuous financial interaction possible, a common discourse among all parties is crucial – in other words, they all need to understand how everyone involved in the interaction thinks, in order to feel confident about what they are trading and trusting of the other parties. You have to understand and abide by a basic business–school discourse on society and markets to make sense and trade on these markets. It is not necessary for you to like it, or find it rational, but you must understand it and act according to it. From afar this system might look like a highly complicated and scientific body of knowledge, but it ultimately boils down to these central collective tenets:

- Markets always drift towards equilibrium, and as financial actors we make markets reach equilibrium faster than they would have done if we had not been there.
- We are all well informed, and act rationally on information indicating price changes for the financial instruments we are in charge of.
- We oil the wheels of the real economy by allocating financial resources to those who have the best use for them – that is, those who pay the most for them.
- We allocate resources more efficiently than politicians do, since we act on economic incentives and seek to maximize profit, while politicians seek to maximize votes.

This is the common discourse, and as long as your actions indicate that you act according to it, you are understood – not necessarily trusted, but understood as acting in a way that is predictably profit-driven, selfish and rational. The 'oiling the wheels' allocation argument is also what legitimizes these markets in their relation to society. Since the values in these markets today are many times larger than those in the real economy, it has become clear that they do more than simply oil the wheels of everyday economic interaction.

The actors

Those doing business on financial markets can be anything from individual day traders logging on to an electronic trading platform to gamble with their savings to institutional investors moving billions between each other. There are, however, a limited number of types of actor that do the bulk of trading and investing on these markets. To understand and be able to influence and change financial markets, it is helpful to understand this typology of actors and what they do.

Banks are important financial actors. The traditional understanding of what banks do is **financial intermediation**: mediating between people with savings that they do not intend to use immediately and those who need to borrow money in the present for investment and consumption. The banks take in people's savings and pay some interest on these deposits, and then lend out to borrowers, charging these a higher interest rate. The difference between the deposit interest payouts and the interest earnings on loans is kept by the banks to finance their own operations and profits. The difference between a bank's financing costs and its earnings from lending is called the **spread**, which is what makes banking profitable. Since depositors normally do not come all at once to withdraw their money, a bank can lend out more than people have saved with it. It needs to keep only a small fraction of the deposited cash to be able to service average daily withdrawals. This is called **fractional banking**, and does not usually lead to problems. In an abnormal situation, however, more depositors than usual might want to withdraw their savings from the bank at the same time, and if there is widespread insecurity about a particular bank's ability to pay back deposits, there might be a 'bank run'. Since fractional banking is normal procedure, almost all banks go bust if they are hit by a large enough bank run. Today, therefore, many states have deposit guarantees for normal bank accounts, such as current or savings accounts, to stave off panic runs and bank crashes in times of financial market problems.

The banking system, as a system, also produces money by **credit expansion**. This is not the illicit printing of money in dark cellars (as some YouTube videos portray it), but results from the circulation of money through the banking system. If you deposit US$1,000 in a bank account, your bank will lend out about US$980 of that. The borrower will then deposit US$950 in another bank, which will lend out US$930 to another borrower, who will deposit US$900 in a third bank, and so on. After your original US$1,000 has circulated through the banking system over the course of a year, it may have resulted in hundreds of thousands of dollars being used in society in different ways. Depending on the **velocity of money** (how fast money circulates in an economy), and how much of their deposits banks are compelled to keep in their vaults, credit expansion happens at a variable pace. Authorities, such as central banks, know this and often plan their interventions in the economy accordingly.

Retail banking is banking for real-world individuals, who deposit savings and borrow money for houses and cars and such. Deposits from this banking by ordinary consumers provide the basis of a bank's financing. **Business banking**, meanwhile, is for firms of all sizes that need to borrow to invest or stock up on intermediate goods and the like, or need a bank to distribute wages to employers, or for other corporate banking services. Business banking overlaps to a large degree with **investment banking**, which constructs and issues (or 'underwrites') bonds for customer firms or for itself, and trades on the stock market and on different derivatives markets on its own behalf, for investors or both. These different forms of banking can be performed by separate banks specializing in the respective activities, or by a single bank with different branches or departments for each activity.

The banking system as a whole is central to the modern project, and under capitalism well-functioning private banks are vital for economic policy. It is through the banking system that monetary policy operates, and that states can finance their lending needs. Employers today pay their employees and suppliers through the banking system; international traders use the banking system for payments; and so on and so forth. The system's importance for economic interaction becomes especially evident during financial crises, and in order to discipline banks and prevent financial crises from happening, they are subject to strict regulation. If you want to open a bank today you will need a special permit; you must show that you have (access to) a sufficient amount of capital to be trustworthy; you must subject your firm to regular inspection by financial authorities; you must strictly follow procedure in your contacts with customers to protect their interests; you must have access to a cash buffer in order to be able to pay unexpectedly large withdrawals; and you must have a system of controls against financial crimes for which people might try to use your bank, such as money laundering, tax fraud or financial market manipulation. Regulations like these exist to safeguard everyday economic interaction against the destructive effects of financial crises and defaults, as well as against criminal and corrupt financial behaviour. Regulations are costly for financial actors, in two ways. First, the control mechanisms that banks must have in place cost money, which the banks could have used more profitably in financial commerce instead of for back-office self-discipline. Second, and more importantly, regulations reduce profits by limiting the trades, positions and contracts you can pursue as a bank. Regulations might stop you from exploiting the full commercial potential in a currency or share trade; they might stop you from lending money to a 'subprime' borrower wanting to buy a house that is likely to rise in value; they might stop you from issuing bonds with future mortgage repayments as collateral; they might forbid you to trade on information that you have but other market actors do not; and so on. There is, therefore, a fundamental conflict of interest between private financial market actors and regulating authorities under capitalism. Regulators try to control the risk of destructive effects on society from financial markets, while market actors want to maximize profits by exploiting the full speculative opportunity they can identify in the market. This tug of war has swung back and forth over the years, with deregulation and free financial markets from the late 19th century until the 1920s, then re-regulation from the 1930s to several decades after the Second World War, and then a new deregulation from the 1980s up until the crisis of 2008. Since this crisis there has been a wave of regulatory measures coming out of the global institutional framework for financial market policy aiming to stabilize globalized financial markets, so far with unclear success. The bulk of these post-2008 regulatory measures concerns banks, since they, especially the larger institutions, are **systemically important** financial actors, and if they run into difficulties the global economy will be in trouble again.

Funds are also important actors. A fund invests to the benefit of those who invest in the fund, with the purpose of making investors' money grow. In addition to this fundamental purpose, funds can have additional objectives, such as promoting sustainable corporate behaviour, supporting and investing in start-up companies, or protecting and enlarging the pool of money allotted for workers' pensions. Pension funds in particular have become big actors on stock markets and other financial markets, simply because of the large number of investors continuously investing in them. As a pension fund buys more shares, it also grows as a corporate owner, and as such expands its potential influence. Not all funds exercise this increased power, but rather sit on their assets and move money to the benefit of their investors. One of the largest funds in the world is the California State Teachers' Retirement System (CalSTRS), which presents itself as an active sustainability-promoting investor (www.calstrs.com). Such **ethical investing** is on the rise, but most funds are still focused on investor return rather than the social or environmental consequences of their investments. Many funds focus on one type of asset and the return this offers, such as interest rate funds, which invest in bonds and bills, or stock market funds, which invest in shares. Some funds can also invest in derivatives related to the instruments they specialize in. Other funds mix different types of asset, so as to maximize returns to investors: if the stock market falls, they move to gold or bonds, and so on. A special type of fund that mixes assets in this way is the **hedge fund**. The typical hedge fund is set up by a group of wealthy individuals, who provide a vast amount of money to a small group of (hopefully) talented traders and analysts, and tell them to make this money grow in whatever way possible. The difference between a hedge fund and an ordinary stock market fund is that the hedge fund, with the more open mandate from its investors, can use a variety of instruments and techniques to 'hedge its bets'. A hedge fund, therefore, will also operate on the stock options market while it invests in shares, and so on. Since hedge funds returned to public attention in the 1980s markets have developed, and today most actors, not least banks, operate in similar ways. As regards regulations, large funds in which the public is invited to invest tend to be regulated more strictly than small funds that are closed to the general public (but this, again, differs between territories and countries).

Stockbrokers might be described as the public face of the financial markets. Their job is typically to buy and sell shares on behalf of customers or employers. Their waving and shouting in front of computer screens and on trading floors has become emblematic of the whimsical emotions and stress in finance. This expressive activity, however, is signalling that they are willing to buy or sell a certain instrument at a certain price, or simply signalling to a colleague that a share price is moving a certain way, information that the colleague can then act on in some way. They may have got an order to buy a share at a certain price, and when the share reaches that price, they signal that they are buying. On a trading floor, such as that of the New York Stock Exchange, the activity as a whole looks insane, but for those involved there is a method and logic to it. A certain frenzy often develops when there are large price fluctuations, because huge losses and gains can materialize during these swings, but this is also part of the culture. Open outcry trading floors have lost much of their importance to financial markets with globalization and digitalization, and a majority of the trades and most of the trading volume is now done from bank offices, over the phone, or by investors and traders placing sell or buy orders on digital platforms. With digitalization has also come high-frequency trading, in which computers react within microseconds to miniscule price changes, and complete fast trades on these very thin signals on their own. Since computers can do many such small trades in a short time, profits can grow very fast. What also happens is that computers amplify price movements by acting procyclically in this mechanical way. What has made this digitalization possible is the development of technical analysis.

Investors and traders on the stock market work with two kinds of analysis: **fundamental** or **technical analysis**. Fundamental analysis is concerned with the fundamentals of the listed corporation, such as its market share, productivity, sales increases, revenue per sold item, patents and other immaterial assets, and so on. When fundamentalist analysts are determining whether to buy, keep or sell shares, they look at the fundamental real-world situation of the corporation and work out what this situation indicates in terms of future dividends from, and price movements of, its shares. This analysis takes some time, and actors considering investing after having done this analysis would normally plan to keep the shares for some time, from a week to a year or more. Technical analysis, on the other hand, does not concern itself with fundamentals, but instead looks at the price curve and what the various bumps, spikes and directions on this curve indicate, as certain figurations of this curve indicate that in X amount of instances, the price will move in a predictable way. What the figurations of the price curve typically indicate in terms of price movements is inferred from how fundamentalists typically behave, so trading based on technical analysis is understood to be a reaction to underlying real-world fundamental developments. Traders working with technical analysis will not concern themselves much with dividends in the coming year, but with price movements in the coming minutes or days. In New York I was once told that "technical analysis is the key to being a trader", meaning that if you want to make big money fast, for yourself or for your employer, you have to work with technical analysis. If your task is to manage funds for rich people over a longer period, then fundamental analysis might be a better strategy, which will also make you rich, though not as fast. With high-frequency trading, and a large army of traders working with technical analysis, most trades on the stock exchange are no longer done on the basis of real-world developments, but on the basis of what others on the market do, so in terms of the number of trades done each day, the stock market is increasingly becoming a self-referential system.

If investors do not want, or are not able, to analyze the fundamentals of an asset they plan to invest in, they can look at the **rating** of the asset instead. Rating is done by rating firms, who supply the market with rating scores that indicate the investment quality of the asset. A credit rating, which is perhaps the most important rating for countries, corporations and citizens, is the score that tells prospective investors and creditors how likely it is that the borrower will not pay as planned. When a corporation issues a bond, it pays a ratings firm, such as Moody's, to rate the bond. The rating firm then performs a thorough fundamental analysis of the corporation, and comes up with a rating that can be anything from BB (junk/risky) to AAA (prime/risk-free). The lower the rating firm deems the risk, the lower the interest rate the issuer of the bond will have to pay. Bonds issued by nation states are rated in the same way, with risky countries (from an investor's perspective) getting low ratings and paying high interest rates, and risk-free countries getting high ratings and paying low interest rates. Even citizens are rated in this way, and in many countries a person's credit rating can be had from a ratings services firm in an instant, such as when a person plans to buy a cell phone or borrow money for a new car. Credit rating has a strong disciplinary effect, because the norms and financial market discourse of the day make up the fundament of the analysis (Sinclair and Thomas, 2001; Gill, 2008). This is quite natural, since investors want the information and credit score that is relevant to them in their daily economic interaction. If countries, corporations or citizens want to avoid higher borrowing costs, they must show that they are not breaking the norms or the normality limits of the discourse. Unorthodox behaviour will be punished by the market, and the first stone is often cast in the form of a worsened credit rating.

The last – but biggest – type of actor in financial markets is nation states, which operate in the financial markets in three ways. First, states are significant actors in the debt markets, borrowing and lending for fiscal policy reasons, to finance public investments, or to place public resources in profitable and secure positions. Some states, especially oil-exporting countries such as Norway or Bahrain, are also major actors on many markets through the funds that handle their oil incomes. Second, states are important by force of their central banks, which run their monetary policies. This task includes issues such as managing the exchange rate, keeping inflation in check, supplying enough liquidity to the financial markets and to the real economy, and surveying and reacting to market developments that will have a bearing on monetary policy. To achieve these tasks, central banks most often have to act **counter-cyclically**, or go against the market, such as when they have to buy their own currency on forex markets if there is a trend towards selling the currency. If the central bank moved with the trend and also sold its own currency, the exchange rate would drop even further and import prices would rise, which would be the same as increased inflation, and would therefore threaten to prevent the central bank from meeting its inflation target. One way to entice the market into buying a specific currency is to raise the interest rate on central bank bonds, which will then affect the general interest rate in the country in question. Monetary policy, as we can see, is very much a matter of balancing different objectives, and central banks do this by operating as an actor on the financial markets, and by adjusting the interest rate to influence the behaviour of market participants. Third, and most importantly, states are the legislators and regulators of financial markets, and as we saw in Chapter 3, all markets get their specific historical form through the institutional order politically constructed in and around them. During globalization, national financial markets were opened up to foreign investment and competition through national institutional changes (Helleiner, 1994). While this was done uniformly on a national level, the result was a market operating on a global scale, so that financial market dynamics in one part of the world came to affect the whole global financial system. Especially influential were those states with principal financial centres (PFCs), such as New York in the US, Frankfurt in Germany and London in Britain. Regulatory changes by states hosting a PFC became this influential, since all other states had to adjust their laws and regulations in order to make their own financial markets compatible with PFC markets (Germain, 1997). If the remaining nation states had not adjusted, their domestic investors and speculators would have perceived the difference as hampering the profitability of their home markets, and would have moved their capital and activities to PFC markets or countries better adapted to their needs. This moving of financial capital was eased greatly by the many national financial deregulations of globalization, and politically supported by the ideology of the time. The full consequences of this global process were hard to perceive in the 1980s, when most of the national legislative and regulatory changes were put in place. Thirty years later the nature of the genie let out of its bottle was clearer.

The 2008 crisis

Two seeds were planted long before the 2008 crisis came into full bloom. The first seed was the invention of the CDS by a group of talented mathematicians at J.P. Morgan in 1997 (Tett, 2010). With the development of an algorithm that could calculate the likelihood that a business would default on its loans, it became possible to construct and price a derivatives instrument related to this risk. The second seed was planted by the Clinton administration, which in 1999 succumbed to intense financial lobbying and scrapped the Glass–Steagall Act in the US. This regulatory change was carried out based on the growing conviction that financial markets served society best if they were allowed to regulate themselves. The ideological truth at the time was that financial market actors were fundamentally rational, and that no rational market actor would trade or deal in a way that put the survival of their employer firm at risk. Additionally, with the growing market in derivatives, which indicated that the market itself could handle and distribute risk, scrapping the Glass–Steagall Act seemed like a rational thing to do. What this law had done since the 1930s was keep retail and investment banking separate. It prohibited investment banking operations (such as bond issuing) using retail banking assets (such as mortgages) as material or collateral. Basically, it stated that you could not sell claims on small businesses and homeowners on to other financial actors, nor could you raise money using the future payments of ordinary workers as collateral. The lesson from the 1930s was that if financial instruments based on ordinary people's lives got caught up in a financial market maelstrom the societal consequences could become devastating. But at the turn of the millennium this was considered impossible, since the financial markets were deemed rational and scientifically much more advanced than they had been 70 years earlier. With the Glass–Steagall firewall between business and retail banking gone, banks' assets became much more liquid, because an ordinary mortgage was no longer merely a future stream of money to plan for; it was also a tradeable asset that you could either repackage and sell, or raise money on. In other words, banks could have access today to resources they had previously had to wait for 20 or so years to get hold of in full. A new source of liquidity had opened up.

The soil where these two seeds were planted was fertile. Money was cheap: interest rates were low, and fell even further after the dot–com crash in 2000, and still further after 9/11 in 2001. Additional liquidity came with George W. Bush's tax cuts and military spending, the money streams of both running through the financial markets. Real estate prices all over the world, and especially prices on private homes, had been rising since the early 1990s, which made the IMF and many others talk of a real estate boom. This boom gave all homeowners an additional sense of wealth, encouraging them to move to larger homes, or consume more on credit secured against their homes, or invest in funds and shares and other financial instruments. As financial markets were deregulated internationally, this dynamic spread throughout the OECD, which resulted in a global business boom. The US drove this boom with its high consumption and military adventures in Iraq and Afghanistan. Rising house prices, in combination with the possibility of using CDSs to insure against borrowers defaulting, led banks to approach new types of borrower with mortgage offers. These 'subprime' borrowers were people that would not have got a bank loan in normal times, due to insecure job situations or bad credit ratings, but now these groups became an interesting opportunity for making use of all the extra liquidity that was sloshing around. The 'subprime' logic was that if one borrower defaulted, the bank could sell the house and get its money back, and if it insured this group of loans (which were at the same time assets) with a CDS, it would be even more secure. Once a bundle of new mortgages had been made out, creditors repackaged these claims in instruments such as collateralized debt obligations (CDOs), sold these and went on another lending spree.

This market liquidity bonanza was fuelled even further by global trade and investment patterns. The US imported much more than it exported, leading to an outflow of money from the US to both Asia and Europe. This stimulated the business cycle around the world. According to standard Economics, a normal country with a huge trade deficit would see its exchange rate fall until imports became too expensive for its citizens to consume, which would then lead to a rebalancing of imports and exports. But that is only the theory, and the US was not a normal country. What happened was that a large proportion of the US dollar export income accumulated in China and Europe found its way back into the US to be invested in government bonds and on the booming financial markets. Even though the US dollar had a floating exchange rate, therefore, the expected depreciation effect on the currency from the trade and budget deficits was neutralized by financial investment flows back into the US, adding further cheap liquidity.

The crisis started to bud in 2007, by which time large groups among the 'subprime' homeowners had run into problems servicing their debts. The banks thus ended up with an unexpected number of houses that they had to get rid of to salvage some money from these non-performing loans. Both the banks and many homeowners struggled to sell these houses at the same time, which led to a fall in house prices, first in the US and then around the world. As a consequence, the collateral for many of the bonds and CDOs issued on the market was no longer sufficient, and the future money flows from homeowners also looked thinner than the original analysis had indicated. In other words, the future was not unfolding in a way that corroborated market valuations. Not at all.

The crisis came into full bloom in September 2008, when Lehman Brothers became unable to sell new bonds and derivatives to finance the payback to holders of older derivatives and maturing bonds. The tacit agreement up until then had been that the state would always come to the rescue of big banks when default was looming, since too much value would be destroyed if they were allowed to default. But the Bush administration did not rescue Lehman, which sent a shock wave through the global financial industry. An informal bond between the state and financial markets had been broken. The panic was somewhat soothed, though not cured, by the rescue of AIG from its CDS adventure, where this firm had taken on much more risk than it could cover once the crisis broke out. The crisis brought the global financial market to a standstill in the autumn of 2008.

What the crisis made evident was that expectations had been inflated to unrealistic and overblown proportions, and that prices had moved upwards with these expectations. It was unrealistic to assume that house prices would rise forever at the same pace. It was unrealistic to think that large groups of relatively poor borrowers would be able to service their mortgage loans, especially as many of these deals were constructed so that costs were low at the start but rose steeply when payback holidays ended. It was unrealistic to believe that there would be enough investors willing to invest in securities consisting of repackaged securities backed by mortgages, in order to finance the maturing of bonds backed by the same type of securities as collateral. The CDS market flourished after 2005, which indicates that many market actors saw that prices had lost contact with reality and wanted to offload risk from their positions. But this only created a false sense of security, merely multiplying the number of interlinkages through which market participants were connected to each other, and increased everyone's dependence on someone else to deliver on their liabilities and risk-carrying promises. At the foundation of this disintegrating, porous financial construction, house prices fell in most countries, investment in real assets slowed to nothing, consumption fell and workers in all parts of the world lost their jobs. In the meantime, financial market actors sat on whatever assets they had left, and crossed their fingers that their customer's customer's borrower would not default in a way that rolled back to them to make their own financial assets worthless. The future was impossible to chart, or bank on, or plan, or discount, or rate. With no clear future, there was no financial activity.

The G20 to the rescue

As no one was lending to anyone at the height of the crisis, central banks stepped in to ensure that there was enough liquidity in society for basic business to function. But this was mere life support, and it was clear that the usual top-level meetings would not suffice to secure a future for the global economy. To cure global capitalism, all the major players would have to cooperate, and both the old and the new industrial and economic powers would need to band together. This they did in London in April 2009, and that meeting marks the political ascendance of new industrial powers such as China and Brazil to a position at top-level global politics. Since both the old G7 and the new powers had to agree on how to handle the crisis, and these were diverse countries with diverse interests, no major global economic changes could be planned or agreed by the diplomats preparing the meeting. Those diplomats I have met, however, are proud that a comprehensive crisis strategy was able to be designed and agreed upon at all, given all these participants.

The crisis strategy encompassed a number of measures and promises. First, the IMF was promised access to an additional US$750 billion if countries should run into payment difficulties. This was to assure global entrepreneurs that they could continue their international business, and that there would be money to pay them even if a country ran into payment difficulties. The Financial Stability Forum, which had been established after the Asian crisis in 1997 to strengthen the 'global financial architecture', was upgraded to a Financial Stability Board (FSB), with the explicit task of overseeing the development of new regulations for global financial markets. The FSB was to be hosted by the BIS, and would work together with this organization and its network to develop new regulations. The G20 also agreed among themselves to abstain from all trade-disturbing protectionist measures in their crisis management, in essence promising to stick to WTO agreements and the applied tariff levels that had existed before the crisis. Some extra billions were also reserved for possible lending to developing countries as necessary, to help them continue trading. Some of the derivatives that had aggravated the risk-taking and the subsequent crisis were to be changed to centralized exchange trading, to increase transparency and oversight. Finally, the OECD countries pledged to abide by IMF advice – which they were not obliged to follow, and indeed mostly neglected, since they all had access to market financing if they needed it. "We call on the IMF to lead us in this endeavour", British Prime Minister Gordon Brown said in the final declaration of the meeting. Getting the G20 members to agree on all this, so that heads of government could be flown in to shake hands and get photographed, was quite the diplomatic achievement. The underlying message of the strategy, however, could be summarized as 'more of the same, but we would prefer it to be in an orderly fashion'.

On the national level, governments had to take a hands–on approach to dealing with the crisis. Banks on the brink of default had to be rescued in various ways, which often proved to be a very expensive task that placed great strain on public budgets. The same budgets had to shoulder the rising costs of people made redundant because of the general recession and the closing down of businesses, and who therefore had to be supported with unemployment insurance or social welfare. In newly industrialized countries without those social security nets, such as China, armies of factory workers were simply locked out of their jobs, which led to a massive exodus to relatives in the countryside. In better–off countries, like the Baltics and Ireland, public workers, teachers, nurses, bureaucrats and others were also sacked or had to accept substantially reduced wages, in order for governments to balance their budgets in this new situation. These cuts were made even more drastic by the fact that official budgets had also been inflated by the swelling liquidity of the early 2000s, and when these budgets were burdened with increased social costs alongside new industry and bank support, workers and public employees were handed the bill. Often these cuts were not enough to balance the budgets, and government debt in many countries, such as Greece and Italy, ballooned, leading to public debt crises and harsh austerity policies that still haunt these countries a decade later.

Central banks took part in crisis management by lowering interest rates aggressively, to the extent that real interest rates first entered negative territory, and after some years a number of central banks even started with negative nominal interest rates. In other words, they had become so eager to pump liquidity into financial markets and the real economy that they charged banks and other financial actors for placing capital in the central banks. As growth failed to pick up, central banks started to buy bonds of various kinds – an activity termed **'quantitative easing'** (QE) – to signal that central banks were making access to liquidity easier simply by expanding its quantity on the markets. A problem was that most of this liquidity did not trickle down to the real economy, but remained on the financial markets and was placed in assets delivering some assured return. Lending to ordinary businesses in crisis-ridden everyday life was too dangerous for many years after the crisis, so actors preferred to invest the cheap liquidity on the stock market or in some emerging market bond or such, where they got at least some return on it. After several years this central bank liquidity stimulus began to produce bubbles, in the form of overinvested bond markets that drove interest rates even lower, pumped up share prices and, in ordinary life, raised house prices back to (and beyond) previous levels. But would this not lead to inflation, the attentive reader might ask? Well, if all this money had ended up in the pockets of ordinary people for buying goods and services, retail prices would have started to rise, which would have constituted inflation as measured on the consumer price index (CPI). However, burgeoning asset prices do not affect the CPI, which means that interest rate and QE stimulus was able to continue without contributing to inflation.

The combination of austerity policies and central bank stimuli led this crisis management to have a tremendous effect on inequality. While workers, public employees and the like saw their wages stagnate or drop and government services and transfers shrink, the upper classes saw their wealth increase when liquidity stimulus and expansion inflated asset values. Those with some income and real estate also had their lives made easier by the lowering of interest rates, car subsidies and other government policies aiming to prop up demand. In short, both the crisis in itself and the crisis management measures aggravated inequality.

Reconstructing global financial markets

There is almost a universal consensus that financial markets need to change. The motives for and ideas behind this view, however, vary considerably depending on ideology and position. Neoliberals and liberals, and others supportive of economic globalization generally, tend to see today's financial markets as too volatile, risky and crisis-prone, and argue that politicians have failed to design an appropriate institutional framework. Exactly how this framework would look is a matter of much debate, but within this camp, financial markets in themselves are viewed as beneficial to society and economic development, and it is believed that we need only to design the right institutional order and framework to realize their full societal contribution and benefit.

For socialists, financial markets are a vital capitalist mechanism securing and maximizing the exploitation of the workers of the world. Financial instruments are symbols for capitalist claims on specific parts of the surplus value that workers produce. A share on the stock market is a claim on the surplus value that the corporation can extract from its employees in the future. A government bond is a claim on the taxes that the state can extract from its citizens in the future, and the interest rate on this bond is an additional work-free reward that the investor can claim simply by having the option to lend money to the state. Other debts work in the same way. In addition to these unjust exploitative mechanisms of financial markets, socialists also view the influence of financial markets as deeply undemocratic. Society is to a large degree shaped by financial capital, since the decisions that capitalists make as regards where and in what to invest influence the lives of a majority of the global population, who have almost no say in the process. From a socialist perspective, corporations should be owned by those working in them, and run for the benefit of the people. Banks should be owned by the public and run democratically, and should serve the interest of the people rather than of their capitalist owners. A socialist reconstruction of financial markets, therefore, would change them completely, and would eradicate much of the interaction we recognize as financial markets.

In the following discussion on how we could reconstruct financial markets, I will focus on the relation between the symbolic level, where instruments circulate, and the real economy. Each financial instrument is a symbol for some kind of relation to the real economy, and establishes a future value that is to be realized performatively in everyday life (Andersson, 2016; Beckert, 2016). It is crucial to analyze how these financial relations might be reconstructed, institutionalized and made to support a just and sustainable global political economy. It is important that a discussion about the role of financial markets does not confine itself to the symbolic level where its signs circulate if we are serious about reconstructing the global political economy.

Reconstructing ownership

A form of ownership contingent to capitalist modernity is the institution of the limited liability company owned by shareholders, which constructs the firm as a separate juridical individual existing independently of its owners. The ultimate moral responsibility for corporate behaviour consequently falls on no individual or group, but instead in a vacuum between management, owners and customers. Proponents of capitalism point to the opportunities this construction opens up for entrepreneurs to finance their creative projects over the stock market, while at the same time standing apart from ill-conceived and growth-hampering interventions from owners and financiers wanting to have it their way. Critics of capitalism instead emphasize the lack of effort that investors put into the firms they profit from, and the fact that the dividends and wealth they enjoy are the products of those working in companies they own but are not accountable for. As we stand on the cusp of a necessary economic reconstruction, with a majority of the biggest companies currently set up as limited liability firms, how to reconstruct the institution of ownership is a natural place to start our analysis.

Problem-solving strategies aimed at retaining the stock market as we know it with some institutional tweaking could start where **ethical investing** is today. As we saw earlier in this chapter, some funds confine their investing strategies to shares in listed corporations that have some sort of sustainability focus in their business model, and these funds are therefore referred to as 'ethical'. It would be a perfectly workable institutional change to rewrite the rules for companies that apply to be listed on a stock exchange to include sustainability clauses, based on the same ethical approach as that of ethical funds. As regards environmental sustainability, this could be done, for instance, by allowing only companies that have a proven positive climate effect to have their shares traded on a stock exchange. For social sustainability, the clause could be that only companies that pay **living wages** wherever they operate are allowed to be listed. You could add that only companies with a proven record of multiethnic and gender-equal employment are allowed onto the stock market. Clauses to ensure economic sustainability could be similar to today's rules about solvency, transparency and jurisprudence, or you could take it further and say that only companies with a proven record of substantial tax contributions to the state and its citizens are allowed to apply. Additions such as these would not change the basic principles of capitalism or its institutional framework, but they would change the corporate behaviour of companies traded on stock exchanges. The owners would still bear little legal responsibility for the companies' behaviour, but the framework for entrepreneurial activities would assure a higher degree of sustainability.

Strictly speaking, there is nothing today stopping a limited company, or any firm, from prioritizing sustainability above profit. Most countries have laws stating that the management of limited companies must act in the interest of their owners, but defining this interest is up to the owners and their board. A company board is fully within its rights to tell management to maximize all three dimensions of sustainability, without prioritizing one over the others. Most investors in a listed corporation today would expect the firm to act only from a profit motive, confined in its actions only by the law and the values of the corporation. While these values might have a certain sustainability dimension, it is dire work to change the norm that puts profit first, hence institutional changes, such as the sustainability conditions for listing the company on a stock exchange discussed in the previous section, might speed up change. They would also, in all likelihood, exert downward pressure on corporate profits, but given the fantastic extent to which money was hoarded by financial actors during globalization (Piketty, 2014), prioritizing their profits is an odd decision when we stand on the brink of an ecological planetary disaster.

A more profound change would be changing the laws regulating liability for company behaviour. It is by no means self-evident that the owners of limited companies should be without legal responsibility for what their companies do; this is a modern capitalist invention. Radical Islamists, for instance, stress that this type of ownership is sinful, and not in accord with their religious ideas about how a morally correct business relation – which the Koran promotes – should be. European green parties have discussed changing shareholding laws so that owners become accountable for their companies' behaviour. If shareholders were legally responsible for what their firms did, it would require much more work and engagement for investors to become owners of a corporation, and if firms broke environmental or labour standard laws, for instance, then owners would have to make good on that. Buying a share would mean that you had the same responsibility as corporate management, but in proportion to how many shares you chose to own. So there are many ways that corporate ownership could be changed without undermining the basic capitalist principle of private ownership of the means of production.

Structurally transformative changes, on the other hand, would mean that shareholding as a primary capitalist principle would be replaced by other forms of ownership. There are many different ideas and historical examples of other ways to organize ownership of production, ranging from Robert Owen's utopian socialist experiments in 19th-century England to worker occupations of factories to continue operations after the owners had abandoned them during the Argentinian financial crisis of 2001. If we look at these examples, there are a couple of overarching principles governing ownership of the means of production in structurally transformative ways. The first and best-known example is the Soviet-style **state ownership** and **central planning**, outlined briefly in the second part of Marx and Engels' *Communist Manifesto* (1848). Under this system the people own the means of production and the state represents the people. Production is organized according to the needs of the people, which are charted and determined by the state, which organizes production to supply the people with the required quantities of all items. This matching of production to the needs of the people needs careful planning, and in centrally planned economies government departments doing this planning tended to become very big and powerful. One positive aspect of this type of central planning was the fact that the large-scale restructuring to meet the needs of the people was done quite quickly. Among the negative aspects was the fact that the state determining the people's needs did not necessarily listen to the people, but, acting on ideological premises, used force to make the people produce what it had decided the people needed. Centrally planned economies, therefore, were often termed **command economies**. Entrepreneurial creativity also tended to get suppressed and stymied within centrally planned economies, though it found an outlet of sorts on the black market that often flourished alongside centrally planned economic interaction. Scientific and technological creativity, on the other hand, did not fare as badly as the entrepreneurial. If we look at capitalist economies, and how they have been built and rebuilt over the last two centuries, we can see a strong element of central planning in the building of welfare states and large private corporations, in the (re-)building of infrastructures and in the political running of national economies in wartime. The pervasive and all-encompassing central planning of the Soviet system, therefore, is not the only version of official/public ownership and central planning. This principle of ownership is still important in many countries for the production of certain goods and services, and will probably be useful in a future economic reconstruction.

Another principle of ownership is that of the commons: a resource such as a sea or a grazing area that can be utilized by the many for their production needs (see Chapter 4). It has long been argued that such collective resources are bound to be overused when they are used by many producers striving to maximize their profits; that they will send too many cattle to graze a commons, for example, and thus destroy it. This argument is called the 'tragedy of the commons'. Elinor Ostrom, however, showed in 1990 that this is not at all what usually happens. What she found was that if there is general understanding and trust between the users of a commons, they tend to develop their own institutional framework for how to use it, and act as a collective for maintaining and developing their common resource. For a long time, the principle of the commons has been intellectually applied to natural resources, but there are several human–made resources to which the principle could also be applied, such as financial transactions systems, human rights law, money, infrastructure and so on. The fundamental prerequisite for collective running of a commons is *trust*, and if the building of commons becomes part of economic restructuring, the building and maintenance of trust between the users of those commons will also be important.

Cooperatives are another widespread form of ownership. The principle of these firms or organizations is that they are owned and run by the participants, sometimes but not always with an elected board that has the mandate to make operative decisions. One type of cooperative that most European readers have probably encountered is the **consumer cooperative**, a product of the labour movements of the late 19th and early 20th centuries. These started as a way to secure access to workers' staple consumer goods, independently of company stores often enjoying a monopoly in small industrial towns. In rich countries today these stores are hard to distinguish from privately owned commercial stores, but they are still formally run as cooperatives. Another common form is the **farmers' cooperative**, often set up to escape the power of buyers and wholesalers on the price and delivery terms for farmers' produce. By setting up a cooperative, farmers get more control over the price and terms of delivery of their produce, and at the same time are able to keep the profits from wholesaling that previously went to the private food industry. In the dairy fridge in your local store, you will most probably find products from a farmers' cooperative, if you read the fine print on the packaging. During the disruption following the 2001 financial crisis in Argentina, many factories were occupied by the workers, who took control of the machines and the buildings and continued to run production under cooperative ownership. Some of these businesses were sold by the previous owners to the workers for a symbolic sum; other occupations were deemed illegal by the former owners, who contested the takeovers in court and called for the police to drive the occupying cooperative out. While these occupations contested the formal institutional order for ownership (and the state did not act exclusively to protect the assets of the owners closing their factories), they also showed the world that workers are able to run modern production.

What these three more transformative forms of ownership show us is that the general modernist paradigm – according to which large companies should be owned by shareholders legally shielded from the real-world operations of their firms – is by no means universal. The global political economy already has successful examples of state ownership, commons and cooperatives, and these can be expanded as forms of ownership, if and when that is required. Getting production organized as independent from the stock market and the pressure to deliver profits with each quarterly report would help industry to achieve sustainability faster than if it continues to work to realize the future profits that are priced into shares by stockbrokers and investors.

Money

Money is a means of communication serving the same function for material communication as letters do for verbal communication. As letters and writing bridge distances in time and space so that people do not need to meet to communicate with language, money bridges distances in time and space so that producers of goods and services do not need to meet to communicate economically. Writing technologizes language and intellectual interaction, while money technologizes work and economic interaction. Money and writing have a common historical origin in the Mesopotamian era mentioned earlier in this chapter. As technologies they subsequently diverged, and technologized their respective areas of interaction and communication. Economic and intellectual interaction are not inherently separate phenomena, therefore, but the social application and institutionalization of their respective bridging technologies has made us understand and treat monetized and written relations as belonging to two different spheres in society. Many economic anthropologists have analyzed and shown how economic and monetized interaction is suffused with social and cultural meaning (Zelizer, 1994; Appadurai, 1996). In this way, money is an important means and technology by which socioeconomic subjectivity is built and exercised. As an institution and technology, money is not synonymous with greed or profit unless we decide that it should be that way. As with grammar in language and writing, institutions and power structures decide how we use money, and that is how it acquires meanings and functions specific to each historical era.

The present connotations of money, therefore, are not written in stone, but can be changed and influenced through ordinary monetary policy, or through other measures external to that field. There is no shortage of ideas if you look around among LETS projects (see Chapter 5), various activist groups, or at the discussion around cryptocurrencies. Money can be used, or not, for what we decide and in ways we agree on (Simmel, 1909/2004). The room for manoeuvre at present for beginning a more profound reconstruction is quite limited, but that is because of the narrow policy space pertaining to economic globalization as we know it (Peterson, 2003; Rodrik, 2011), and if that institutional order changed, money could be changed in multiple ways depending on national preferences.

The institution particularly important for money and monetary policy is of course the **central bank**. In a future reconstruction of the global political economy, central banks will need to be included and used to ensure that monetary policy is geared towards sustainability. The independence from political influence that they were granted during the 1990s will probably be reversed – especially if Economics generally, and monetary policy particularly, loses its status as an apolitical field, and is instead brought back under the banner of political decision-making. When this is done, central banks can no longer be left with the responsibility for running these policies and financial surveillance 'technically', as if they were physics laboratories or plumbing structures. One international institution well worth analyzing is the BIS. This Swiss bank, set up by central banks in 1930, is a kind of central bank for the central banks. Apart from functioning as a clearing centre for claims and liabilities between central banks, it also serves as a meeting place for central bankers, where they get together every two months to discuss current trends in the world economy and how these can be dealt with in monetary policy and financial regulation terms. The common understanding that is achieved during these meetings influences how the world economy develops, but the meetings are removed from democratic scrutiny. Since central banks were made independent from governments, this BIS interaction has become even more secluded from general and political influence and accountability (Andersson, 2016b). Opening up the structure of the BIS will be necessary to make reconstruction effective, because otherwise common understandings reached in the BIS might result in independent central banks counteracting economic policymaking, making fiscal and institutional measures ineffective with monetary and financial policy instruments, such as interest rate changes or forex market operations.

Conceptually, the activity of central banks collaborating through the BIS is an example of political issues being **rendered technical** (Li, 2007) and **depoliticized**. During the neoliberal globalization era monetary policy was removed from the political agenda because the discourse held that fighting inflation should be the overarching goal of monetary policy, and central banks got the job of achieving this technically. A typical move during any struggle for discursive hegemony is to establish a dominant understanding of an issue and then remove it from the political agenda to put it in the hands of experts to deal with (Mouffe, 2005). Even though the issue may still be politically charged for many, the institutional order resulting from this move shields the matter from political influence and change. In a reconstruction of the global political economy many issues related to financial markets, not just monetary policy and the role of the BIS, will need to be **repoliticized** (de Goede, 2004) – that is, brought back onto the political agenda to be dealt with as political, not technical, issues.

Cryptocurrencies such as Bitcoin represent a move in the opposite direction. Their proponents highlight the unpolitical and institutionally homeless nature of this money as a form of economic freedom. There is no central bank that issues cryptocurrencies, no state that can regulate their use for certain markets or purposes; instead every user is free to choose how to use them. They get their ephemeral but agreed-upon value from the use of so-called **blockchain technology**. It is this technology that allows the holders of cryptocurrencies to operate without a central bank. Each transaction needs to be digitally confirmed by all other holders of the cryptocurrency around the world. When the whole chain has confirmed (or blocked) the buyer and the seller and their deal, the deal takes place (or not). This is naturally a comparatively slow technology, because of the many computers and holders connected to it, and can only manage something like seven deals per second globally. It has also become a completely unsustainable energy consumer, the Bitcoin computers consuming as much electricity as the whole of Denmark. Nouriel Roubini also argues that cryptocurrencies quickly became centralized under unaccountable private actors seeking to maximize their own profits by controlling large sections of the data traffic in their closed networks (Roubini, 2018). The freedom that cryptocurrency proponents lauded in the early days of Bitcoin, therefore, seems to have become a chimera. For our purposes, an additional issue is the absence of an institutional framework that could inscribe cryptocurrencies into everyday life according to some political and social logic. This absence leaves cryptocurrencies devoid of any ability to stimulate or discourage different forms of economic interaction in a controlled fashion. Money and monetary policy have always been important instruments for achieving macroeconomic and political outcomes, and this instrumentality is lost with cryptocurrencies and blockchain-based economic interaction. Unless the political scope is widened to take this issue into account, blockchain technology will not be able to solve or even engage with any of the problems that global economic reconstruction needs to address.

Debt

'Debt' is also an elusive term, worthy of conceptual problematizing in our reconstruction of the global political economy. What makes debt socially and intellectually problematic is its three-dimensional character. The first dimension is the everyday meaning of the term: the idea that we owe someone money that we are expected to pay back in the future. The second dimension is debt as a social obligation. These social obligations reach out from the past, through the present and into the future. In everyday life these obligations normally function in a social fabric that evens out the burden of obligations over time, through some form of reciprocity. It is only if someone in a relation does not reciprocate that we start to perceive some kind of debt building up over time. The third dimension, related to the second, is that of the moral dynamics around debt. In the English language 'debt' and 'guilt' are two different words with separate meanings, but in German (as in several other languages) there is only one word for both concepts: *Schuld* (Graeber 2011). English makes a distinction between the economic relation in which one party owes the other party something, and the moral or religious burden a person carries after having behaved immorally. The distinction is not unknown in Germany or Sweden; its two sides simply do not have their own words. As debt functions today, in the relation between financial markets and the rest of society, these three dimensions are at play at the same time, although they are emphasized differently and to varying degrees in different instances of this relation.

On financial markets, between different speculating actors financing themselves, the first dimension of debt comes to the fore. Debt is simply a contract establishing monetary claims and liabilities between parties for a specific period, with interest earned by the creditor as remuneration for taking part in this relation. Even though these financial actors often try to establish rapport and trust between one another, it is primarily a business relation without deeper everyday social obligations. Even debt relations between financial and real-economy actors, such as between banks and homeowners, are still business transactions. In such cases, however, the social obligations of the homeowners, and how they have previously delivered on similar obligations, become a matter of financial and econometric adjudication, with the purpose of setting the prices the debtors will have to pay the banks for the entering into the debt relations. The first and second dimensions get intertwined, with the two parties approaching each other from their respective standpoints with their specific interests in the relation. The assessment of debtors' **credit scores**, which determine whether they are **creditworthy**, is done for financial market purposes, to determine the financial risks incurred by creditors with particular debts. The everyday behaviour that prospective borrowers have to give proof of to be creditworthy, however, needs to conform to standards and norms that creditors – and financial markets generally – understand and approve of. In this way, debt acquires a social disciplinary function, similar to IMF surveillance on the international level (see Chapter 3).

The third discursive and linguistic – perhaps even religious – dimension of debt serves to ensure everyday life functions while subjected to debt burdens and interest payments. The basic human principle of reciprocity, in combination with the normative overlap of debt and guilt, fosters a strong social norm in most modern societies that people must repay their debts (Graeber 2011), at least ordinary people in their everyday lives. In financial markets there is a rule of thumb that assumes a certain proportion of outstanding debts will not be repaid, and interest rates and fees are adjusted to cover this. A debt not repaid is the same as the loss of an asset, and some assets are bound to be lost. If the same phlegmatic attitude towards debt took hold among ordinary people in everyday life, the financial system would be endangered and the future priced into debt-based assets would not materialize. To help the financial market and its creditors uphold this norm in everyday life, modern states have laws regulating the fulfilment of debt contracts, as well as authorities assisting creditors with foreclosure routines and other ways to get hold of debtors' assets and money. As the numerous financial crises over the last decades have shown, huge asset losses on financial markets mean downturns, recessions and a loss of growth. This stands in stark contrast to the regular debt forgiveness practiced in ancient Mesopotamia, where at the start of each year rulers cancelled all farmers' debt to creditors in order to maintain social stability (Hudson, 2018). The rationale for this debt forgiveness was that if a clean slate was not offered to farmers every now and then, all land would end up in the hands of creditors, which would be followed by widespread poverty and the endangerment of social stability. So in this low- or no-growth society, debt had to be cancelled in order for resources to remain where people made good use of them. Today's financialized capitalism employs the opposite logic thanks to its growth and profit imperative. As Piketty's observation $r > g$ (income from financial capital ['return'] is higher than growth over time) implies, an increasing share of the world's wealth is ending up in financial markets. At the heart of this process, the norm that ordinary people must repay their debts creates and sustains the future extrapolated by debt markets.

Could we resurrect the Mesopotamian debt cancellation tradition? Strictly speaking, a parliament can give its government, head of state or central bank the right to cancel the debts of people by deciding on such a law. Whether the actor given this power would use it wisely or not, whether it would produce constructive and positive outcomes, and whether anyone would be willing to lend money and face the increased risk are issues worth pondering before resurrecting this tradition. A Mesopotamian debt cancellation would shift the risk of moral hazard to the borrowers, who would be incentivized to take on more debt than they are able to repay. On the other hand, laws and regulations could mitigate both kinds of moral hazard, by regulating behaviour in financial markets and outlawing certain debt relations and actions altogether.

One thing that has been deemed immoral for long periods of history is **interest** on money loans. Within Christianity and Islam there have been bans on lending money to be repaid with interest. I have already mentioned Islamic views on ownership and shareholding, and a similar relation is also in force as regards debt: you are not allowed to profit from participating in economic interaction only with your money; you have to participate socially and materially too. The Islamic ban on interest is not a ban on rich people using their money profitably; it is a ban on profiting from their money without committing to the actual activity in which their money is used. Even if interest today is quite trivial for most people, there is something to learn from this norm of committing to the object of your investment. Similar commitment norms could be inscribed into institutional frameworks for debt relations and debt market interaction. Viewed differently, paying interest might be the most efficient way to free borrowers from the influence of creditors, and it is unclear whether society would be better off if creditors were deeply engaged in the real interaction that their money was financing (the 1980s examples of IMF and World Bank engagement in developing countries would suggest not). Either way, interest on money loans is usually subject to regulation and law in one form or another, and this is important to include in our reconstructive analysis.

In the deregulated and crisis-prone financial environment of today, the norm has for some time held that interest rates should be set by market participants according to the principle of supply and demand. After the subprime crisis of 2008, it became clear that this bred deceitful and usurious lending behaviour among creditors, ensnaring borrowers in complex debt relations that they could not service once the nature of the deals became clear. Such practices can be outlawed without touching the charging of interest in itself. Many countries also have, or have had, **interest rate ceilings**, establishing a highest legal interest rate that banks and other lenders can charge. Such ceilings often lessen the incentives for private creditors to make out loans, and they have often been used in combination with some public, official distribution of credit to projects deemed politically attractive. IMF auditors typically want to minimize political influence on credit distribution in member countries, arguing that it leads to corruption and suboptimal (in market terms) allocation of credit. These reservations are logical and correct from an IMF perspective, but throughout history many states have allocated credit politically during industrialization or reconstruction phases in their development. China, for instance, has used politically distributed credit from its state-owned banks to finance commercial as well as infrastructural investments, and this has been pivotal to the country's phenomenal economic growth and its crisis management post-2008 (Walter and Howie, 2011).

In summary, debt is what we make it. And which of its three dimensions (the synthetic market dimension, the everyday dimension or the moral dimension) we allow to influence its institutionalization the most is a political decision. Over the globalization decades financial markets and their synthetic perception of debt have dominated legislation and understanding of debt. There is nothing stopping us from letting the everyday version of debt, or the religious, dominate institutional design and economic interaction in our reconstructive analysis. What constitutes moral hazard ultimately depends on the morality that is written into the institutional framework for debt and finance.

Endemic risks

Since deregulation, national financial markets have been connected in a single global system of financial markets, a system that instantly reacts as one organism on information that influences its pricings and extrapolations. Financial markets have seemingly become a trans-territorial phantom state (Thrift and Leyshon, 1994), a separate 'virtual' economy functioning on its own terms above the productive and reproductive economies (Peterson, 2003), unconstrained by national borders or physical geography. Since the values of all assets in this economy are based in the extrapolated future, there is an inherent risk accruing to all its assets. If the future priced into the assets unfolds in a way that fails to materialize the expected profits, asset prices will fall. When asset prices fall, the savings in everyday life will be partially or completely erased. This means that the system as such must be managed and regulated so that its risks do not spill over into the real productive economy and hit people with little or no stake in this economy. So far this management has not been very successful.

Self-regulation was proved misguided and dysfunctional by the crisis of 2008, when market actors did not behave as the discourse at the heart of this strategy stipulated. Markets are not always efficient, and market actors are not necessarily rational. The previous strategy − regulating individual entities to make them behave responsibly and produce attractive societal outcomes − was not sufficient either. The dot-com bubble at the turn of the millennium was proof that even if you could regulate bank behaviour, as the Glass–Steagall Act did, you cannot stop individual investors paying ludicrous prices for overhyped financial assets (Galbraith, 1993). When many actors are caught up in the same hype, you get a market that extrapolates an unrealistic future. When this future does not become real, a large proportion of the value evaporates into thin air. Investors then have to resort to those assets of theirs that are available today, which means that money and values in the current real economy will be used to cover their loss of future value. Financial market risk, therefore, ultimately tends to be borne by people in the everyday life of the real economy. Not least when states use public funds to mitigate financial crises, there has been a tradition of 'socializing the losses', meaning cutting down on welfare and public works to pay for the bailout of financial actors. The political logic for this is that the costs of these bailouts are lower than the macroeconomic costs of letting systemically important financial institutions (SIFIs) go bust. Allowing big actors, like Lehmann Brothers, to default has widespread consequences, and saving SIFIs will cost less than letting them fail. The way you save flailing SIFIs, however, can be more or less expensive, more or less smart, and it appears that the saving of financial institutions after 2008 was particularly stupid and expensive (Stiglitz, 2010).

Derivatives do not change this ultimate financial dependence on everyday life to realize the future priced in by the markets. What derivatives do is redistribute risk among financial actors. If the future does not unfold as expected, they make sure that it is not the investor sitting on the affected asset that loses, but someone else on the market. The loss is the same, however. Derivatives also reduce investor diligence, since financial positions can be made less risky by derivative hedging. You do not have to check your trading partners as carefully, and can invest in riskier assets and use more leverage, than would have been 'rational' without derivatives. As the debt crisis of 2008 shows, derivatives can lead to market-endemic moral hazard, aggravating the overall systemic risk that financial speculation poses to the real productive economy.

The problem-solving reforms following the 2008 crisis were called 'macroprudential regulation', to indicate that regulators were addressing the financial system at the macro level (Baker, 2013). Under closer scrutiny, however, these new regulation packages do not address aggregate financial markets, but mostly take the form of tighter regulation of individual financial actors. SIFIs in particular have been subjected to increased capital and reserve requirements, intended to allow them to better withstand future financial crises (Kranke and Yarrow 2019). This failure to remould the relation between financial markets and the productive economy is a case of **path dependence**. The institutions entrusted with the mandate to design and enforce new regulations did not have the powers to erect new institutional frameworks, and it is not clear whether they had a deep restructuring in mind or not. Once the new regulations started to take form, SIFIs were identified as the most important risk bearers, which led the stabilization of these institutions to be seen as the primary method of stabilizing the global financial system (Kranke and Yarrow, 2019). A redesigning of the relation between the globalized financial market and everyday life would have required the proactive engagement of legislators – that is, the parliaments of the G20 members – since these were the bodies that had the direct power to change how financial markets relate to the real economy. States, however, were busy with national crisis management, and bided their time while Basel III was crafted within the BIS network, subsequently to be introduced across all member countries. So the design task and the implementation power ended up in different institutional places, resulting in compromises that have reduced systemic risk somewhat by placing additional restrictions and reserve requirements on certain private institutions. The intrinsic risk of financial markets and its relation to everyday life remain largely unchanged.

It is precisely this market relation to everyday life that we should focus on first if we want to reconstruct the exposure to this risk. The risk that everyday life will fail to materialize the priced-in future is carried by both financial actors and people in everyday life. If the share price of a corporation falls, this first hits investors in the form of asset loss, after which those who work at the corporation are sacked or pushed to work harder or reorganized, in an effort to recreate an extrapolated future that can support a higher share price and higher future dividends. With derivatives, investors can rid themselves of some of this risk, but few equivalent manoeuvres are available in everyday life. There are unemployment benefits and health insurance schemes, but those are not available to everyone affected. They are also indicative of substantial real-life disruptions, whereas derivatives are risk-mitigating instruments for the financial positions of investors, who typically have the means to handle life disruptions.

This is a question of justice, and of who should bear the ultimate responsibility for financial values and the accruing risks.

A problem-solving measure that would make risk distribution fairer would be to reduce the number of derivatives available on the market, with the aim of making all investors bear the risk associated with their positions themselves. This would reduce the moral hazard that derivatives markets produce in financial markets generally, and confine risk to the financial instruments that accrue it. Such a measure might lead to a reduced 'risk appetite', but as Best (2010) notes, it is not certain that market actors want to, or can, follow new regulations of this sort. A reduction in the number of available derivatives instruments might lead to other risk-spreading behaviours, motivated by alternative portfolio strategies.

Another problem-solving move would be to re-regulate financial flows between countries, to reduce the contagion effect on financial markets. Contagion occurs when risk perception – real or imagined – starts to increase among financial actors. When such contagion takes hold, countries get hit by capital flight regardless of whether the feared risk is present in those countries or not (Best, 2010). With restrictions on financial flows, such as those in place during the Bretton Woods exchange rate era, risk perception would not lead to the same contagious capital flight, which could give states more room to pursue political and economic development on their own terms. In today's deregulated environment the implementation of this kind of regulation would benefit from international coordination, to avoid the risk of forerunner countries getting disproportionately hit by capital flight during the implementation period. On the other hand, as long as everyday life is protected from the repercussions of this flight, the future of the real economy (and those values based on it) could quite possibly be left more or less intact.

A critical transformative measure regarding financial risk would be a general safeguard regulation between financial markets and everyday life, of the same nature as the Glass-Steagall Act, but universal. Glass-Steagall erected a firewall between retail banking and business banking, and similar firewalls could be erected between workers and shareholders, between homeowners and mortgage lenders, between states and bond investors, and so on. Such regulations would shift the power from investors to workers, homeowners and states, and the investor community would naturally perceive these regulations as a loss of status and economic freedom. The benefit would be an everyday life less susceptible to the whims of finance.

The critical measure that would reduce financial risk the most, of course, would be to outlaw financial speculation and market arbitrage altogether, and tie all financial interaction to real production and everyday life directly. This would not free everyday life from economic risks – there would still be weather events affecting agriculture, business downturns and the like – but it would limit the extent to which everyday life was exposed to the repercussions of financial market panics and crashes. It would also deny investors – large and small alike

– the opportunity to benefit from financial market manias and bull markets. Since values produced in these manias and bull markets represent goods and services not yet produced and consumed, this loss might be negligible from an aggregate perspective, even if certain investors might lose significant assets. From an ecological sustainability perspective, producing all goods and services priced into inflated asset values is exactly what the planet does *not* need.

Conclusion

Several researchers stress the philosophical axiom that the future does not exist yet and is unknown to us, and that we therefore cannot know the true value of extrapolations in financial markets. As a consequence they stress that financial markets operate with 'fictitious' assets (Beckert, 2016), and that prices and values are 'self-referential' (Palan, 2015). This harsh truth requirement is correct in a philosophical sense, but everyday life does not work according to such philosophical truths, but rather according to what can reasonably be expected to happen. Farmers sow in the spring because summer will most likely come; bakers bake because people can reasonably be expected to want bread tomorrow too; toy corporations place orders with Chinese subcontractors because they expect gifts to be given to children next Christmas; and so on. Since financial values are founded on what will be achieved in everyday life in the future, they are valuations of what can reasonably be expected to happen, not truth claims in themselves. For shares, bonds, derivatives and other financial assets to retain their values, however, achievements in everyday life must make them come true. Production and commerce must be managed so that this happens. The fear of falling asset values locks the world – politicians, investors, savers and firms alike – onto the historical trajectory of financial extrapolations. The relations between financial markets and everyday life that financial instruments establish will need to be reconstructed with the rest of the global political economy. It will be hard to cater for present financial market interests and values during a reconstruction of the global political economy, because a reconstructed global economy will put us on the path towards a different future.

Further reading

A classic critical introduction to financial markets is Doug Henwood's *Wall Street: How It Works and for Whom* (1998), at the end of which he presents some ideas on how to make finance serve people better. Of the flood of books dealing with the financial crisis of 2008, Gillian Tett's *Fool's Gold* (2010) is worth mentioning for its insightful inside report on how the invention and use of derivatives inflated asset values of all kinds before the crisis. In 2010, Joseph Stiglitz published *Freefall: America, Free Markets, and the Sinking of the World Economy*, in which he delivers a scathing criticism of neoliberalism and deregulation, and sketches a Keynesian alternative for the global economy. A collection of post-structuralist writings on the 2008 crisis and capitalism is Fumagalli and Mezzadra's *Crisis in the Global Economy* (2010), in which these European political economists of the left critically analyze 2008 as part of a wider crisis of late capitalism. For the regulation and governance of global finance, Randall Germain's *Global Politics & Financial Governance* (2010) is a seminal work, informatively presenting the mechanisms of and various attempts at financial governance, and emphasizing the vital role of the nation state in the re-regulation of global financial markets. Groundbreaking research on how financial market analysts construct probable futures is Stefan Leins' book *Stories of Capitalism* (2018), in which the author follows analysts in a Swiss bank and explains how their narratives shape the ways investors and savers relate to the market and to society. To keep track of developments on the financial markets, two obvious websites are those of the IMF (www.imf.org) and the BIS (www.bis.org). Publications such as *World Economic Outlook* and *Financial Stability Report* on the IMF home page present an aggregate financial picture of the global economy. The home page of the BIS offers more fine-grained and specialized research on financial markets, with the aim of helping central banks and regulators understand developments (financial and general) in the global economy. Both these organizations are very mainstream in a discursive sense, and following them gives you an idea of where the mainstream is moving. Some material on these pages requires a certain amount of specialist knowledge, but you can usually find an explanation of specialist concepts and terms on sites such as Investopedia (www.investopedia.com) or Wikipedia (www.wikepedia.org). On money and debt specifically, David Graeber's *Debt: the First 5,000 Years* (2011) has become a key node in the debate, and his friend and economic historian Michael Hudson's *...and Forgive Them Their Debts* (2018) seems to be acquiring a similar status. And, of course, the whole debate has been revolutionized by Thomas Piketty's *Capital in the Twenty-First Century* (2014), which establishes with clarity and irrefutable economic statistics that if left to itself, the financial system always claims an increasing share of the value produced in the real economy.

7

Globalized Production

To avoid planetary disaster, a reconstruction of globalized industry is necessary. During the globalization era TNCs have restructured themselves into hierarchical networks of **global value chains** (GVCs). With great ingenuity the flow from raw materials and manual labour at the beginnings of these GVCs to supermarket shopping and consumption at the ends of them has been reconstructed to deliver great profitability to shareholders and an avalanche of goods to consumers. Hundreds of millions of sweatshop jobs have been created in the process, which has reduced poverty levels in several industrializing countries. Deep economic interdependence, central to the discourse of the global institutional order (see Chapter 3), has been achieved, and countries today rely on this global production system for their provision and economic development. All productive activities, from corporate boardrooms to everyday chores, are tied to this global industrial production order. And the whole system runs on fossil energy. It has to change.

In this chapter we will first see how firms have globalized, and then discuss ways their production might be reconstructed to make it socially, economically and ecologically sustainable.

What is a firm?

In 1937 Ronald Coase pointed out a paradox of current economic theory. On the one hand, it was built on the market principle, and trusted the price mechanism to allocate society's production and resources according to supply and demand. On the other hand, the firms in this market internally functioned like command economies according to the rationale and will of the entrepreneur. If the market is so great, Coase seemed to be asking, why do we have companies? Why can the interaction currently organized via central planning inside firms not be market-driven? Coase's answer was that **transaction costs** would be too high. It would be exceedingly expensive to negotiate and buy every production factor at market prices in market transactions on a daily basis. It is much more efficient to organize complex production activities in the form of centrally planned economies, with the help of long-term contracts that give the entrepreneur, within defined limits, access to an individual's labour or another firm's patent for as long as the contract is valid. Entrepreneurs construct their firms by contracting labour, immaterial rights and other production factors to what they already own, such as land, materials and financial capital, in long- or short-term contractual relationships. Good entrepreneurship, then, can be said to consist in creative and productive central planning of these relationships, so that the firm produces efficiently and distributes its products and services to markets where they can attract and fulfil consumer demand.

To understand the globalization of production that has taken place since the 1970s, we must understand how firms such as TNCs have changed their principles of ownership and their contractual relations in order to be profitable. In conceptual terms, this change can be described as a shift from a Fordist to a post-Fordist mode of industrial production.

The end of Fordism

Modern industrial production began with the partition of craftsmanship, as in the classic example of Adam Smith's needle factory, where each task was done by a single person in a line of workers who did not have to know any skills other than those necessary for the tasks they were assigned. This **division of labour** allowed the factory to produce more items faster than would have been possible if everyone had performed all the tasks needed to produce needles in individual workshops. Goods produced in modern factories were increasingly produced on **assembly lines**, with automated movement of the items under production from one worker to the next. Building such factories required large investment, but once a factory had produced enough to finance this investment, huge profits could be made by producing massive quantities of identical goods for large consumer markets. This is known as **returns to scale**. Henry Ford, the car manufacturer, became synonymous with this form of industrial production in the early 1900s, when he flooded the growing American car market with comparatively inexpensive cars.

At the heart of Fordism was the combination of the assembly line's division of labour and Taylorist scientific management of large-scale industrial production. In 1911 Frederick Winslow Taylor published *The Principles of Scientific Management*, a manual for the central planning of efficient industrial production that was read and applied all over the world, even in socialist command economies. Given the assembly line's division of labour, each worker in a factory could be taught a few scientifically precise actions and tasks, and when many workers did their respective tasks with speed and precision, the factory would become efficient. Taylorist central planning required a fairly large cadre of bureaucrats, time-study personnel, middle managers and the like, all of whom reported to the headquarters, where another cadre of bureaucrats, economists, management specialists and engineers oversaw the scientific planning of the organization to maximize efficiency and profitability.

The required investments to build and maintain large Fordist industries grew so large that they had to be discounted over several business cycles, and this naturally created additional risk for entrepreneurs. From the 1930s until around 1980 industrial interests and the growing welfare states enjoyed a symbiotic relationship, with the welfare state guaranteeing a floor of demand by means of health and social insurance and unemployment benefits for workers, alongside government procurement adjusted to meet the needs of national industries. This floor of demand ensured that during business downturns there would always be enough demand to keep industries operating, which made the financing of large industries over several business cycles possible. In return industrialists promised an ordered relation to trade unions, and agreed to pay minimum wages and various health and social insurance fees for their workers. Within the relatively closed national economies of the era, this symbiosis could be handled productively with Keynesian fiscal and monetary policies. Taylorist central planning within firms, meanwhile, found a constructive counterpart in the social engineering of the welfare states.

In the middle of the 1970s this form of industrial production developed serious profitability problems, for three main reasons. The first was that the rebuilding of war-torn countries was finished. The additional demand, both public and private, that the war had created disappeared, and the extra workers and additional capital that firms had employed to meet this demand were still weighing on the corporate books.

The second reason was that the Keynesian symbiosis between corporations and welfare states stopped working when economies internationalized in accordance with the global institutional order. The propping-up of consumer demand using welfare mechanisms no longer supported national industries and jobs. Swedish parents were not using their child benefits to buy clothes sewn in Borås or Norrköping, but to buy those from Portugal or Algeria. Internationalized production of consumer goods made demand stimulus 'leak out' of the countries trying to use it to support their industries. Firms themselves had also internationalized, and often ran operations in several locations outside their home countries. States that tried to create investment and jobs by directly supporting firms, in the form of investment subsidies, procurement or cheap government loans, often saw this stimulus being used for automation, international investments and a slimming down of domestic employment. In summary, neither supply-side nor demand-side stimulus was able any longer to provide the increase in jobs and investment they had done previously.

The third reason was a crisis in Taylorist central planning. Under Fordism, corporations had diversified into additional types of production, internationalized their operations and integrated many of their suppliers into their corporate structures through ownership. Fordist firms had developed into large international conglomerates, still run with central planning as coherent organizations. This high degree of organizational complexity had led to swelling bureaucracies and proliferating levels of management, continuously adding costs that swallowed an ever larger portion of corporate earnings. The cost of managing the Taylorist command organizations of Fordist firms was beginning to eat away at profits.

In summary, then, the completion of post-war reconstruction, the dysfunctional Fordist-Keynesian symbiosis and the crisis of Taylorist scientific central planning together added up to a crisis in which industries had to reorganize in order to restore profitability. In the terms established in Chapter 6, shareholders and other investors needed industry to reorganize to recreate a future of profits and growing asset values. Politically, institutional changes supportive of this reorganization had to be implemented, and associated changes in welfare regimes and employment policies put in place. The reorganization of corporate industry to address the three causes of its unprofitability in the 1970s is what gave us the globalized production of today. In the remainder of this section I will first describe the corporate measures undertaken, followed by the main political changes pertaining to this reorganization.

One corporate reform was to create 'flat organizations', meaning that operative decision-making would be made not at corporate headquarters, but in departments and factories by those close to the relevant activity. A typical operative decision might be, for instance, 'How many extra workers do we need over the next two months to secure timely delivery of item X?' The mandate to change the way in which a certain product was produced, sold or distributed was passed on down the hierarchy. In this way a great deal of bureaucratic work in the multilevel chains of command could be spared. As a consequence many middle managers and clerks were sacked during the 1980s and 1990s, which created a lot of problems, but also saved a lot of money. Headquarters were shrunk to only a fraction of their Fordist size, since only strategic decisions were to be taken there. Strategic corporate decisions addressed such questions as, 'In which kind of medicine should we invest our research funds over the next five years?' or, 'Where in our organization should we place the production of the next medium-sized car?' In a metaphorical sense we can describe this change as a shift in corporate central planning from a Soviet/Stalinist model to a Yugoslav/Titoesque form of central planning, with greater freedom in the lower ranks of the hierarchy. Headquarters continued to control the means of production and had the final word on what and how much should be produced, but not on how this should happen on the factory floor.

Another reform was to simplify or streamline corporate structures, and get rid of firms that had been bought for diversification. The reasoning for this was that even if a diversified conglomerate could survive multiple business cycles with some branches delivering profit when other branches did not, the costs of productive and financial coordination often exceeded the gains from this risk-spreading. Stock markets also liked shares that were easy to analyze and whose future was relatively simple to extrapolate. This simplification of corporate structures, therefore, contributed to rising share prices.

Part of the streamlining of corporate structures involved looking over the production structure under corporate ownership, and closing down or selling those operations that were not delivering a profit of their own accord. While Taylorist central planning aimed to ensure profits based on the productivity of the whole organization, this reform was carried out based on the principle that all departments and divisions should be productive and produce at competitive costs. 'If a division cannot be profitable in itself', ran the logic, 'we will close it down and place that production with a subcontractor'. **Outsourcing** therefore became an important part of corporate restructuring, and simpler forms of production that were not strategically important for the corporation were placed, for a specific task over a specified period, with another firm.

Typical Fordist industrial organizations were built by setting up and buying production capacity in order to internalize profit and maximize scientific management control. In contrast, **post-Fordist** organizations are built on the basis of more short-term and specific contractual relations between global corporations and subcontractors around the world, to maximize organizational flexibility and cut costs. By getting rid of permanently employed workers, as well as machines and real estate, corporations assured their owners that in the next business shift or downturn they would be able to reorganize or cut costs much faster by renegotiating contracts with their Chinese or Mexican subcontractors than by reorganizing self-owned productive capacity in their home countries. This also freed up capital tied up in machinery and buildings, and reduced the permanent expenses related to labour. Stock market sentiment in the 1990s was so focused on this that share prices received a boost as soon as a firm announced plans to outsource production – especially if it was to China.

The globalization of production was complicated, and many corporations went through this shift without delivering profits to their owners during the period of reconstruction. The social capital built up by mid-level management disappeared when organizations were slimmed down and flattened, and when the so-called 'soft knowledge' of forepersons and workshop clerks did not oil the wheels on factory floors and in offices, many organizations had to bring back discharged employees on a temporary basis as consultants, just to get operations working. With time, new forms of control and self-discipline were disseminated with new management philosophies, most notably that of '**lean production**', inspired by the culture in the Japanese factories of Toyota. Lean production aims at devolving control of the work process to individual sections of plants, so that foreperson oversight and centralized surveillance can be reduced. As regards quality control, for instance, each worker and each station on the assembly line is expected to take responsibility for this, and to make sure no defective items leave a station. No more emissary Taylorist quality controllers; workers must run their own quality control checks, and if something goes wrong, they or their stations are expected to fix it on their own so that the overall organization continues to function as planned. Each worker, station, workshop and subcontractor therefore bears the responsibility for the quality of their own work, and heavy penalties can be levied against workers and subcontractors who deliver faulty items into the firm's GVC.

The classical Fordist production site was the plant, the steel mill, or the car or garment factory, owned and operated by a single firm producing their products to the benefit of consumers and for the profit of owners. Globalized production is not built like this. Instead production is organized in GVCs, arranged like loose networks stretching around the globe. Each part in these networks has its temporary role and position in corporate production specified in contracts. Subsidiaries or subcontractors in a low-cost country must deliver items to the GVC according to a contract negotiated when they join the chain. The sections of these contracts concerning the price of each item are particularly important, and price pressure has encouraged global corporations to locate as much of the value chain as possible in countries with low wages. Cheaper labour means that larger profits can be made, and corporations are constantly hunting for new locations that promise to bring labour costs down. These savings are not necessarily reflected in retail prices.

But labour cost is not the only important issue when constructing a GVC and contracting out different areas of production. It is also crucial that production is located such that each component can be brought to the site smoothly, and that the assembled (or sown, or welded, or moulded) product can leave the site and be transported to the next link in the value chain without problems. The production location must therefore be near a well-functioning infrastructure that allows fast and frictionless transport in and out. Skilled workers might be poorly paid in one location, but if a firm's products end up stuck in containers for several months after they have left the factory, this delay will mean that financial capital is bound up in products that are not delivering profit. If transport is also unpredictable, a sudden disruption of deliveries might endanger the whole value chain. Even if some workers are better paid than those in another location, therefore, firms might prefer to locate production where labour costs are higher, if the better infrastructure in this area means fast and predictable deliveries to and from the production site.

Another clause in many contracts with subcontractors concerns yearly price decreases. The logic for this is that a subcontractor can be expected to learn to produce the item more efficiently each year, and the contracting TNC wants part of the resulting profit in the form of lower prices for itself. There is consequently a downward pressure on wages, or increased pressure on labour productivity, inscribed into the contract relations of GVCs.

Another typical clause concerns flexibility, where a subcontractor agrees to change production in accordance with how well an item sells. Especially in the electronics and textiles industries, which deal in design- and fashion-sensitive products, these clauses are prevalent. Thanks to information and communication technology, information on items sold can reach headquarters extremely rapidly. This information is instantly relayed to the subcontractor, which is contracted to speed up or slow down production as demand for the product changes. If a new gadget becomes fashionable, the workers will have to put in a lot of overtime to uphold the contract; if its design or function do not attract much demand, workers will lose their jobs. Paying workers below the living wage is a way to uphold flexibility, since workers will depend on overtime to support their families and themselves. If an item sells well, a subcontractor or subsidiary will be able to squeeze more overtime out of employees that depend on overtime for their survival, without taking the risk of hiring more workers representing higher permanent costs.

One type of clause that has become common during the last few decades of globalization relates to the provision of adequate working conditions, the prohibition of child labour, free unionization and gender equality. These additional clauses are the product of anti-sweatshop campaigns run by NGOs like CorpWatch and Amnesty International, who have lobbied against degrading, dangerous and unsanitary working conditions at the lower end of GVCs, sometimes instigating or threatening consumer boycotts that can hurt profitability. Corporations have included clauses like these into their contracts as part of their **corporate social responsibility** (CSR) policies, and this has meant some change for the better, but the overall logic of GVCs is the same, and their influence on the other clauses of the contracts that give rise to this logic is minor.

The construction of GVCs today is done through **sourcing**, which means that the top-level management of TNCs analyze and make decisions on where to locate the different parts of the GVC. In this they strive for maximum profitability of the value chain as a whole, but this is not achieved by scientific management, as under Taylorism, but through competition between different potential sections of a chain, which are invited to bid for a place in it. This bidding decides who gets the contract; several such contracts then make up a GVC constructed to produce a specific sports shoe, cell phone or car, for example. Once each section of the value chain is contracted, the computer networks of all sections are connected, and headquarters has as good an overview as at any time under Fordism, which allows it to oversee and manage production. When the new sports shoe, cell phone or car has been designed and produced, a new value chain may be constructed, with some new sections and some old ones. The changes depend on how subcontractors and subsidiaries have performed before, and the potential they have for performing well in this new GVC. The deterritorialization of production consists in this shift from geographically discernible plants and sites to flexible and hierarchical global networks overseen and managed through strategic decision-making at the headquarters of TNCs. Efficiency in this new form of production is achieved not primarily through scientific management, but through competition among the different sections within and outside the value chains. Competition takes place everywhere, on all levels – and if you are not competitive as a seamstress, consultant or subcontractor, or even as a location, you fall out of the network. Exclusion materializing as cancellation of contract relations gives post-Fordism its dynamic and exploitative nature. The price reduction on consumer goods, such as electronics, clothes and food, that this reordering has led to has served to keep rich-world inflation in check, and also to maintain Northern life styles for the working and middle classes, which have seen their real wages stagnate during globalization.

Around the turn of the millennium globalization of production was accomplished, and corporations began to deliver fantastic profits to their owners. Especially during the boom years up until the crisis of 2008, GVCs produced garments, electronics and other consumer items like never before, and met increasing demand from the global upper class, mostly in the North but increasingly also in industrializing countries in the South. As we saw in the previous chapter, trade and profits quickly picked up again after the crisis, even if sales were lower. In the post-crisis environment competition to be included in the GVCs stiffened, which gave global TNCs the ability to negotiate even more profitable contracts with subcontractors and workers. Over the decade since the crisis global corporations have done very well and delivered good profits to their owners, and stock market values have reached record highs, while GVCs have kept operating and relocating across the globe to maintain and prop up the future extrapolated in asset prices.

Post-Fordist political dynamics

The globalization of production and post-Fordist management has meant a shift of power over industrial development from nation states to TNCs. Corporate production is not built on specific sites or owned by those controlling what gets produced, but is instead organized as global, contractual, short-term and flexible network relations between different actors. This makes a country's industrial production very hard to control or direct by political fiat. Instead states have to compete with each other to attract foreign investment, and support local firms to enable them to win market shares or contracts with global TNCs. As early as 1991 Stopford, Strange and Henley noted that 'states cannot direct anymore, they can only bargain'. To strengthen this bargaining capacity, most states have embarked on a re-/deregulation trajectory of a similar nature to the 'corporate friendly' institutional changes of the SAP era (see Chapter 5), spurred by globalizing production and competition.

One common institutional change has been the construction of **export-processing zones** (EPZs), also known as special economic zones or free-trade zones. There are thousands of these zones around the world. The general trend over the globalization era has been towards regulatory changes that have favoured private industry, as can be seen in the *World Investment Reports* from UNCTAD over the last several decades. The zones are constructed with all the infrastructure that the country in question can afford, modified to meet as many demands as possible from potential investors. This includes efficient transport, good telecommunications, stable and plentiful supplies of electricity and other types of energy, water, and sewage and sanitation developed enough for the industries the country is trying to attract. An EPZ is typically given a more modern and efficient infrastructure than the rest of the country. Institutionally an EPZ has regulations and laws catering for what foreign investors are likely to want. These might include lax labour laws that make it easy to hire and fire workers, tax holidays of five to ten years for corporate tax, free repatriation of profits for foreign investors to the home country of the TNC, and investment subsidies to entice foreign investors and national industries to build in the EPZ. Many countries implement the regulatory changes on a nationwide scale, and construct EPZs only in a material infrastructural sense, as starting areas for industrialization and the inclusion of the country in globalized production. A well-educated and disciplined labour force is also very attractive for global industry, which means that small, weak or government-controlled trade unions are also an asset for a country setting up an EPZ.

The feminization of the labour force (as discussed in Chapter 2) has been a significant feature of the globalization of production. In every industry – from textiles to electronics to guitars to cars to toys – women have entered factories on a massive scale. From a corporate perspective there are a number of factors in favour of employing women rather than men for manual work. Women are, as a result of a global patriarchal history, paid less than men for the same work. Girls are traditionally raised to heed the words of men and their elders, and to put the needs of others ahead of their own, which makes women on average less troublesome than men on the factory floor. They are not unionized to the same degree as men, which makes them accept lower wages and harder working conditions than unionized male labour tends to do. In many countries there is a tradition for women to work for some years before marriage, which gives the employer additional flexibility in the form of a steady outflow of workers leaving to marry. In all countries where men are traditionally the primary breadwinners of their households, women are seen and treated as a labour reserve that can be used at low cost whenever needed. When there is no longer any industrial need, women are discharged and expected to return to the 'home', considered their rightful place in society (Peterson, 2003; Benería et al, 2016).

When patriarchal discourses, traditions and laws around the world make women ideal flexible workers in globalized networked production, and women are hired in unprecedented numbers, this rearranges the material base of patriarchal gender systems. As women start to receive their own incomes, and often become the primary providers for households, husbands lose a traditional power instrument that gave them control over their families and the freedom to cater for their own needs. As we saw in Chapter 2, men around the world have to live up to masculine norms and traditions in new and different ways when they lose this role as primary breadwinner. This loss of power leads many men to attempt to recover their traditional role and position through other means than economic ones. Religious radicalization and nationalist movements have been platforms for this recovery. Donald Trump's misogynistic conservatism and India's Hindu nationalism are examples of patriarchal political trends gaining traction from the reorganization of economic gender roles under globalized production. These conservative trends, of course, contain elements other than this reaction to rearranged gender roles, but their political dynamic can hardly be understood without this gender dimension.

What women make of this new economic role differs depending on where they live and who they are. In some countries, such as South Korea, women's new role as workers important to national industry and development allows them to form trade unions of their own, and to begin to renegotiate an unfavourable gender system and their position in it. In other countries, such as Mexico, patriarchal norms prevail and encourage the serious gendered mistreatment of women workers, thus preserving local patriarchy within globalized production. As Marchand and Runyan showed, there is also a very mixed picture on the individual level (Marchand and Runyan, 2010). While some women use their incomes to save and build a life of their own after having worked in global production for a period, others spend their entire working lives in sweatshops, sustaining their families on small incomes, able to change neither their economic situation nor their gender position.

In terms of equality, proponents of globalization argue that women are escaping old gender roles and becoming individual economic agents and subjects (Sachs, 2005). A CSR officer of a TNC would probably say that a single mother is better off working with them, having her child in their day care, than she would be in her home village without her job. On a macro level, the millions in Asia who have left a life of absolute poverty and joined the growing middle class are often credited to this globalization of production. Critics of global capitalism instead point out that this is merely the merging of two exploitative systems, with women in the global South recruited as cheap labour to raise the profit on items that global corporations sell to the global upper class (Peterson, 2003). Intersectional criticism takes this even further, claiming that globalized production works like this because of an acceptance of exploitative patriarchal oppression of the daughters of 'others', while 'we' would never want our own daughters to work in a Cambodian or Ethiopian sweatshop.

Clusters and regions

The geography of global production is not truly global. What has happened is that high-value and low-value production have ended up in different parts of the world. High-value production, with high-level knowledge and high capital content (such as engineers and IT consultants working with expensive high-tech stuff) is done in clusters in the North such as Silicon Valley, Northern Europe or the Tokyo area. Here corporations have access to highly qualified labour and consultants, needed for design, research and product development. Universities in the vicinity provide young recruits for the corporation, or highly qualified flexible labour. When many firms locate to the same area, this creates **network value**: workers are able to move from firm to firm, required skills can be found on a temporary basis quickly, collaborations can be negotiated and established between firms close to each other, and infrastructure is generally well maintained by the municipality or region in question. This type of production is what Northern countries compete to attract.

Low-value production, on the other hand, is done in the South or in places like Eastern Europe, by low-skilled manual labour, often in EPZs. These production sites are located in logistical proximity to the North, in accordance with post-Fordist GVC logic. This is the type of production that developing and industrializing countries compete for. Countries that are successful typically have EPZs on the coast, so containers filled with consumer goods can be shipped easily to markets in the North, or are located just across the border from large markets so that trucks can take products directly to wholesalers inside the OECD market. Evidently, large sections of the planet are outside global production, in both the North and the South. This may be because there are no consumers or workers in these areas, or because of geographical circumstances making them unattractive – or very often both at the same time.

As a consequence of this, the **global labour force** has segmented into three groups: the **strategic group**, the **flexible group** and the **irrelevant group** (Cox, 1995). The strategic group consists of individuals who have some knowledge or skill that is strategically important for the high-value production of TNCs. These individuals are therefore able to find jobs in clusters in the OECD, where they are either permanently employed and well paid inside corporate-owned production, or they move around as expensive consultants, applying their skills and knowledge to specific issues and tasks that corporations need people from outside to deal with. This group have the ability to plan for their economic future, and can walk into a bank and negotiate a mortgage with no collateral other than themselves. This is the group that TNCs want to sell to, and who demand the items on which TNCs make their largest revenues, such as new cars or the latest high-end cell phones. Around 10 per cent of the global population belongs to this group, with the growing middle class in Asia replacing the shrinking middle classes in the US and Europe in terms of consumer demand. The global market segment of attractive consumers, therefore, is not growing.

The second group, which is growing, consists of workers who are flexible in a highly quantitative sense. They have jobs as long as subcontractors in their country manage to land contracts with TNCs, and when this does not happen they are out of a job. They also work in the service sector developing around the strategic group, catering for private needs in households, or performing the tasks that firms outsourced during reconstruction, such as cleaning, invoicing or local transport services. These are the new jobs created during the globalization era. They are poorly paid, with short-term and insecure contracts (if there are written contracts at all), on jobs that are often dangerous, stressful and dirty. This group drifts in and out of these (not very good) jobs as global production changes and moves over the planet. They are not very attractive consumers, and since they have no stable financial future, banks do not find them good customers or borrowers.

The irrelevant group is approximately the same size as the flexible group. They are termed 'irrelevant' because they have no role to play in globalized production. They are not relevant as labour for several and often overlapping reasons: they may be living in the wrong areas; they may have poor health; they may be subjected to racist exclusion; or they may not have any of the skills demanded by the present corporate hiring regimes. These reasons for labour irrelevance also make them unattractive as consumers, not to mention banking. They may have resources in the form of land, skills or knowledge that is valuable from a broad human perspective, but given how globalized production works, these resources cannot be brought to any productive use that might make this group relevant in today's capitalist understanding.

While these groups exist all over the world, the proportions between them differ from North to South. Northern countries often have large sections of their citizens in the strategic or flexible groups, while most people in Southern countries are in the irrelevant or flexible groups. All national development policies, in North and South alike, are aimed at pushing as large a section of the population as possible higher up this ladder. Rich countries expand their PhD training programmes to attract research-intensive industry to their clusters of high-value production. China and other industrializers work to move from low-value to high-value production by acquiring as much technology and expertise as possible, while expanding their universities and sending students and researchers abroad to learn and practice. Poor countries establish EPZs and enter free-trade agreements and taxation treaties with rich countries, in order to attract investments that might lift their population from global economic irrelevance to some form of economic inclusion in the global industrial pecking order.

To conclude the first section of this chapter, I would like to point out a contradiction in this globalized industrial provision system: the global 'metabolism'. On the one hand, TNCs have become very skilled at utilizing all opportunities that globalization has produced, so as to benefit from wage differences, productivity increases, EPZ offerings and the like around the world. This has led to stagnating wages for the working and middle classes in the rich world, leaving only the richest 10 per cent in the world as attractive and bankable consumers. On the other hand, globalized industry has become exceedingly efficient at producing goods at low cost. TNCs are hunting after the same 10 per cent of the global population, because the items they can sell to this group are those that deliver the highest returns. The gargantuan level of consumption discussed at the very beginning of this book, therefore, is upheld by a global production system commercially focused on a limited and static group of attractive consumers. This becomes a contradiction because the consumption capacity in such a limited group is finite: there is a limit to the size of car you can drive; to how big a house you can live in; to how many electrical appliances you can operate comfortably in everyday life. But in order to keep TNCs profitable and hiring, politicians around the world have pampered this group with neoliberal policy for decades, hoping to accelerate their consumption and investment to stimulate GDP growth. This policy seems to have run its course, for three reasons. First, the present type and level of production and consumption is far beyond planetary ecological limits. Second, inequality within countries is becoming politically untenable, leading to all kinds of populist reaction, of which some have especially nasty historical roots. Third, it is not working very well. GDP growth is not stimulated by channelling more money to the rich and their firms. The additional money the rich get from such policies today is saved on the financial markets, propping up inflated asset prices even further without adding very much demand to the economy. More money received by firms is doled out to owners, and not spent on investment, because production capacity today is sourced, not built. Money is not trickling down in the global political economy after industrial globalization. It is floating upwards.

Reconstructing global production

In 1999 at the World Economic Forum in Davos, UN Secretary-General Kofi Annan invited the elite of the global economy to 'embrace, support and enact a set of core values in the areas of human rights, labour standards and environmental practices.… You can uphold human rights and decent labour and environmental standards directly, by your own conduct of your own business'.[1] Businesses should not wait for national legislation to embrace these values, Annan urged, but should adapt their operations of their own volition wherever they did business. Firms were invited to sign up to the UN Global Compact (www.unglobalcompact.org) and agree to follow its ten principles, providing regular reports on their progress in adapting to these principles. No retributive mechanisms came with this membership, but Annan and the UN trusted civil society and media organizations to report on breaches of the principles and hold culprit firms accountable to the public, their owners and customers. Twenty years later, 10,000 companies are members of the Global Compact, and have agreed to adapt their businesses to incorporate these values and principles. Activities are updated along with general developments, with businesses today declaring how they intend to contribute to the Paris Agreement on climate change by defining individual corporate pathways to zero carbon emissions in the future, for example, or how they are adapting their operations to the SDGs. In a similar vein members are also expected to explain how they are working to uphold and further human rights and labour standards where they and their subcontractors operate. The Global Compact has become an institution defining and developing the discourse of CSR.

CSR is the current global manifestation of the inherent angst of capitalism. Throughout industrialism capitalists have always been torn by the moral dilemma of exploiting workers and polluting the earth to maximize profit, while at the same time aspiring to be moral people and good citizens (and perhaps even pass through the eye of a needle after death). In the 1990s, when globalization was radicalizing corporate activities and states were running a 'race to the bottom' in terms of allowing corporations to exploit workers and destroy nature to an unlimited degree, CSR became a means of establishing an informal baseline, a level playing field, for how low TNCs would be allowed to sink morally. Ethics officers began to be hired and codes of conduct were introduced, which put some limits on how far firms would go, especially in poor countries hosting FDIs. The values and ethics of CSR are not very complicated; in philosophical terms they are more like 'good manners' of everyday life. What is complicated is incorporating CSR into capitalist industrial organizations, which often run environmentally dangerous operations with exploited labour in countries with questionable political systems. Since globalization, much of this production is done by subcontractors, which complicates the question of moral responsibility and accountability even further, as chains of command become opaque in networked production with devolved operative decision-making. CSR can make a difference, however, in a problem-solving way.

If the ten principles of the Global Compact were made defining features of global production, it would change capitalism as we know it. Firms are centrally planned economies constructed by means of ownership and contracts; firms could therefore institutionalize the ten principles by making them fundamental parts of their contracts with employees, suppliers and subcontractors. The contracting TNC would then have to oversee all actors within its networks to ensure that they upheld and realized those principles. The management of a TNC has the highest authority over the network it constructs, so theoretically it could make ideal human rights, labour standards and environmental sustainability come true within its sphere of influence. In most jurisdictions top-level management of a company has the legal space and opportunity to do whatever it finds most appropriate, so the institutional hurdles are low for delivering in full on the Global Compact principles and taking full corporate social responsibility. Why has this not happened?

The reasons why corporations do not act justly and sustainably are structural. The most important reason has to do with ownership. Since the neoliberal turn of the 1980s, the first responsibility of corporate leadership has been to deliver the highest possible dividends to owners and shareholders, under the assumption that the riches of the owners will 'trickle down' in the form of investment and consumption, creating jobs and growth and promoting general welfare. Firms listed on stock exchanges have to be 'shareholder-friendly', meaning that an increasing proportion of their revenue goes to shareholders instead of towards investment and salaries. TNCs therefore have to weigh the costs of CSR against the overarching interests of their owners, and if CEOs want to stay in their jobs, they need to keep the boards and the owners happy. As a result, a firm is only as sustainable as its owners allow it to be, and if the owners believe that the firm is no longer being 'friendly' to them, they will replace the CEO.

The second structural reason limiting how sustainable firms can be is the fact that they have to keep their owners happy by maximizing revenue in a colonial, racist, patriarchal and unequal world, and utilizing the opportunities presented by these circumstances. As we saw in Chapter 6, share prices are based on extrapolated profits, and these extrapolations are based on firms utilizing the opportunities that exist in this world, not in the decolonized, non-racist and egalitarian world envisaged by SDG values and the Global Compact. The more society's savings and wealth are invested in assets based on these extrapolations, the more dependent society becomes on profits from 'business as usual'. As long as this time-based macro-dependence persists, CSR and the Global Compact cannot become anything more than icing on the cake of globalized production: tasty, but superficial. There are, however, several possibilities for problem-solving reform of globalized production that would allow firms to become sustainable faster and in a more profound sense.

The **business model** approach, which some firms are already practising (such as 'Fair Trade'), is to change production mode. Instead of maximizing returns to scale in global networks and churning out price-competitive staple goods, with all the social and environmental damage that this causes, the sustainable business model calls for producing what is possible within the limits of social and environmental sustainability, and then passing the increased cost on to consumers in the form of higher retail prices. This will make demand fall, but if a large enough group of consumers is attracted by the changed (probably higher) quality of the goods, and the sustainability of the model, this mode of production has proved to be commercially viable. An additional benefit of this strategy would be that falling demand would reduce the environmental costs of production, simply because it would reduce the number of consumer items sold. The business model approach can be productively combined with politically institutionalized cap-and-trade systems (see Chapter 3), even if these were expanded to include inputs damaging the biosphere and not just emissions, as existing systems do. When the business lobby greeted the Paris Agreement with satisfaction, this was the approach it had in mind. It allows global production to continue in its present capitalist form, with some tweaks to cater for increased sustainability in line with the Global Compact, which most TNCs are already subscribing to in any case. If a business model is inherently unsustainable, however – such as extracting and selling as much fossil fuel as possible, or selling as many light weapons as you can manage – a few tweaks and a cap cannot make it just or sustainable. Banning and phasing out such trades will be more appropriate.

The **degrowth** approach is different from the business model approach, in that it starts from a specific critique of the growth paradigm. As we saw in Chapters 4 and 5, growth has been an integral part of the modern project, and we have grown accustomed to think of GDP growth as a societal necessity. Degrowth proponents (Jackson, 2009; Kallis et al, 2012) argue that we have to break with this belief and shrink production and consumption to sustainable levels. It will not suffice to apply the environmentally best technology to production in its present form, because GDP growth is adding to our ecological footprint at a faster pace than technological change is reducing it. We need both technological change and degrowth. Büchs and Koch (2017) identify three main perspectives on degrowth, based on the system–reform, the anti-capitalist and the alternative-open positions on the issue. Whereas system reform can reasonably be understood as discursively equivalent to Cox's problem-solving theory, the anti-capitalist and the alternative-open positions both qualify as belonging to Cox's critical theory (see Chapter 1). What these three positions have in common is a firm belief that we have to rebuild global production to function without growth, or leave the growth imperative behind and embark on a post-growth development trajectory. System-reformist post-growth is often designed with a strong dose of Keynesianism, in which capitalist ownership and traditional markets are retained, while sustainability is pursued through the strengthening of the welfare state, stricter and deeper regulation of production, and a publicly driven technological shift. This reform would disconnect GDP growth from societal well-being. While some sectors might grow on the basis of necessity, the general political focus on capitalist GDP growth would become irrelevant to policy. Anti-capitalist post-growth, on the other hand, views capitalism as incompatible with societal well-being, and holds that as long as the global economy works according to capitalist exploitation of labour, we will have an unjust, socially and ecologically destructive form of growth. When those in control of capital are also allowed to control the use of labour and land in society, the capitalists' drive to enrich themselves at the cost of nature and their fellow human beings will prevail. In order to free people from exploitative structures, and to save the biosphere, capitalism has to be rebuilt into a system in which capital is owned collectively, its use circumscribed by ecological and social sustainability institutions, and socioeconomic interaction must be driven by needs, creativity and reciprocity instead of individual gain. The alternative-open position on post-growth does not focus specifically on anti-capitalism, but instead on the core values and functions that would be needed in a post-growth society. Basic human needs, creativity and reciprocity are cornerstones of this perspective as well. Based on these cornerstones, proponents of this perspective sketch a variety of possible institutional orders that would be conducive to well-being in a post-growth society. These models are often characterized more by their ecological and social characteristics than their economic features, containing many creative ideas about cooperatives, recycling and reciprocity, and more rarely drawing a straight line from the capitalist global mode of production to a post-growth, deglobalized mode. The most valuable common contribution from these perspectives on degrowth or post-growth is their attack on GDP growth as a central feature of an economy. Once we free ourselves from growth as a prerequisite for societal well-being, the policy space available for creative and reconstructive thinking and design of industrial production – global or not – expands considerably.

What's in a firm?

During the neoliberal globalization era, the entrepreneur ascended to iconic status, and the firm became his (yes, 'his') revered vehicle. Much of the de- and re-regulation that took place during this era was corporate- and investment-friendly, creating a favourable environment for corporate profit generation. This was done under the assumption that there were creative entrepreneurs in every centrally planned bundle of contracts that constituted a firm, and that they would bring development and growth through their companies to a country going through this de- or re-regulation. Many Southern countries adapting their economic structures during the Washington Consensus era found that firms often did not have any entrepreneurs in them, but that these firms were rather hit-and-run constructions, allowing business people to extract resources out of a country without leaving much economic development behind in return. Many Northern countries undergoing analogous de- and re-regulation experienced similar disappointment regarding job and welfare growth, when footloose TNCs took advantage of the opportunities presenting themselves in the wake of neoliberal adjustment. This has led to a broad critique from many quarters regarding the political shift in favour of corporations (Klein, 2007; Wilkinson and Pickett, 2009; Crouch, 2011).

If we take Ronald Coase (1937) seriously, and understand firms as centrally planned economies existing as bundles of contract relations, then it is worth contemplating what a 'firm' is, and to what degree this institutional entity in itself can be held responsible for the way that the global economy has developed. As Handy (2002) writes, firms do not exist primarily to make profit, but to relate constructively to needs and demands in society. If this constructive relation also results in business profit, then the firm ideally uses this to develop the constructive relation even further. Neoliberal regulation has created an environment in which firms are used in a profit-maximizing way, conflating the institutional construction of 'the firm' with economic creativity itself. A prerequisite for the continued existence of a firm is that its earnings are enough to maintain a constructive relation to society, but as Adam Smith and many others have argued, when profit is the overarching motive, firm activity happens at the expense of society in general, thus reducing the overall productivity of society's resources (Smith, 1776).

Reconstructing the corporation

During globalization corporations have gained increased political leverage in several ways. The political system in the US, which hosts many of the largest TNCs, has changed so that campaigns and politicians are financed by corporations, who are subsequently included in the design of policy before it is presented to Congress. The lobbyists have moved from the lobby to the back room, most obviously in the US, but also in many other countries (Crouch, 2011). The embracing of CSR and the Global Compact by most TNCs has established a general perception that the business world is already busy adjusting for sustainability. This perception is largely misguided, as corporations are still primarily operating to maximize profits for their owners, and CSR is no hindrance to their utilizing all structural opportunities to maximize revenue, amounting to little more than the selective tweaking of their standard business models. The crisis management after 2008 had an overarching focus on corporations, propping them up with subsidies and support in the belief that they would drag Northern economies out of the recession. Catering for corporate needs with public funds and political measures, therefore, was prioritized over social needs and the necessary shift to sustainable production, with the hope that once corporate profitability was restored, firms would use these resources for sustainable restructuring. During the decade after the crisis profits have been fantastic, but new sustainable business models and changed production modes are still waiting to be applied. In the meantime inequality is increasing, and climate emissions are at record levels. Putting TNCs centre stage politically while hoping that their CSR departments will create sustainability is clearly not working. A more profound political change, involving formal institutional frameworks with new industrial economic and social policies, is needed.

From a neoliberal viewpoint raising taxes or tightening laws and regulations for corporations has been regarded as risky, as they might lead to financial and corporate flight. Unless all similar nations enact the same legal changes at the same time, parliaments and politicians are reluctant to make any changes affecting corporate profits in their countries. Institutional changes driven by the WTO or the EU have been regarded as safe, since they affect all member countries of these organizations in similar ways. Today both the WTO and the EU are having severe coordination problems, so waiting for global or regional solutions may take a long time. Two countries, China and the US, have walked their own path, and from these special cases we can discern what we can do while waiting for a global treaty on sustainable production to take effect. The US has started to prosecute TNCs with operations and institutional presence in the US for corruption crimes committed in countries all over the world. Similar legal options could be institutionalized by all countries and used for sustainability purposes. If a TNC with a presence in your country is not paying a living wage to workers somewhere in its GVC, you can take it to court and have it fined in your home country. If a TNC is polluting and damaging the biosphere by running its global network on dirty energy, it can be sued in any country where it has a legal presence and be forced to change its energy use. Several environmental activists are already doing this in courts around the world, and parliaments have the sovereign right to pass laws that make unsustainable corporate actions and activities illegal, regardless of where in the world they happen. If a TNC wanted to have a presence in a particular country, it would have to follow the laws of this country throughout its GVC. Organizations such as the WTO, the IMF or the European Commission could of course strengthen and streamline the nature of such legal changes, but there is nothing stopping individual nations from writing and using such laws, as the corruption cases in the US show.

The possibility of influencing corporate investment and behaviour is also starkly displayed by Chinese industrial policies. When China opened up to foreign investment, TNCs flocked there to profit from millions of well-trained and eager workers and wage levels lower than they could have dreamed. To give TNCs access to this tremendously cheap labour, the Chinese state, mostly in the form of provincial governments and municipalities, imposes conditions such as Chinese-majority ownership, local access to technologies and patents used in any production facilities, co-financing of infrastructure, domestic content in inputs, and various other conditions. Access to labour, which pulled corporate production to China in the 1990s, has today been coupled with another pull factor: access to the growing Chinese consumer market. The strength of these pull factors gives a large country like China, and its provinces and cities, extra bargaining power. Even when Chinese government involvement goes against the intents and articles of WTO treaties, there is not very much an investor or another country can do. The Chinese state is still sovereign over its territory, and as long as corporations are willing to invest in and trade with China, you would need a military blockade of Chinese harbours to stop this from happening. In principle, however, there is nothing stopping other countries from treating corporate investment in a similar way. China shows that it is possible to influence how, under what leadership and in which forms industrial production happens. It is not that this does not happen all over the world already, for regulation and official approval have considerable influence on production everywhere; it is the degree and radicalism of Chinese influence over production that inspires. That China has this influence over investment and production makes it evident that politics can direct corporate investment and production, if it sets out to do so.

But if we squeeze global corporations like this, will they not move elsewhere? Well, yes, they may. It is important to remember that the imperative of supporting corporations politically and economically is a product of the neoliberal era and globalization, and the fear of losing corporate presence in a country is rooted in a discourse that depicts market forces propelled by private entrepreneurs as the only major constructive force of history. Given experiences such as Chinese state-led growth or Ellen Johnson Sirleaf's renegotiation of Liberian mining concessions with TNCs, among many other examples, there are strong indications that this fear is misguided or plain wrong. Corporations in most cases have strong incentives to keep operations going, and if they decide otherwise and move, the country they leave often has access to enough competence and resources to set up production to provide for the necessities lost when a TNC emigrates.

Squeezing big firms might also slow corporate as well as GDP growth. If we accept that GDP growth is a superficial expression of societal development, slower growth or even a recession might not be a bad thing. In environmental terms it would mean that less stuff was produced and consumed, and consequently that our ecological footprint shrank. As regards ecological sustainability, therefore, it might be a benefit. What would become a vital issue if growth slowed down or a recession hit is the social consequences of lower growth: the question of which groups should carry the economic burden, and how.

In all the crises of the globalization era it has been the working and middle classes who have carried the heaviest burden. The neoliberal macroeconomic argument for this has been twofold. On the one hand, the argument runs, the working and middle classes make up a majority of the population, therefore the economic burden can be distributed over many individual households, which will make it bearable on an individual level. On the other hand (and in line with the idolization of the firm), corporations and financial wealth are not touched because that would reduce their capacity to lead us out of crisis. The austerity policy founded on this discursive construction has been applied time and again, from the 1980s up until today, with increasing inequality, a shrinking middle class in the OECD, and stagnating or falling real wages for everyone without higher-level education. This economic policy has become so ingrained in politicians – from the centre of the ideological spectrum all the way to the right – that even when the IMF and the OECD, as well as world-renowned liberal economists such as Paul Krugman and Joseph Stiglitz, argue strongly for increased government spending to get out of post-crisis stagnation, politicians in Europe and the US continue to lower taxes for corporations and the rich, while cutting down on welfare and public works. Austerity has become a value in itself, to be promoted whenever a country's competitiveness in the global economy is up for discussion, and it has so far always been the workers and the public servants who are told to tighten their belts and accept deteriorating job security and stagnating wages. That major global institutions and economists no longer support this strategy does not necessarily diminish the political and argumentative value of spreading such arguments. As long as 'austerity' circulates in the political debate as the dominant method for dealing with economic crises, everyone involved in the debate can be forced to talk about it. This discursive dominance serves the political interests of corporations and investors at the expense of workers and civil servants, even when the policy makes little conventional economic sense (Hopkin and Rosamond, 2018). Breaking with this fixation with 'austerity', and bringing fiscal policy and the state into the debate as a legitimate participant in the reconstruction of global production, will be important, especially in light of the many popular uprisings across the world – including the Brexit campaign, the Yellow Vests of France, democracy activists in the DR Congo and Lebanon, and strikes among textile workers in Bangladesh – and the strengthening of populist political parties of various ideological blends. There is clearly little will or capacity among the working and middle classes to bear the burden of another crisis, nor for further austerity politics, for the sake of a neoliberal global version of the modern project that is no longer delivering on its promise.

Technology and reconstruction

GVC production functions because of cheap and readily available energy, mostly fossil. This energy is required for everything from the extraction of raw materials to production, transport, use, consumption and disposal. Increased energy prices would therefore slow down global production, and increase the price of everything produced in GVCs. Such price increases can happen because of decisions on the production side, or through political decisions. A global carbon tax, should a UN climate meeting decide in favour of one, would therefore not only raise the cost of transport in globalized production, but would also lead to a fall in demand for goods and services. If old fossil-based energy technology became expensive, the theory has it, creative entrepreneurs would supply us with some other, cleaner and cheaper form of energy. There are other forms of energy production making their way into markets everywhere, such as solar panels and windmills, but the global production networks still operate using fossil fuels, because that is the energy available to make them work now. And it is not very likely that any corporation will take the financial risk of launching a new form of energy, for as Bill Gates says: 'There is no fortune to be made from it' (Bennet, 2015). The time span for introducing energy innovations, making them commercially viable, and establishing market presence and widespread distribution is simply too long for private corporations. They cannot be trusted or expected to solve the issue of clean energy for global production, and global producers will not trust them to supply this energy until it is completely certain that it can be relied upon to make the GVCs function. The technology for clean energy has to be invented, introduced, and maintained by governments and states. While inventions have not been in short supply, introduction and implementation is still happening on only a limited scale, in a handful of countries.[2] Until some new forms of energy come to dominate global markets, globalized production will continue to release carbon dioxide and its equivalents into the atmosphere, strengthening the greenhouse effect and changing the biosphere. There is no alternative to fossil fuels if GVCs are to remain operational in the meantime.

A factor delaying sustainability change in production, and political measures that might foster it, is the idea that this change should come in the form of new gadgets and appliances produced for profit by private firms. The electric car is emblematic of this fixation. It seemingly solves an environmental problem with private motoring, and at the same time keeps global production structurally unchanged while opening up new business opportunities. The ecological effect of simply replacing private fossil-driven cars with electric ones on a global scale, however, would be disastrous – not least since the mining for all the rare earth metals needed for the batteries would have huge negative sustainability effects, ecological as well as social. The eastern DR Congo, from where much of these metals come today, is an example of this. The immense human suffering here can be attributed for the most part to a long history of civil wars and corruption, but even if the mining here was done within stable institutions and according to CSR values, it would still weigh heavily on the environment both locally and globally. And that is just the batteries; the rest of an electric car is produced in the same way as its fossil-driven counterpart, with all the associated environmental damage. A life-cycle analysis shows that this swap to electric vehicles would not be a big enough change to make today's transport patterns sustainable. It will never be a very good idea to send individuals off in private metal contraptions at high speed. It consumes too much energy over the life cycle of each machine, regardless of the type of energy that propels them, and the opportunity cost of using scarce energy resources for such transport is high and will continue to increase for the foreseeable future. But as long as the iconic image of the firm and its entrepreneur remains politically untouchable, debate about and planning of sustainable production will be sidetracked by this fixation with more or less hypothetical gadgets that profitable corporations produce and sell. Technological change is vital, yes. But it needs to be part of a broader and deeper change in global production to make a substantial ecological difference.

Approaches to the planning of this broad and deep change in global production have been presented in several places throughout the previous chapters. In Chapter 2 we encountered life-cycle analysis, EROEI and other concepts relevant for global production. In Chapter 3 we discussed the political construction of markets, and how both national and global markets can be influenced through institutional changes and political will. In Chapter 4 we analyzed how global trade, and the different ways it might be regulated, are also vital instruments for the reconstruction of global production. Chapter 5 elucidated how development thinking today must be global, and how 'overdevelopment' in the North is the major environmental threat to the planet, while poverty in all its forms needs to be addressed to produce social sustainability and justice. In Chapter 5 I also discussed the problem of the global upper class, and how the Southern development experience teaches us that this class needs to be handled carefully. Chapter 6 examined financial markets and the time-based macro-dependence between global production and financial extrapolations, a dependence that locks the global political economy onto the unsustainable development path of creating and securing asset values on a future extrapolated by the financial market. This chapter has dealt with the understanding of what a firm is, and how global corporations utilize openings offered by globalization in the global political economy to maximize profit. We will also discuss the degree to which CSR can change corporate behaviour, and how easily sustainability and justice can (or cannot) be reconciled with the logic of GVCs.

Everyday life is where the global political economy happens and materializes, and its meaning and discursive power evolve in the interplay between global economic processes and our local lives. The material and social activities that bring the global political economy to its final fruition belong to both globalized production and everyday life at the same time. To conclude this discussion on political change in globalized production, we need to return to the framework introduced in the first two chapters and the intersectional matrix through which global capitalism is woven into everyday life.

Gender, class and racism

As has been shown throughout this chapter, globalized production relates to the intersectional matrix in two ways. On the one hand, it exploits the multiple inequalities and oppressions it finds in its search for increased revenue; on the other hand, it destroys the social fabric where these inequalities and oppressions are rooted. But it does not replace them with any alternative liveable social system or culture. Instead people are left to rebuild liveable societies on their own in the rubble of precolonial and capitalist cultures, simply by surviving with some amount of beauty and joy in their lives while trying to make ends meet as best they can. Very often we have few or no alternatives; remember Butler's observation that 'subjection exploits the desire for existence'. While proponents of industrial globalization often take pride in the destruction of oppressive social structures, they are less proud of footloose capital's negative effects on social sustainability. As people struggle to rebuild good everyday lives, they very often find themselves up against the same oppressive powers once more, as a result of a global production system functioning in accordance with these powers. In a reconstruction of globalized production these forms of oppression needs to be addressed, and there are a number of analytical approaches to this.

Affirmative action is a strategy used by some firms and public employers as part of their CSR policy to address the problems of racism and patriarchal oppression. This means that when recruiting, they actively seek to employ people from groups under-represented in the firm, usually women or ethnic groups traditionally excluded from jobs of a certain kind. In an equal society all firms would have a representative cross section of all groups in society on all corporate levels, and affirmative action is an attempt to achieve this within the centrally planned economies of individual firms. On the level of the individual firm it may make recruitment less racist and misogynistic, but it changes little as regards the economic mechanisms created by colonial and patriarchal structures.

Another problem with affirmative action is its politics of representation, which has a tendency to make people ambassadors for values and interests they do not necessarily sympathize with. From a performativity viewpoint, we can say that the colour of your skin does not make you more or less racist; your biological sex does not make you more or less patriarchal; your class origin does not make you more or less revolutionary; rather, it is how you relate to and interact in these oppressive structures that determines these qualities. Affirmative action shines a light on how employers relate to these structures in their recruitment and workplace routines, which is important and brings about some degree of change. The substantial structural change required for social sustainability and justice in globalized production, however, is not going to come about any time soon through affirmative action in TNCs.

The organizations best positioned to speak for workers' rights and justice in globalized production are **trade unions**. Historically, unions have been important drivers of changing labour standards in the North, and also in the construction of welfare states during the 20th century. Trade unions represent the interest, needs and values of their members, ideally also in a democratic way, so that the pressing issues affecting workers are taken up by union representatives and lead to collective pressure on employers. During the era of Fordism this pressure could be very effective, and led to significant improvements in working conditions, wages and benefits. This was particularly the case when political parties based in labour movements were in government, and pressure could therefore be exerted from both trade unions and the state. A marked effect of globalization and post-Fordist production has been a weakening of trade union power, first because of political attacks on union power, such as in Thatcher's Britain, and second because of the networked and footloose organization of production. While unions could credibly threaten to go on strike and hurt capitalist interests when firms were confined to their home nations, today firms can credibly threaten to offshore production to (another) low-cost country through outsourcing or by setting up shop in an EPZ, thus making union members redundant if the pressure becomes too hard from an entrepreneurial perspective. This structural change has reduced the direct power of trade unions, and even though they are still active politically to further the interests of workers, they have lost relevance for ordinary employees. Union bargaining power on behalf of the precariat is perceived as weak, so people do not join trade unions to the same degree as during Fordism. From a global perspective trade unions are still important, and the harassment and killings of union leaders in Cambodia, China, Vietnam, Honduras and many other low-cost countries bear witness to the threatening influence that industrialists, and some states, ascribe to free trade unions. As feminist development economist Naila Kabeer said to me once, "We should not stop buying sweatshop products, because these jobs are important for the women workers, but we should combine our purchases with active support to the trade unions speaking for and working in the interest of sweatshop workers". International collaboration among national trade unions within the same industry has long been part of globalization, as a continuation of the traditional international solidarity among labour movements. But even when unions work together, the Fordist degree of direct union power is hard to achieve and exercise in today's GVCs. Union power is still exercised primarily within firms or plants, and on a national level.

Within the UN system the ILO works to further the implementation of decent labour standards, with a tripartite approach involving states, employers and trade union representatives. As UN bodies go, the ILO can only advise, coordinate, research and further mainstream official discourse, and it is on a national level that labour standards have to be improved. All nation states that have ratified the International Covenant on Economic, Social and Cultural Rights (ICESCR, based on the second half of the Universal Declaration on Human Rights) have agreed to allow workers to associate in trade unions in order to bargain collectively for improved wages and labour standards. Most states have also adapted their legislation accordingly, but in many places there is not enough institutional capacity or will to ensure that firms comply with the laws, which gives entrepreneurs latitude within their companies to treat workers in whichever way they find most profitable. In many instances this means violating their human rights while paying them measly wages. Half the purpose of SDG 8 is to promote decent work; the other half is growth. As we have seen in this chapter, corporate growth and decent work do not fit naturally together. For this to happen, trade unions are important actors.

Consumer power is another influence on global production. In the North today there is a strong trend among entrepreneurs to offer sustainably produced goods and services. There is also vocal demand among some consumers, or a certain market segment, for sustainable products. Various sustainability brandings, with accreditation and monitoring mechanisms attached to them, are used to attract attention in this market segment. This trend is making some difference to those involved in production – although only a qualified difference. First, since the goods and services offered to consumers are supplied through the networks of global production, structural change driven by consumer choices is a slow process. Second, since more ethical market choices tend to cost more than unethical ones, consumer power in this sector is exercised primarily by comparatively well-off consumers. This means that most people are unlikely to prioritize ethical consumption with their limited resources. Third, consumer power is exercised through the price mechanism, which is a very blunt form of communication with producers. When this signal originates from a limited market segment, the critical traction of consumer choices becomes even weaker and more blurred. But at certain junctures consumer power is important, such as when environmental or child labour scandals break in the media and consumer boycotts follow. This potential for consumer punishment appears to be a stronger disciplinary force for corporations than individual consumer choices. Corporations exposed to retail consumer demand also tend to have stronger and more transparent CSR policies, and this correlation can be attributed to the fear of consumer boycotts.

During globalization, and the general ideological shift to a more individualist society that has accompanied it, consumption has become a vital form of identity construction and expression. In Northern societies people shop, eat, dress, exercise, and carry out many other everyday activities in their capacities as consumers. The many different ways people do this are markers for who they are, or want to be. Corporations therefore do extensive research to be able to catch shifts in identification processes, along with other trends, in order to adapt to the resulting new consumer demand.

Identification through consumption, and willingness to express one's identity through the economic dynamics driving globalized production, is vital for keeping GVCs operating. It is our continuous, everyday participation in the global economy, as producers, owners, investors *and* consumers, that allows TNCs to realize the economic future that keeps owners more or less happy. Accelerating profit-making in globalized production is necessary for financial growth and stability, and that means that consumption also needs to accelerate. But thanks to globalized production, different consumer groups are drifting so far apart that we are approaching the situation set out in the IMF warning mentioned at the very beginning of this book: global inequality is becoming so acute that it is hurting growth. The social effects of economic globalization are beginning to threaten the profitability of global corporations.

Revolution is the classical Marxist answer for what might come after a crisis of overproduction. The working class has been so exploited that it no longer constitutes an attractive market for the goods and services of capitalist production. The purpose of a Marxist revolution is to give the proletariat, which has no ownership or control over the means of production or its own labour, control over the factories, the banks, the mines, and all other means of production and finance. After having taken control of the means of production, Marx expected, the proletariat would use this control to create an equal society, where all individual needs are catered for by collective decision-making for the freedom and full self-realization of each individual (see Chapter 2). This vision is attractive and somehow impractical at the same time. The current examples we have of successful worker control of the means of production have not been achieved through revolutions in the Marxist sense, but through quiet civic organizing, sometimes in combination with civil disobedience. The classical Marxist revolutions, such as the Soviet system or those in Cuba and Angola, are today either dissolved, or in a state of decay and authoritarian corruption and inequality. Taking control of the means of production in many instances has shown itself to be feasible, practical, and conducive to sustainability and development, but while doing so through Marxist revolution is an effective way of breaking up colonial political relationships, it has not proved very good for establishing sustainable and just societies.

Conclusion

The post–Fordist mode of organizing industrial production has changed how firms operate, and in their globalization the command economies of post–Fordist networks has very successfully exploited inequalities in wage levels and other production factor differences all over the world. TNCs are approaching a point where they are becoming the victims of their own successful reorganization, as the competition between countries, workers and subcontractors that adds to their profits is also driving down wages and aggravating inequality. New markets with new consumers in Asia are replacing disappearing markets in US and Europe, and the attractive market of the top 10 per cent is getting saturated. In the meantime we have to participate in the circuits of globalized production if we want to lead an ordinary everyday life. By structural fiat, therefore, we are performing a capitalist logic that is dragging the planet towards ecological disaster. Throughout this book I have presented different ways to break with this logic and change these structures, and in this chapter we have moved from CSR to Marxist revolutionary takeover of the means of production.

Humans are creative, and this is expressed through our work, through production and economic interaction, and to some extent also through consumption. The home for much of this creativity today is the firm, and if we change how firms function and operate, locally as well as globally, this creativity will be worth cherishing and developing. When we reconstruct production, we need to break with the post-Fordist accelerated exploitation of colonial and patriarchal inequalities, but much of what is needed to build a better social metabolism is already at hand. The nation state has many practical institutional features that can be used. Workers, engineers, designers, waiters, cleaners and teachers all possess knowledge and skills that will continue to have creative productive applications. The vital aim of reconstruction is not to establish a particular format of production, but to ensure that just and sustainable production is achieved, and that people find this new mode of production meaningful and possible to live and love in.

Further reading

Two books have been formative for the debate on globalized production, TNCs and post-Fordism. The first is Naomi Klein's *No Logo* (2000), which presents a broad analysis of how sweatshop squalor hangs together with rich-world consumerism through capitalist exploitation and cultural and political processes around brands and TNCs. Klein's sharp critical analysis in this book had a tremendous influence on the global justice movement. The second is Peter Dicken's textbook *Global Shift: Mapping the Changing Contours of the World Economy* (7th edn 2015), which is one of those global textbooks that influence generations of students and academics. In this book Dicken presents a mainstream explanation of how TNCs function in a globalized world. How corporations invest and move in the world is reported on in UNCTAD's yearly *World Investment Report*, which in 2019 focused on special economic zones and the ways countries use these to try to attract investment, with variable success. The reports are downloadable for free from www.unctad.org, where a great many investment and trade statistics can also be found. In civil society CorpWatch has become an important player, holding TNCs accountable for their actions in relation to human and social rights as well as the environment. Their critical research and journalism can be found at https://corpwatch.org. Finally, to get an idea of what is happening in the corporate world, it is instructive to read a company report and the *Financial Times* every now and then.

Do Not Waste a Crisis

I started this book with a figure from the *Economist*: 23 per cent of global consumption over the last 2,000 years happened between 2001 and 2010. This gargantuan level of consumption is not tenable: the resulting climate change and biological degradation is quickly pulling us towards planetary disaster. An economic crisis is the fastest way to achieve drastic emission reductions and put the global economy on track to realizing the Paris Agreement on climate change. The only dips in the steeply rising emissions curve correlate with the economic crises of the early 1990s and 2007–8. Biodiversity, climate stability and ecological sustainability in general would benefit greatly from a really severe economic crisis in the near future.

In an article written early in the last crisis, Widmaier et al (2007) explain how wars and economic crises provide openings for designing and building radically changed political economies. They also convincingly show that this design and implementation cannot be understood only as the result of elite decisions, or structural circumstances, or popular will. What happens in a crisis is that several agents and interest groups struggle over how to interpret the structural and political circumstances, and then out of this debate and political struggle a response to the crisis is forged by institutional, material, political and economic measures. Wars and crises are 'what agents make of them' (Widmaier et al, 2007, p 757). Severe economic crises can offer ideal opportunities to change political economies, as many of the structural and discursive nuts and bolts of the capitalist system are loosened or broken. G20 diplomats were quite proud in 2010 to have screwed the whole global political economy together again in the same way as before the crisis (with some new washers and buffers in the construction, such as Basel III). Philip Mirowski (2014) has described how neoliberal politicians and a select group of economists managed to preserve the neoliberal global economic order, even after the crisis of 2007–8 had seemingly delegitimized it and its economistic discourse. As we approach the next crisis – which will come – we need to start planning how to get out of it, how to prevent the economic powers of the present order monopolizing the agenda, and how to reconstruct the global political economy so that it becomes socially and ecologically sustainable.

In this last chapter I will return to the themes of the previous chapters, and discuss how to make the most of the next economic crisis. What openings and opportunities can be utilized to construct a just, fair and ecologically tenable global political economy? History teaches us that such reconstruction is possible. It also teaches us that there are no magic bullets, and that one size does not fit all. There are, however, valuable ideas and experiences that will be useful in the reconstruction.

Sustainable finance?

We start with financial market reconstruction for two reasons. First, the next crisis will most likely break out as a crisis in financial markets, either as a 'Black Swan event' when markets go unpredictably crazy, or as a 'Green Swan event' (Bolton et al, 2020) when climate change or ecological disaster results in unforeseeable economic adjustments. Second, a financial crisis creates an ideal opportunity for reconstruction, since it erases many values based in the future, which in turn makes the future easier to rewrite and revalue. Firms, finance ministries, banks, central banks and workers are no longer obliged to realize the same future as the one priced into financial assets before the crisis. There are four vital financial market decisions to make when restarting the economy.

The first decision will relate to how we should handle the values lost in the crisis. Should we prop up the banks and other institutions whose solvency rested on financial extrapolations of the many different financial assets and instruments? This was the strategy after the 2008 crash, and it was widely criticized for being excruciatingly expensive and for leading to unjust redistribution of public funds into the coffers of private financial actors. As I discussed in Chapter 6, the logic for not allowing banks to default is that this would eradicate a great deal of value. However, vital banking functions can be taken over by the state, as demonstrated by the Swedish government after a real estate crisis in the early 1990s, and the lost wealth of private investors can stay, well, lost. If the priced-in future is not going to happen, the values based in this future will never become real. The upper class will have to live with that, and make do with the wealth they still have.

The second decision will be how to refinance society – that is, how to feed money into the economy to make it function again. If you siphon this liquidity through the financial market, you can trust financial actors to absorb large chunks, and only a trifle of the funds will reach firms and people in everyday life and the real economy. This is what happened with QE money in the 2010s. Frances Coppola (2019) instead advocates a 'people's quantitative easing', which would consist of feeding money into the economy via fiscal policy channels or simply transferring cash from central banks directly to citizens. This would lead to a fairer sharing of the burden of the crisis, and a faster remedying of its negative social effects. A people's QE would also restart the economy 'from the bottom up', from the sphere in society where real–world sustainability is achieved. This would mean that everyday life could be put on a trajectory towards a sustainable future. Moreover, instead of trying to secure values based in a future that would wreck the planet, everyday economic interaction would gradually realize a sustainable future that could be banked on, discounted and amortized. If we decided such financial relations to the future were to be part of the package, that is.

The third decision will relate to how we should deal with financial risk. As discussed in Chapter 6, financial market actors are not always the most apt to handle risks related to the future. A clean–up in the derivatives markets, where handling and redistributing financial risk takes place, might also be called for. This would reduce the level of moral hazard endemic to the market, so that investors would not expect someone else to clean up their mess when their investments did not deliver profits as planned.

The fourth decision will concern ownership of economic assets, and whether this ownership should really be part of financial market interaction. Are private financial actors really the best holders of claims on ordinary people's future income, as with mortgages? Or should homes be financed in another way? Are shareholders the best group from whom to recruit the boards that will decide on what to produce in our mines and factories? In many previous crises the answer to such questions has been 'no', and states have taken over ownership of private assets. This has been a way to secure vital societal functions and retain productive capacity. After a financial crisis and a stock market crash, there will be a chance for a widespread reshuffling of asset ownership, and for a general reconstruction of the principles of ownership that we discussed in Chapter 6.

These four decisions are only entry points into the reconstruction of financial markets after the next crisis. Financial actors have gained a lot of power during the globalization era, and financial market logics have penetrated ever more spheres of everyday life. In general terms, this power and its discourse will be a vital part of reconstruction, and a 'definancialization' of the global political economy will most probably be the result of shifts in power and logic, away from financial gain and towards some kind of sustainability. As Happer (2017) writes, financial actors have a huge influence over the political agenda, not least through the media, and it will be of great importance not to let financial interests control the reconstructive agenda after the next crisis.[1]

Just, sustainable global production

The next crisis will slow down consumption and industrial production. This is good. More than half of greenhouse gas emissions stem from industrial production. So an economic crisis will slow our drift towards ecological disaster, and the more a crisis can lower production and consumption, the better. It is not the economic slowdown or financial crisis *per se* that is a problem; the problem is how you allow the crisis to hit along social divides and for different groups and countries. If you let unemployment soar and poverty spread because of the crisis, then you have problems of justice and social sustainability. Restarting production after the crisis, therefore, needs to be done in such a way that it becomes compatible with both social and environmental sustainability.

As we discussed in Chapter 7, TNCs can be influenced and adjusted, and after the crisis their receptivity to influence may probably increase. Historically, TNCs have been regarded as crucial for GDP growth and job opportunities. But if we put production on a steady-state or post-growth trajectory after the crisis, the role for global corporations in national developmental policy will shrink or even disappear. This will mean that the negotiating power of TNCs will diminish. In a sustainable global political economy, if that is what we aspire to create after the crisis, private central planning within corporations will have to adjust in at least three ways.

The first adjustment will be a shift to renewable energy sources and most likely much higher energy costs. Since cheap fossil energy has fuelled GVCs until now, the GVC mode of organizing production will suffer a severe blow. Transport costs of GVC items have so far been only a small fraction of final consumer prices, but with scarce or rationed energy and rising energy prices, transport costs will add considerably more to final consumer prices. Producing on the other side of the world will in many cases become prohibitively expensive. If emission fees and ecological footprint tariffs are levied on production and final consumer prices, it will make GVC products even costlier. This adjustment to new energy prices and reduced energy availability will cause a break-up of many GVC networks.

The second adjustment will concern the global labour force and the availability of cheap and competent labour. After the 2008 crisis, corporate profit bounced back quite rapidly, partly because contract relations in GVCs could be renegotiated and production costs brought down even further. This translated into suppressed wages and harder working conditions on factory floors around the world. The Chinese development experience with rising wages and scarcity of labour and garment worker strikes in countries like Bangladesh and Cambodia show that the era of abysmal international wage differences is coming to an end. Labour exploitation, if that continues at all, will have to soften. We are already seeing previously off-shored production move back to the US and European mainlands. Consumer demand for ethically produced products is feeding into this adjustment. After the next crisis the strategy of paying living wages and treating workers decently, instead of aggravating exploitation, will be a counterintuitive corporate strategy. Corporations will therefore have to be nudged and pushed to adopt this strategy, and legislators and government agencies will need to side with unions to give it traction. A first step towards social and ecological sustainability in global production is living wages and decent conditions for GVC workers, because this will make prices rise and demand fall, and hence push down the bulimic consumption and related ecological footprints of shoppers in the rich world.

The third adjustment will be a new societal role for business. If we restart global production 'from below', on a similar basis to that of 'people's QE', and put global industry on a trajectory towards the realization of the UN's SDGs, there will be much less political space for private entrepreneurship. During the globalization era, the 'firm' and its owners were seen as the primary constructive historical force. But a firm is just one among many possible ways to organize production and human creativity, and if justice and sustainability are our primary goals, other institutional constructions for production might be more effective. TNCs and other large private centrally planned economies will have to prove they are worthy of continuing operations, or they will have to be closed down. If a firm is not fit to keep operating, but its production is societally important, there are many other ways to get this production done. After the next crisis, it will be more important to maintain vital production than to save the firms that controlled it before the crisis.

Will globalized production disappear? Probably not. There will be many items that need materials from international markets for their production, and there will be a need for foreign skills when reconstructing society to achieve sustainability. So networks such as GVCs will probably continue operating, but in new ways. If we accept that it is not the size of a system, but the flows within it, that determine its sustainability, then it is possible to imagine GVCs operating sustainably. If social and ecological sustainability become the primary objectives of GVCs, and profit to shareholders secondary or tertiary, their continued operation may even be beneficial.

Treaties for sustainable trade

Since the Bretton Woods Conference in 1944, the global order has been politically constructed to increase international trade. The WTO still has a mandate to further this. In light of the chaotic nationalistic and mercantilist international trade of the 1930s, this is understandable. After the next crisis we can expect countries to embark on different trajectories towards a more or less sustainable reconstruction of their economies. It will be important to establish collaboration between states and regions striving to reconstruct sustainably, and to establish routines for collaboration and trade to foster this. Trade barriers such as infant–industry tariffs, labour standards and environmental production standards will be important instruments to fend off competition from predatory TNCs and countries. Mercantilist and profit-maximizing trade policies that benefit a country's national TNCs, which have characterized WTO negotiations as well as bilateral or regional free-trade agreements, may become irrational after a reconstruction of GVCs and TNCs. Countries would benefit from entering sustainability agreements for productive collaboration, instead of free-trade agreements negotiated to achieve continued growth and corporate profits. As Stephen and Parizek (2019) show, the WTO's institutional structure for international trade is already drifting towards economic and political irrelevance, and after the next crisis there will be an opportunity to establish an institutional order for trade based on sustainability and social justice – either by changing the WTO and existing treaties, or by forging new treaties on the basis of social and ecological necessities. The saying from the 1990s that 'global problems need global solutions' is probably going to be refuted by groups of countries pushing ahead for sustainable trade collaboration. Other countries will try to squeeze the last drops of fossil profits out of the existing global political economy, and continue down the capitalist free-trade path. Two or more trade orders are likely to evolve, according to the logic of a multipolar world that is already in the offing (Acharya, 2018). As long as the difference in economic interaction is not securitized, and military and nationalist radicalization such as that in the 1930s is kept at bay, different trade policies can most probably coexist peacefully after the next crisis.

Post-crisis markets

We know that markets are what we make them, and in Polanyi's terms we should reconstruct post-crisis markets so that market mechanisms get 're-embedded' in the social fabric. But what exactly does that mean today? There is no 'original' society left, no 'authentic' culture that can close the societal metabolism in its embrace. What we have are culturally different versions of capitalist modernity, where people are doing their best in their multicultural everyday life.

The 're-' in re-embedding cannot mean a return to a pre-market 'authentic' cultural past, but a circumscribing of the market mechanism into socially beneficial and democratically constructed confines within each society. If we accept that countries will go different ways after the crisis, then there is room for national democratic debates on how to create sustainable economies. In these economies the market may play different roles depending on what the electorate and politicians decide. Market mechanisms may pervade everyday life to different degrees, from total central planning to complete laissez-faire, and as long as this happens within ecological planetary boundaries it will be democratically fine. Local political economies would get embedded in society in many different ways, each serving to create a sustainable societal metabolism compatible with local everyday life. This sounds mushy, I know, but not much mushier than the SDGs, which all countries have agreed to realize. The next crisis will reduce emissions and help countries move more quickly towards realizing the climate-related SDGs and the Paris Agreement. The crisis will also create policy space to deal with the other SDGs.

The most pain and suffering created by economic crises has normally been inflicted on people with limited means to weather those crises in everyday life.

Even if the upper classes may lose most money in absolute terms per person, the harshest social effects of an economic crisis are felt elsewhere and by others. In the intersectional matrix, the effects of crisis hit downwards along each axis, with the result that women, working-class people, people of colour and so on bear a heavier burden in relative income terms. To secure social sustainability and a viable crisis response, these tendencies need to be counteracted with economic measures in the next crisis. Such measures could involve people's QE, public ownership takeovers, or fiscal and monetary redistribution, as indicated earlier. Apart from making more economic sense than propping up financial values, such measures will also cause less pain and suffering than the austerity policies pursued after the crisis of 2008. Measures of this kind can be constructively combined with national, legal or global initiatives to reconstruct industrial production for ecological sustainability. Many jobs will be created in the rebuilding of energy systems, the establishment of new forms of transport, the reconstruction of habitation and so on.

Conclusion

Love practice would be a very fruitful corrective after the next crisis: politicians, bureaucrats and other powerful actors need to scrutinize crisis-induced measures in terms of their effects on love in everyday life. Measures that diminish or threaten everyday love and people's capacity to love must be avoided, to avoid endangering social sustainability. Whenever I have presented this love argument at seminars, listeners have protested and said that "people won't endure anything just because politicians focus on love". That is of course correct. Love in itself is not the answer, but I am sure it can be a vital corrective for post-crisis policies and economic reconstruction.

Institutional change during the globalization era has moved markets to become more individualist and utilitarian, and the enrichment of oneself has been hailed as the motive force for the creative entrepreneur, who is expected to elevate society to the next level of mass consumption. This institutional order is not compatible with planetary survival; nor is it supportive of justice, fairness or social sustainability. I don't even think it is built on an accurate depiction of economic creativity and entrepreneurship in everyday life. When you talk to entrepreneurs, they most often talk about things like dedication, creation, networking, social relations, capabilities and the like. Most entrepreneurs also toil with their ideas and companies for a substantial time before any enrichment whatsoever happens, if it ever happens. In other words, they like what they do, and they do it because they think it will be meaningful and good in people's lives. Economic creativity is not alien to bell hooks' love practice, unless it is institutionalized to be that way. That is why the love practice needs to be a corrective when we restart the global political economy after the next crisis.

Notes

Chapter 1

1   In the 1980s and 1990s, GPE was called 'International Political Economy'. Since then the world has globalized, and there is no longer any clear division between national and international economic and political forces. In this book I therefore use 'Global Political Economy' as the name for the discipline, in line with most recent textbooks.

2   The basic principles of both versions of GPE can be summarized as a series of obligations on researchers to: be transparent about their selection of methods and use of theories and concepts; account for and show how they arrived at a certain result; be prepared for and open to critical scrutiny of their work; and be prepared to share their work with other researchers and the general public.

3   Many other theorists have written on power, including Max Weber, Emile Durkheim, Iris Marion Young, Steven Lukes, Anthony Giddens, Thomas Hobbes, Plato, Aristotle, Thucydides and many more. While all these have contributed tremendously to social science and democracy, I present power conceptually using the thinkers discussed in this chapter because they have written good and accessible theory on these four forms of power. As can be seen in Thucydides' writings from 400 BC, these forms have always been part of the study of power in some way.

Chapter 2

1   There is a debate about whether Kipling wrote the poem as a satire, or as a sincere ode to colonial armies and the imperial project. Readers are invited to find out for themselves: the poem is available in many places online, including: 'Modern History Sourcebook: Rudyard Kipling, The White Man's Burden, 1899' (nd) *Fordham University* [online], available from: https://sourcebooks.fordham.edu/mod/Kipling.asp

2   Fanon's *The Wretched of the Earth* was written during the Algerian War of Independence, and the writing is coloured by the colonial brutality of this conflict. Fanon has in some quarters been misunderstood as promoting violence as a general tool in antiracist struggles (and Jean Paul Sartre's foreword aided in this misconception). But there is an important distinction between anticolonial liberation wars and antiracist political struggles and policies, and for the most part it is the former in which Fanon advocates violence as a tool.

3   Love is not unknown to neoliberal economists such as Gary Becker or Paul Frijters. When these figures include love in their marginalist models, however, it is presented as determined by the utilitarian individualism of the theory. Frijters, for instance, argues that 'we love people and entities because our unconscious mind has tried to strike an implicit bargain with them' (Frijters, 2013, p 30). Defining love in this way subsumes it under economistic rationality, and misses most of the social universe that hooks and Butler engage with.

4   *New Political Economy* and *Feminist Economics*, along with many other academic journals, have online paywalls. Abstracts of articles tend to be open-access, but if you want to read the full texts you often have to log in via a university or library, which then also needs to have a subscription to the journal in question. Sometimes the author of an article has produced a non-academic

text with the same argument that can be found on a freely available website, so this may be worth a try if you are unable to access the journal text.

Chapter 3

[1] In 2005 the General Assembly agreed on the 'responsibility to protect' (or R2P, as it is called), which states that if a state cannot protect its citizens against human rights violations, genocide or war crimes, then the UN has the right to intervene. This has been the norm throughout UN history, but with R2P it has been set out clearly in a convention. The final object of security, therefore, has become the individual human.

[2] An African social vision was formulated in 1966–7 by Julius K. Nyerere (1968), who sketched out a socialist vision that subsequently became important for Tanzanian economic development. In 1902 anarchist philosopher Peter Kropotkin wrote *Mutual Aid: a Factor of Evolution* (available at www.gutenberg.org), a collection of essays on anarchist economic and social organization. Walden Bello, Vandana Shiva, Samir Amin, Rajni Kothari and many other scholars have discussed how colonial and imperial capitalism might be toppled or transformed so as to bring about development and improve well-being in Southern countries, based on equality principles and local social institutions.

Chapter 4

[1] An oft-cited figure for average tariff levels in 1947 is 40 per cent, but this figure has not been confirmed, and Bown and Irwin (2015) have found that the records for core GATT countries indicate that the average tariff applied was 22 per cent.

Chapter 5

[1] As the philosophy and discourse of the Enlightenment was gradually inscribed into the institutional structure of nation states, this idea created a bond between political power and scientific inquiry. This bond stands out starkly in Adam Smith's *Wealth of Nations* (1776), but is also visible in the visionary dimension of Marx and Engels' *Communist Manifesto* of 1848 or Léon Walras' economic marginalist works from the second half of the 19th century.

[2] https://avalon.law.yale.edu/20th_century/truman.asp

[3] The 'real interest rate' is the difference between the nominal interest rate – the percentage fee on the debt that the bank wants in remuneration each year for lending the money – and the inflation rate. Since inflation hollows out the value of the debt stock each year at a certain percentage rate, just as it hollows out money's worth generally, the actual long-term cost of a loan is the real interest rate, and not the nominal interest rate.

[4] Purchasing power parity is a model for recalculating prices and incomes to make them comparable across countries.

[5] While the Bretton Woods institutions have influenced development thinking and policy a great deal over the last several decades, I do not include them in this ODA discussion since they are not, strictly speaking, development organizations. The IMF is designed to stabilize the international system of payments, and the World Bank is a bank. You might argue that the loans from the IDA section of the World Bank are on non-commercial terms, and the 'gift component' in the financing of these loans by rich donor countries is listed on the ODA budgets of those countries. But the IDA is also a lender, and therefore does not offer assistance in the popular altruistic sense of the word.

Chapter 6

[1] Moral hazard as a concept is used most often in relation to reckless lending by banks, who count on governments bailing them out in times of crisis. Recklessly lending too much money to actors who are likely to default on the loans is easier if you can count on states, or multilateral institutions like the IMF, to bail you out if things go wrong.

Chapter 7

1 Kofi Annan, 31 January 1999, Davos. Annan's speech was disseminated as UN Press Release SG/SM/6881 and is available at https://www.un.org/press/en/1999/19990201.sgsm6881.html.

2 How this tendency should be interpreted, and how much hope it should raise, is a matter for debate. Stephen Bell (2020) interprets it in a much more positive way. He has also found several positive indications of state–market collaboration to implement and commercialize sustainable energy technology.

Chapter 8

1 On legislative changes proposed by financial actors and other members of the commercial class, Adam Smith wrote that such a proposal must be treated with great caution, since 'it comes from an order of men whose interest is never exactly the same with that of the public, who have generally an interest to deceive and even to oppress the public, and who accordingly have upon many occasions, both deceived and oppressed it' (Smith, 1776, p 359).

References

Acharya, A. (2018) *The End of American World Order* (2nd edn), Cambridge: Polity.

Aganbegyan, A.G. (1988) *The Economic Challenge of Perestrojka*, Bloomington: Indiana University Press.

Albin, C. (2001) *Justice and Fairness in International Negotiation*, Cambridge: Cambridge University Press.

Amin, S. (2004) *The Liberal Virus: Permanent War and the Americanization of the World*, London: Pluto Press.

Andersson, E. (2012) 'Who needs effective Doha negotiations, and why?', *International Negotiation*, 17(1): 189–209.

Andersson, E. (2016a) 'Everyday futures: the foundation of financial market stability in the performative social present', *Real-World Economics Review*, 75: 126–34.

Andersson, E. (2016b) 'Monies that matter, on the discursive power of the bank for international settlements', *Globalizations*, 13(2): 203–16.

Appadurai, A. (1996) *Modernity at Large: Cultural Dimensions of Globalization*, Minneapolis: University of Minnesota Press.

Bachrach, P. and Baratz, M.S. (1962) 'Two Faces of Power', *The American Political Science Review*, 56(4): 947–952.

Bairoch, P. (1993) *Economics and World History: Myths and Paradoxes,* Hemel Hempstead: Harvester Wheatsheaf.

Baker, A. (2013) 'The new political economy of the macroprudential ideational shift', *New Political Economy*, 18(1): 112–39.

Beckert, J. (2016) *Imagined Futures: Fictional Expectations and Capitalist Dynamics*, Cambridge, MA: Harvard University Press.

Bell, S. (2020) 'The renewable energy transition energy path divergence, increasing returns and mutually reinforcing leads in the state–market symbiosis', *New Political Economy*, 25(1): 57–71.

Bello, W. (2002) *Deglobalization: Ideas for a New World Economy*, London: Zed Books.

Benería, L., Berik, G. and Floro, M.S. (2016) *Gender, Development, and Globalization: Economics as if All People Mattered* (2nd edn), London: Routledge.

Bennet, J. (2015) 'We Need an Energy Miracle', Bill Gates interviewed in *The Atlantic*, 2015(11): n.p.

Best, J. (2010) 'The limits of financial risk management: or what we didn't learn from the Asian crisis', *New Political Economy*, 15(1): 29–49.

Boettke, P.J. and Heilbroner, R.L. (2019) 'Economic system', in *Encyclopædia Britannica* [online], 9 January, available from: https://www.britannica.com/topic/economic-system

Bolton, P., Despres, M., Perira da Silva, L.A., Samama, F. and Swartzman, R. (2020) 'The Green Swan: Central banking and financial stability in the age of climate change', Basel: BIS.

Bourdieu, P. (1985) 'The social space and the genesis of groups', *Theory and Society*, 14(6) 723–744.

Bown, C.P. and Irwin, D.A. (2015) *The GATT's Starting Point: Tariff Levels Circa 1947 NBER Working Paper No. 21782*, Cambridge, MA: National Bureau of Economic Research.

Bregman, R. (2016) *Utopia for Realists: The Case for a Universal Basic Income, Open Borders, and a 15-Hour Workweek*, translated by E. Manton, [no place]: The Correspondent.

Büchs, M. and Koch, M. (2017) *Postgrowth and Wellbeing: Challenges to Sustainable Welfare*, Cham: Palgrave Macmillan.

Butler, J. (1993) *Bodies That Matter: On the Discursive Limits of "Sex"*, New York: Routledge.

Butler, J. (1997) *The Psychic Life of Power: Theories in Subjection*, Stanford: Stanford University Press.

Butler, J., Laclau, E. and Žižek, S. (2000) *Contingency, Hegemony, Universality: Contemporary Dialogues on the Left*, New York: Verso.

Carson, R. (1962) *Silent Spring*, reprint, London: Penguin, 2015.

Chang, H.J. (2002) *Kicking Away the Ladder: Development Strategy in Historical Perspective*, London: Anthem.

Chang, H.-J. (2010) *23 Things They Don't Tell You about Capitalism*, London: Allen Lane.

Coase, R.H. (1937) 'The nature of the firm', *Economica*, 4(16): 386–405.

Collier, P. and Hoeffler, A. (2004) 'Greed and grievance in civil war', *Oxford Economic Papers*, 56(4): 563–95.

Connell, R.W. and Messerschmidt, J.W. (2005) 'Hegemonic Masculinity: Rethinking the Concept', *Gender & Society*, 19(6): 829–859.

Coppola, F. (2019) *The Case for People's Quantitative Easing*, Cambridge: Polity.

Cox, R.W. (1981) 'Social forces, states and world orders: beyond international relations theory', *Millennium*, 10(2): 126–55.

Cox, R.W. (1983) 'Gramsci, Hegemony and International Relations: An Essay in Method', *Millennium*, 12(2): 162–75.

Cox, R. (1995) 'Critical political economy', in B. Hettne (ed.) *International Political Economy: Understanding Global Disorder*, London: Zed Books, pp 31–45.

Crenshaw, K. (1989) 'Demarginalizing the Intersection of Race and Sex: A Black Feminist Critique of Antidiscrimination Doctrine, Feminist Theory and Antiracist Politics', *University of Chicago Legal Forum*, 1989(1): 139–167.

Crouch, C. (2011) *The Strange Non-Death of Neoliberalism*, Cambridge: Polity.

Dahl, R. (1957) 'The Concept of Power', *Behavioral Science* 2(3): 201–215.

Dahl, R. (1961) *Who Governs? Democracy and Power in an American City*, New Haven, Conn.: Yale University Press.

Davis, A.Y. (1981) *Women, Race & Class*, New York: Random House.

de Goede, M. (2004) 'Repoliticizing Financial Risk', *Economy and Society*, 33(2): 197–217.

de Goede, M. (ed.) (2006) *International Political Economy and Poststructural Politics*, Basingstoke: Palgrave Macmillan.

de Soto, H. (2001) *The Mystery of Capital: Why Capitalism Triumphs in the West and Fails Everywhere Else*, London: Black Swan.

Dicken, P. (2015) *Global Shift: Mapping the Changing Contours of the World Economy* (7th edn), Los Angeles, CA: Sage.

Doganova, L. (2018) 'Discounting the future: a political technology', *Economic Sociology*, 19(2): 4–9.

The Economist (2011) 'Two thousand years in one chart: an alternative timeline for the past two millenia', 28 June, https://www.economist.com/graphic-detail/2011/06/28/two-thousand-years-in-one-chart.

Faludi, S. (1999) *Stiffed: The Betrayal of the Modern Man*, London: Chatto & Windus.

Fanon, F. (1961) *The Wretched of the Earth*, translated by C. Farrington, reprint, London: Penguin, 2001.

Fanon, F. (1967) *Black Skin, White Masks*, New York, NY: Grove Press.

Farid, M., Keen, M., Papaioannou, M., Parry, I., Pattillo, C., Ter-Martirosyan, A. et al (2016) *After Paris: Fiscal, Macroeconomic, and Financial Implications of Climate Change, IMF Staff Discussion Note SDN/16/01*, [no place]: International Monetary Fund.

Foucault, M. (1971) 'The Order of Discourse', inaugural lecture delivered at the Collège de France, *Social Science Information*, 1 Apr, 10(2): 7.

Frank, A.G. (1966) *The Development of Underdevelopment*, Boston, MA: New England Free Press.

Freeman, M. (2017) *Human Rights*, Cambridge: Polity.

Frijters, P. with Gigi Foster (2013) *An Economic Theory of Greed, Love, Groups and Networks*, Cambridge: Cambridge University Press.

Fumagalli, A. and Mezzadra, S. (2010) *Crisis in the Global Economy: Financial Markets, Social Struggles, and New Political Scenarios*, translated by J.F. McGimsey, Los Angeles: Semiotext(e).

Galbraith, J.K. (1993) *A Short History of Financial Euphorias*, New York, NY: Whittle.

Gallagher, K.P. (2008) 'Understanding developing country resistance to the Doha Round', *Review of International Political Economy*, 15(1): 62–85.

Garcia, E., Martinez-Iglesias, M. and Kirby, P. (eds) (2017) *Transitioning to a Post-Carbon Society: Degrowth, Austerity and Wellbeing*, London: Palgrave Macmillan.

Gelfer, J. (2014) *Masculinities in a Global Era*, New York, NY: Springer.

Germain, R.D. (1997) *The International Organization of Credit: States and Global Finance in the World-Economy*, Cambridge: Cambridge University Press.

Germain, R. (2010) *Global Politics and Financial Governance*, Basingstoke: Palgrave Macmillan.

Gill, S. (2008) *Power and Resistance in the New World Order* (2nd edn), Basingstoke: Palgrave Macmillan.

Gilpin, R. and Gilpin, J.M. (1987) *The Political Economy of International Relations*, Princeton: Princeton University Press.

Gilroy, P. (1993) *Black Atlantic: Modernity and Double Consciousness*, London: Verso.

Goodhart, D. (2017) *The Road to Somewhere: The Populist Revolt and the Future of Politics*, London: Hurst.

Graeber, D. (2011) *Debt: The First 5,000 Years*, New York: Melville House.

Haberl, H., Fischer-Kowalski, M., Krausmann, F., Martinez-Alier, J. and Winiwarter, V. (2011) 'A socio-metabolic transition towards sustainability? Challenges for another Great Transformation', *Sustainable Development*, 19(1): 1–14.

Handy, C. (2002) 'What's a business for?', *Harvard Business Review*, December: 49–55.

Hanlon, J., Barrientos, A. and Hulme, D. (2010) *Just Give Money to the Poor: The Development Revolution from the Global South*, Sterling, VA: Kumarian Press.

Happer, C. (2017) 'Financialisation, media and social change', *New Political Economy*, 22(4): 437–449.

Helleiner, E. (1994) *States and the Reemergence of Global Finance: From Bretton Woods to the 1990s*, Ithaca, NY: Cornell University Press.

Henwood, D. (1998) *Wall Street: How It Works and for Whom* (rev. edn), New York: Verso.

Hettne, B. (1990) *Development Theory and the Three Worlds*, Harlow: Longman Scientific and Technical.

Hettne, B. (ed.) (1995) *International Political Economy: Understanding Global Disorder*, London: Zed Books.

Hettne, B. (2009) *Thinking about Development*, London: Zed Books.

Hickel, J. (2017) *The Divide: A Brief Guide to Global Inequality and Its Solutions*, London: William Heinemann.

Hochschild, A. R. (2000) 'The nanny chain', *The American Prospect*, 11(4): 32–36.

Hochschild, A.R. (2016) *Strangers in Their Own Land: Anger and Mourning on the American Right*, New York: New Press.

Hoogvelt, A. (2001) *Globalization and the Postcolonial World: The New Political Economy of Development* (2nd edn), Basingstoke: Palgrave.

hooks, b. (2000) *All about Love: New Visions*, New York: HarperCollins.

Hopkin, J. and Rosamond, B. (2018) 'Post-truth politics, bullshit and bad ideas: "deficit fetishism" in the UK', *New Political Economy*, 23(6): 641–55.

Hudson, M. (2018) *...and Forgive Them Their Debts: Lending, Foreclosure, and Redemption from Bronze Age Finance to the Jubilee Year*, Dresden: ISLET.

Hull, J.C. (2018) *Options, Futures, and Other Derivatives* (10th edn), New York: Pearson.

IMF (International Monetary Fund) (2017) 'Fiscal Monitor: Tackling Inequality, October 2017', Washington DC: International Monetary Fund.

Jackson, T. (2009) *Prosperity without Growth? The Transition to a Sustainable Economy*, London: Sustainable Development Commission.

Kallis, G., Kerschner, C. and Martinez-Alier, J. (2012) 'The economics of degrowth', *Ecological Economics*, 84: 172–80.

Keynes, J.M. (1923) *A Tract on Monetary Reform*, London: Macmillan.

Kim, S.Y. (2010) *Power and the Governance of Global Trade: From the GATT to the WTO*, Ithaca, NY: Cornell University Press.

Klein, N. (2000) *No Logo: Taking Aim at the Brand Bullies*, Toronto: Knopf.

Klein, N. (2007) *The Shock Doctrine: The Rise of Disaster Capitalism*, New York: Picador.

Kothari, R. (1995) *Poverty: Human Consciousness and the Amnesia of Development*, London: Zed Books.

Kranke, M. and Yarrow, D. (2019) 'The global governance of systemic risk: how measurement practices tame macroprudential politics', *New Political Economy*, 24(6): 816–32.

Krugman, Paul (2008) 'Dead Doha', *The Conscience of a Liberal*, blogpost, https://krugman.blogs.nytimes.com/2008/07/30/dead-doha/.

Langley, P. (2008) *The Everyday Life of Global Finance: Saving and Borrowing in Anglo-America*, Oxford: Oxford University Press.

Leins, S. (2018) *Stories of Capitalism: Inside the Role of Financial Analysts*, Chicago: University of Chicago Press.

Li, T.M. (2007) *The Will to Improve: Governmentality, Development, and the Practice of Politics*, Durham, NC: Duke University Press.

Loomba, A. (1998) *Colonialism/Postcolonialism*, London: Routledge.

Lukes, S. (2004) *Power: A Radical View*, London: Macmillan/Red Globe Press.

MacKenzie, D. (2006) *An Engine, Not a Camera: How Financial Models Shape Markets*, Cambridge, MA: MIT Press.

Malhotra, K. et al (2003) *Making Trade Work for People*, UNDP/London: Earthscan.

Marchand, M.H. and Runyan, A.S. (eds) (2010) *Gender and Global Restructuring: Sightings, Sites and Resistances* (2nd edn), London: Routledge.

Marx, K. and Engels, F. (1848) *Manifesto of the Communist Party*, available at marxists.org, Moscow: Progress Publishers.

Marx, K. (1859) *A Contribution to the Critique of Political Economy*, Moscow: Progress Publishers.

Merleau-Ponty, M. (1973) *The Prose of the World*, edited by C. Lefort, translated by J. O'Neill, Evanston, IL: Northwest University Press.

Mirowski, P. (2014) *Never Let a Serious Crisis Go to Waste: How Neoliberalism Survived the Financial Meltdown*, New York, NY: Verso.

Mitchell, W. and Fazi, T. (2017) *Reclaiming the State: A Progressive Vision of Sovereignty for a Post-Neoliberal World*, London: Pluto Press.

Motesharrei, S., Rivas, J. and Kalnay, E. (2014) 'Human and nature dynamics (HANDY): modeling inequality and use of resources in the collapse or sustainability of societies', *Ecological Economics*, 101: 90–102.

Mouffe, C. (2005) *On the Political*, London: Routledge.

North, D.C. (1990) *Institutions, Institutional Change and Economic Performance*, Cambridge: Cambridge University Press.

Nove, A. (1989) *An Economic History of the U.S.S.R.* (2nd edn), London: Pelican.

Nyerere, J.K. (1968) *Freedom and Socialism. Uhuru na Ujamaa: A Selection from Writings and Speeches, 1965–1967*, Dar es Salaam: Oxford University Press.

O'Brien, R. and Williams, M. (2016) *Global Political Economy: Evolution and Dynamics* (5th edn), London: Palgrave.

OECD (2018) 'Launch of ODA figures 2017' (remarks by Angel Gurria) OECD, Paris, 9 April 2018, https://www.oecd.org/development/launch–of–oda–figures–2017–france–april–2018.htm.

Ostrom, E. (1990) *Governing the Commons: The Evolution of Institutions for Collective Action*, Cambridge: Cambridge University Press.

Ostry, J.D., Loungani, P. and Furceri, D. (2016) 'Neoliberalism: oversold?', *Finance & Development* (June), pp 38–41.

Palan, R. (ed) (2013) *Global Political Economy: Contemporary Theories*, London: Routledge.

Palan, R. (2015) 'Futurity, pro-cyclicality and financial crises', *New Political Economy*, 20(3): 367–85.

Peterson, V.S. (2003) *A Critical Rewriting of the Global Political Economy: Integrating Reproductive, Productive and Virtual Economies*, London: Routledge.

Piketty, T. (2014) *Capital in the Twenty-First Century*, translated by A. Goldhammer, Cambridge, MA: Belknap Press.

Pirie, I. (2011) 'The political economy of bulimia nervosa', *New Political Economy*, 16(3): 323–46.

Polanyi, K. (1944) *The Great Transformation*, reprint, Boston: Beacon, 1968.

Polaski, S. (2004) 'Protecting labor rights through trade agreements: an analytical guide', *Journal of International Law and Policy*, 10(13): 13–25.

Ramo, J.C. (2004) *The Beijing Consensus*, London: Foreign Policy Centre.

Ravenhill, J. (2016) *Global Political Economy* (5th edn), Oxford: Oxford University Press.

Rodrik, D. (2011) *The Globalizaton Paradox: Why Global Markets, States, and Democracy Can't Coexist*, Oxford: Oxford University Press.

Rodrik, D. (2017) *Straight Talk on Trade: Ideas for a Sane World Economy*, Princeton, NJ: Princeton University Press.

Rostow, W.W. (1990) *The Stages of Economic Growth: A Non-Communist Manifesto* (3rd edn), New York: Cambridge University Press.

Roubini, N. (2018) 'Blockchain isn't about democracy and decentralisation – it's about greed' *The Guardian*, 15 October 2018.

Ruggie, J.G. (1998) *Constructing the World Polity: Essays on International Institutionalization*, London: Routledge.

Sachs, J. (2005) *The End of Poverty: How We Can Make It Happen in Our Lifetime*, London: Penguin.

Sandbrook, R. (2003) *Civilizing Globalization: A Survival Guide*, Albany: State University of New York Press.

Scholte, J.A. (2008) 'Looking to the future: a global civil society forum?', in J.W.St.G. Walker and A.S. Thompson (eds) *Critical Mass: The Emergence of Global Civil Society*, Waterloo, ON: Wilfrid Laurier University Press, pp 231–50.

Schuurman, F.J. (ed.) (1993) *Beyond the Impasse: New Directions in Development Theory*, London: Zed Books.

Sen, A. (1999) *Development as Freedom*, New York: Bantam.

Sennett, R. (1999) *The Corrosion of Character: Personal Consequences of Work in the New Capitalism*, New York: W.W. Norton & Company.

Simmel, G. (1909/2004) *The Philosophy of Money*, London: Routledge.

Sinclair, T.J. and Thomas, K.P. (eds) (2001) *Structure and Agency in International Capital Mobility*, Basingstoke: Palgrave Macmillan.

Skeggs, B. (2005) 'The Making of Class and Gender through Visualizing Moral Subject Formation', *Sociology*, 39(5): 965–82.

Smith, A. (1776) *The Wealth of Nations*, reprint (3 vols), edited by A. Skinner, London: Penguin, 1986.

Standing, G. (2014) *The Precariat: The New Dangerous Class*, London: Bloomsbury Academic.

Stephen, M.D. and Parizek, M. (2019) 'New powers and the distribution of preferences in global trade governance: from deadlock and drift to fragmentation', *New Political Economy*, 24(6): 735–58.

Sterner, T. and Coria, J. (2013) *Policy Instruments for Environmental and Natural Resource Management* (2nd edn), New York: RFF Press.

Stiglitz, J.E. (2010) *Freefall: America, Free Markets, and the Sinking of the World Economy*, New York NY: W.W. Norton.

Stopford, J.M., Strange, S. and Henley, J.S. (1991) *Rival States, Rival Firms: Competition for World Market Shares*, Cambridge: Cambridge University Press.

Strange, S. (1988) *States and Markets: An Introduction to International Political Economy*, London: Pinter.

Taylor, F.W. (1911) *The Principles of Scientific Management*, New York, NY: Harper & Row.

Tett, G. (2010) *Fool's Gold: How the Bold Dream of a Small Tribe at J.P. Morgan Was Corrupted by Wall Street Greed and Unleashed a Catastrophe*, New York: Free Press.

Thrift, N. and Leyshon, A. (1994) 'A phantom state? The de-traditionalization of money, the international financial system and international financial centres', *Political Geography*, 13(4): 299–307.

Tilley, L. and Shilliam, R. (2018) 'Raced markets: an introduction', *New Political Economy*, 23(5): 534–43.

Truman, H.S. (1949) 'Inaugural address', 20 January, https://avalon.law.yale.edu/20th_century/truman.asp.

UNCTAD (2017) *World Investment Report 2017*, Geneva: United Nations.

Wacquant, L. (2007) 'Territorial Stigmatization in the Age of Advanced Marginality', *Thesis Eleven*, 91(1): 66–77.

Wallerstein, I.M. (1974) *The Modern World System 1: Capitalist Agriculture and the Origins of the European World-Economy in the Sixteenth Century*, New York: Academic Press.

Walter, C.E. and Howie, F.J.T. (2011) *Red Capitalism: The Fragile Financial Foundation of China's Extraordinary Rise*, Singapore: John Wiley & Sons.

Werner, T.L. (2015) 'The war on poverty and the racialization of "hillbilly" poverty: implications for poverty research', *Journal of Poverty*, 19(3): 305–23.

White, R. (1975) 'A New International Economic Order', *International and Comparative Law Quarterly*, 24(3): 542–552.

Widmaier, W.W., Blyth, M. and Seabrooke, L. (2007) 'Exogenous shocks or endogenous constructions? The meanings of wars and crises', *International Studies Quarterly*, 51(4): 747–59.

Wilkinson, R. and Pickett, K. (2009) *The Spirit Level: Why More Equal Societies Almost Always Do Better*, London: Allen Lane.

Williamson, J. (1990) 'What Washington means by policy reform', in J. Williamson (ed.) *Latin American Adjustment: How Much Has Happened?*, Washington, DC: Peterson Institute for International Economics.

Woods, N. (2006) *The Globalizers: The IMF, the World Bank, and Their Borrowers*, Ithaca, NY: Cornell University Press.

Young, I.M. (2006) 'Responsibility and global justice: a social connection model', *Social Philosophy and Policy*, 23(1): 102–30.

Zelizer, V.A. (1994) 'The creation of domestic currencies', *American Economic Review*, 84(2): 138–42.

Index

A

across the board approach 66
affirmative action 171–2
Africa 98
agape 26
agenda power 9
Agreement on Trade-Related Aspects of
    Intellectual Property Rights (TRIPS)
    49
Agreement on Trade-Related Investment
    Measures (TRIMs) 49
agricultural subsidies 70, 105
aid for trade 76
Albania 23
Albin, Cecilia 82
alienation 22, 26–7
alternative-open post-growth position 164
altruism 103
American International Group (AIG) 120,
    130
Amnesty International 155
Annan, Kofi 161
anthropology 21
anti-capitalist post-growth position 164
anti-sweatshop campaigns 155
anywheres versus somewheres 24
apartheid 28
applied tariff levels 66
Argentina 136, 137–8
    coupon system 108
Aristotle 26
Article IV consultations (IMF) 46
Asian Infrastructure Investment Bank (AIIB)
    98
assembly lines 150
asset prices 144
austerity 101, 132, 168

B

Bachrach, P. & Baratz, M.S. 9
bank runs 123
banking
    credit expansion 123

economic importance 124
origins of 116
post-financial crises 178
    see also central banks
banks 123–5
    financial intermediation 123
    subprime borrowers 129–31
    systemically important financial actors 125
bargaining parties 67
Barre, Siad 86
Basel III 145
Beijing Consensus 97–8
Bello, Walden 82, 108
Belt and Road Initiative 98
Benería et al. 17, 38
Best, J. 146
Beyond the Impasse (Schuurman) 112
bilateral free-trade agreements 73–4
bilateral ODA 106
biofuels 33
biosphere 31, 32
BIS (Bank for International Settlements) 139
Black Atlantic, The (Gilroy) 39
black bloc 69
black pride movement 36
Black Skin White Masks (Fanon) 39
Black Swan event 178
blockchain technology 140
Bolsa Familia programme 104
bonds 47, 118, 127
bound tariff levels 66
Bourdieu, Pierre 24
Brazil 104
Bretton Woods 3, 44–5
    exchange rate system 51, 52
Brexit 75
Brown, Gordon 132
Büchs, M. & Koch, M. 164
budget balance 90–1
Buen Vivir 107
bureaucracy 94
business banking 123–4
business model approach 163

Butler, Judith 27, 38
  The Psychic Life of Power 38

C

Cairns Group 70
California State Teachers' Retirement System
    (CalSTRS) 125
Cancun (2003) 70–2
cap and trade systems 56
Capital in the Twenty-First Century (Piketty)
    148
capital market 117–18
capitalism 17
  alienation 22
  conflict with religion 42–3
  consequences of growth 1–2
  crises 22–3
  and CSR 162
  expansion of production 43
  exploitation 22
    of social inequalities 19
  inequality 100
  and markets 59
  ownership of companies 134
  state, control of 21–2
carbon tax 57, 169
Carson, Rachel 87
cash transfers 103–6
  channelling through women 104
Castro, President Fidel 86
central banks 116–17
  acting counter-cyclically 127–8
  bonds 118
  crisis management 132–3
  depoliticization 139–40
  independence 139
  liquidity stimulus 133
  loans 118
  and money 139
  political issues rendered technical 139–40
  quantitative easing (QE) 133
central planning 60–1, 136–7, 149–50
  Taylorist 150–1
    crisis 151–2
Césaire, Aimé 36
Chang, Ha-Joon 82
change 1–13
  institutions 4–7
  power 7–10
charity redistribution 102–3
Charter of the United Nations 43
China 72, 143
  inward foreign investment 167
  relationships with developing countries
    97–8

unemployment post-financial crisis (2008)
    132
chlorofluorocarbons (CFCs) 77–8
civilizational idea 83
class 21–4
  Marxism 21
  origins of 24
class conflict 22
Clean Development Mechanism (CDM) 76
clean energy 169
Club of Rome 87
clusters 158–61
Coase, Ronald 149, 165
Cold War era 86
collateralized debt obligations (CDOs) 130
collective action 81
colonialism 20, 21, 36
  European powers 83
colonies, former *see* developing countries
colonization 25
colonized people, scientific depiction of 21
Columbus, Christopher 20
command economies 136
commercial considerations 65
commons 81, 137
communism 23, 136
Communist Manifesto, The (Marx & Engels)
    136
company behaviour 135–6
comparative advantage in production 49, 63
Comprehensive and Progressive Agreement
    for Trans-Pacific Partnership (CPATPP)
    74
conditionalities 89–90, 104–6
  see also SAPs (structural adjustment
    programmes)
consensus 66
consumer cooperatives 137
consumer power 173–4
consumption 52–3, 91
  between 2001 and 2010 1, 177
  and central planning 60
  during globalization 174
  identification through 174
  luxuries 43
  reducing 99, 109, 164
  of the upper classes 57, 160–1
contagion 146
controlling units 9, 10
cooperatives 137
COP 21 (21st Conference of the Parties) 10
Coppola, Frances 178
corporate behaviour 134
corporate leadership 162
corporate production 156

corporate social responsibility (CSR) 155,
155, 162–3
corporations
    consumer power 173–4
    diversification 151–2
    profitability 166
    reconstructing 166–9
    support for post-crises 168
        financial crisis (2008) 166
    see also firms; TNCs (transnational
        corporations)
corporatist role of states 84
CorpWatch 155
corruption 94
cotton farmers 70–1, 73
counter-cyclically, acting 127–8
Cox, Robert, W. 6–7, 26
credit default swaps (CDSs) 120, 128–30
credit expansion 123
credit market 117–18
credit ratings 127
credit scores 141
creditors 118
creditworthiness 141
Crenshaw, Kimberlé 24–5
crises see financial crises
Crisis in the Global Economy (Fumagalli and
    Mezzadra) 148
A Critical Rewriting of the Global Political
    Economy (Peterson) 38
critical theory 6
cryptocurrencies 140
cultural capital 24
culture 21
currencies 120
currency speculation 121
customs unions 67

D
Dahl, Robert 9–10
Davies, Angela 39
de Beauvoir, Simone 35–6
de Goede, Marieke 9
debt 19, 87–91, 117–18, 140–3
    crisis 89
    three-dimensional character 140–2
debt crisis (1982) 53, 54
debt forgiveness 141
Debt: the First 5,000 Years (Graeber) 148
debtors 118, 120
decolonization 36
decommodification of everyday life 30
definancialization of global political economy
    179
Deglobalization (Bello) 82
degrowth approach 79, 109–11, 164

delinking development strategy 80
demarketization 61
democracy 59–60
dependency school theorists 85
depoliticization 139–40
deposits 123
deregulation 93
derivatives 19, 119–20, 144–5, 146, 179
devaluation 92
developing countries 84
    as commodities producers for industrial
        rich 85
    deteriorating Terms of Trade 85
    relations to China 97–8
    export incomes 97
    import substitution industrialization (ISI)
        86
    inspiration of dependency school and post-
        Marxist analysis 85–6
    institutional problems 85
    interest rates on loans 89
    macroeconomic development 86
    underdevelopment 85
    see also Third World countries
development 83–6
    Beijing Consensus 97–8
    debt trap 87–91
    degrowth and the upper-class problem
        109–11
    designing a modern project 98–9
    lessons from SAP era 96–7
    overdevelopment in the North 86–7
    poverties 99–108
        cash transfers 103–6
        charity redistribution 102–3
        conditionalities 104–6
        income poverty 99–100
        international redistribution 106
            bilateral ODA 106
            multilateral aid 106
            tied aid 106
            untied aid 106–7
        official redistribution 103
        post-development 107
        poverty-alleviating redistribution 103
        public goods 103
        redistribution 102
        relative deprivation 100–1
        socialist perspective 107–8
        subsidies 105–6
        taxes, redistribution of 104–5
        universal basic income (UBI) 103–4
    SAP reconstruction 90–6
    Truman's speech 83–4
Development as Freedom (Sen) 112

Development Economics research (World Bank) 48
Development Theory and the Three Worlds (Hettne) 112
Dicken, Peter 175–6
difference-equality strategy 36
difference feminism 36
digitalization 126
direct power 9–10
discourse analysis 8–9
discrimination 20, 25
discursive power 8–9
distributive justice 35
dividends 117
division of labour 23, 150
Doha Development Round (DDR) 49, 69–70
double movement 62
Democratic Republic of Congo 170

E
ecological destruction 1–2
ecological footprint 32–3, 58
ecological sustainability 168
economic growth 1–3, 49
    slowing of 168
    see also output
economic interaction 5
economics 6
Economist 1
education 92
electric cars 169–70
emerging markets 69
emission rights 76
Encyclopaedia Britannica 15
energy 169
    clean 169
    efficiency 169
energy return on energy invested (EROEI) 33
Engels, Friedrich 22, 23, 136
Enhanced Structural Adjustment Facility 95
Enlightenment 21
entrepreneurship 150, 165
environmental capital 77
environmental sustainability 86–7
    see also sustainability
equilibrium 122
equity 117
Escobar, Arturo 107
essentialism 36
ethanol 33
ethical consumption 173
ethical investing 125, 135
Ethnic and Racial Studies 39
EU (European Union)

institutional sustainability changes 166
everyday life
    reconstructing 27–31
    risk of financial markets 145–6
    see also political economy of everyday life
exchange rates 45, 46, 51
    adjustments 121
    Bretton Woods system 51, 52, 116–17
    competitive 92
    floating 52, 117
    multilateral 52
    US dollar 51, 52
exploitation 22
export-processing zones (EPZs) 156–7
export tariffs 92
externalities 2, 76–7
extradiscursive 9

F
Fanon, Frantz 36, 185n2
    Black Skin White Masks 39
    Wretched of the Earth, The 39
farmers' cooperatives 137
farming 80
feminine characteristics 25
feminism 36
Feminist Economics 38
fictitious assets 147
financial capital 134
financial crises 22–3, 124, 177–8
    burden borne by working and middle classes 168
    environmental benefits of 177
    just, sustainable global production 179–81
    post-crisis markets 182–3
    support for corporations 168
    sustainable finance 177–8
    treaties for sustainable trade 181–2
financial crisis (2008) 125, 128–31
    G20 rescue package 131–3
financial instruments 115–21
    bonds 118
    credit default swaps (CDSs) 120, 128
    debt 117–18
    derivatives 119–20, 144–5, 146
    gold standard 116–17
    IOUs 116
    money 116, 120–1
    shares 117, 119
    swaps 119–20
financial intermediation 123
financial markets 115
    actors 122–8
        banks 123–5
        funds 125

nation states 127–8
    stockbrokers 125–6
debt 140–3
endemic risks 143–7
financial crisis (2008) 128–31
financial instruments 115–21
G20 131–3
global, reconstructing 133–4
logic of 121–2
money 138–40
perceived as rational 129
post-crisis 182–3
reconstructing ownership 134–8
reconstruction 178–9
repoliticization 140
self-regulation 144
socialist perspectives on 133–4
socialist reconstruction of 134
financial risk 179
financial speculation 146
Financial Stability Board (FSB) 131–2
Financial Stability Forum 131
financial stabilization 89
financialization 115
firms 149–50, 165, 175, 181
    internationalization of 151
    shareholder-friendly 162–3
    structural limitations of CSR 162–3
flat organizations 152
flexibilization 24
flexible group 159–60
food sovereignty 80–1
Fool's Gold (Tett) 147
Fordism 150–6
    diversification of corporations 151–2
    see also post-Fordism
foreign direct investment (FDI) 93–4
forex market 116, 120–1, 127–8
and Forgive Them Their Debts (Hudson) 148
formal institutional order 29
formal institutions 5
fossil fuels 32, 56, 77, 78, 169
Foucault, Michel 7, 9
fractional banking 123
Frank, Andre Gunder 85
free market 5
free-market ideology 51–2
free trade 49, 63
    mobilization against 68
    prevailing 73–5
    reframed as a technical issue 67–8
free-trade areas (FTAs) 67, 74
free-trade zones 156–7

Freefall: America, Free Markets, and the Sinking of the World Economy (Stiglitz) 147–8
Friedman, Milton 53
fuel taxes 57
Fumagalli, A. & Mezzadra, S. 148
fundamental analysis 126
funds 125

G
G20 group 73, 131–3, 177
G77 35
Gates, Bill 169
GATT (General Agreement on Tariffs and Trade) 49, 64
GDP (gross domestic product) 1, 74, 101, 161, 164, 165, 168
gender 16–20
    affirmative action 171–2
    oppression, fighting 35–7
    productive economy 17–19
    reciprocity 16
    reproductive economy 16, 18
    virtual economy 19–20
Gender, Development, and Globalization (Benería et al.) 38
gender inequality 19
General Agreement on Trade in Services (GATS) 49
General Assembly (UN) 43, 44, 186n1
Geneva (2008) 72–3
geopolitics of poverty 84
Germain, Randall 148
Germany 45
Gilroy, Paul 39
Gini coefficient 100
Glass–Steagall Act (1933) 128, 146
Global Compact (UN) 161–2, 163
global economic order
    change 51–4
    multinational economic institutions 44–50
    multinational institutional system 43–4
    nation states 41–3
    reconstructive lessons from the 1970s and 1980s 54–5
    solving problems 55–60
    transformation of market structures 60–1
global economy
    colonialism 20
    and everyday life 15–16
global free-trade regime 64–7
global labour force 159–60, 180–1

global metabolism 160
global North, overdevelopment 86–7
global political economy
    big GPE perspective 6
    interdisciplinary perspective 6
    Political Science and International
        Economic 6
    theoretical objectives 6–7
Global Politics & Financial Governance
    (Germain) 148
Global Shift: Mapping the Changing Contours of
    the World Economy (Dicken) 175–6
global social market approach 54
global South
    feminists 27
    see also developing countries
global value chains (GVCs) see GVCs (global
    value chains)
globalization 2–3, 17, 30, 61, 68, 112
    from below 181
Globalization and the Postcolonial World
    (Hoogvelt) 112
globalized production 149
    affirmative action 171–2
    business model approach 163
    clusters and regions 158–61
    consumer power 173–4
    contradiction 160–1
    crisis 151–2
    degrowth approach 164
    end of Fordism 150–6
    exploitation 158
    feminization of the labour force 157
    firms 149–50, 165, 175
    flat organizations 152
    flexibility 154–5
    global labour force 159–60
    GVCs (global value chains) 154, 155–6
    headquarters, reduction in size 152
    just and sustainable 179–81
    lean production 153–4
    loss of social capital 153
    outsourcing 153
    post-Fordism 153, 156
        political dynamics 156–8
    reconstructing corporations 166–9
    reconstructing global production 161–5
    reorganization 152
    revolution 174
    streamlining corporate structures
        152–3
    technology and reconstruction 169–71
    trade unions 172–3
    yearly price decreases 154
gold standard 116–17

government procurement 71
GPE (global political economy) see global
    political economy
Graeber, David 148
Gramsci, Antonio 26
Great Society welfare programme 52
Great Transformation, The (Polanyi) 62
green room deliberations 67
Green Swan event 178
greenhouse gas emissions 33, 56
growth see economic growth
guilt 29
GVCs (global value chains) 149, 154, 155
    competition 155–6
    energy costs 180
    infrastructure 154
    and labour costs 154
    sourcing 155

H
Haberl et al. 31
Handy, C. 165
Happer, C. 179
hedge funds 125
hegemony 26, 51
Henwood, Doug 147
Hettne, Björn 112
Hickel, Jason 109
high-frequency trading 126–7
high mass consumption 83
high-value production 158–9
Hochschild, Arlie Russell 27
Hoogvelt, Ankie 112
hooks, bell 26
Hudson, Michael 148
hyperglobalization 59

I
identification through consumption 174
IMF riots 91
imperialism 21
import substitution industrialization (ISI) 86
import tariffs 92
income poverty 99–100
income tax 57, 105
independence 49
    of colonized countries 84
India, in WTO negotiations 72–3
industrial development 86–7
industrial technology 87
industrialization 63
inequality 2, 100
    post-financial crisis (2008) 133
    in wages 17
inflation 88, 133

informal institutions 5
informalization 24
initial public offerings (IPOs) 117
institutional capacity 29
institutions 4–7
interest on money loans 142–3
interest rate ceilings 143
interest rate funds 125
interest rates 53–4, 88
    control of money supply 88
    increased 88–9
    negative 132
    supply and demand 143
International Bank for Reconstruction and
        Development (IBRD) 47, 51
International Centre for Settlement of
        Investment Disputes (ICSID) 49
International Covenant on Economic, Social
        and Cultural Rights (ICESCR) 173
International Development Association (IDA)
        48
international exchange rate 45
International Finance Corporation (IFC)
        47–8
International Labour Organization (ILO) 39,
        173
International Monetary Fund (IMF) 2, 3,
        45–7, 52, 53
    conditionalities 89–90
    managing debt crisis 89
    rescue package (2009) 131–3
    see also SAPs (structural adjustment
        programmes)
international redistribution 106
international trade 92–3
Internet 68
intersectional justice 36–7
intersectionality 24–5, 27–8
investment banking 124
investment-friendly climate 93–4
IOUs 116
irrelevant group 159, 160
Islam 135–6, 142

J
Jackson, Timothy 39
Japan 17
J.P. Morgan 128
just prices 60
justice 179–81
Justice and Fairness in International Negotiation
        (Albin) 82

K
Kabeer, Naila 172–3
Keynes, John Maynard 101
Keynesian macroeconomic programmes 52
Khor, Martin 82
Kicking Away the Ladder (Chang) 82
Kipling, Rudyard 25, 185n1
Klein, Naomi 3, 78, 175
knowledge production 8–9
knowledge, upper classes 111
Kropotkin, Peter 186n2
Krugman, Paul 73, 168
Kyoto Protocol (1997) 76

L
labour exploitation 180
labour force, feminization of 157
labour standards 78
lawmakers 5
laws 29, 58–9
lean production 153–4
Leeson, Nick 120
legitimacy of taxes 57–8
Lehman Brothers 130, 144
Leins, Stefan 148
LETS (local exchange and trading systems)
        108
Li, Tanya Murray 37
life-cycle analysis 32–3
lifestyles 31
limited liability 134, 135–6
living wages 135
loans 46, 48, 88, 118
    increased interest rates on 89
local currencies 108
love 25–7, 183, 185n3
love ethic 26
love practice 38
low-value production 159

M
MacKenzie, Donald 3
macroprudential regulation 145
Marchand, Marianne & Runyan, Anne 17,
        18, 158
marginal tax rate 57
market activities 77
market arbitrage 146
market expansion 30
market logic 30
market risk 144
market society 61
market, the
    equilibrium 53
    freedom from state intervention 53

marketization 61
markets
    and capitalism 59
    and democracy 59–60
    reconstructing 55, 59
    transformation of structures 60–1
Marshall Plan 51
Marx, Karl 22, 23, 136
Marxism 21
    alienation 22, 26–7
    class conflict 22
    communist revolution 23
    exploitation 22
    revolution 174
masculine characteristics 25
means of production 136, 174
Merleau-Ponty, Maurice 2
Mesopotamia 116, 138, 142
metal coins 116
Mexico 74, 158
middle classes 22, 24
military strength 23
Millennium Development Goals (MDGs) 99
Mobuto Sese Seko 86
modernization 83
modes of production 23
monetarism 53–4, 88
monetary policy 45, 128, 139–40
money 116, 120–1, 138–40
money supply 88
Montreal Protocol (1987) 77, 78
moral hazard 120, 142, 145, 146, 179, 186n1
most-favoured-nation (MFN) 64
multilateral aid 106
multilateral economic institutions 44–50
    free trade and growth 49
    GATT (General Agreement on Tariffs and Trade) 49
    International Monetary Fund (IMF) 3, 45–7
    World Bank 47–9
multilateral institutional system 43–4
Multilateral Investment Guarantee Agency (MIGA) 48–9

N
nation states 41–3
    construction of 42
    financial markets 127–8
    non-intervention, principle of 43
    regulation of economic interaction 42
national treatment 65
nationalism 2
NATO (North Atlantic Treaty Organization) 51
Nazi Party 45

needs fulfilment 86
Negritude project 36
neoliberalism 53, 54
network value 159
New International Economic Order (NIEO) 35, 79
New Political Economy 38, 39
New York Stock Exchange 126
Nixon, President 52
No Logo (Klein) 78, 175
non-industrialized countries *see* developing countries
non-intervention principle 43
non-tariff barriers (NTBs) 64–5
norms 8–9
North *see* global North
North American Free Trade Area (NAFTA) 74, 75
Nyerere, Julius K. 186n2

O
OECD (Organization for Economic Co-operation and Development) 39
off-setting deals 119
official development assistance (ODA) 48, 84, 106–7
official redistribution 103
oil crisis (1973) 52
    lessons from 54–5
OPEC (Organization of the Petroleum Exporting Countries) 52
oppression 25, 26
options 119
Ostrom, Elinor 81, 137
output
    ecological consequences 1–2
    unequal distribution of wealth 2
outsourcing 153
overpopulation 87
Owen, Robert 136
ownership 30–1, 134–8
    alternatives to capitalism 136–7
    commons 137
    company behaviour 135–6
    of economic assets 179
    shareholder responsibility 136
ozone layer 77–8

P
paper money 116
Paris Agreement (2015) 10, 163, 182
particularism 58
path dependence 145
patriarchal gender norms 25
    loss of male economic power 157–8

new economic role for women 158
patriarchal norms 18, 37
    political trends 158
patriarchy 27
Pax Americana 51
Peace of Westphalia (1648) 41, 42
pension funds 125
people's quantitative easing 178–9
Peterson, V.S. 16, 17, 19, 116
    *A Critical Rewriting of the Global Political
        Economy* 38
petrodollars 88, 89
philia 26
phrenology 21
Piketty, Thomas 115, 141, 148
Pinochet, General Augusto 86
Polanyi, Karl 5, 62
political costs 91
political dictators 86
political economy of everyday life 15–39
    class 21–4
    ecological footprint 32–3
    energy return on energy invested (EROEI)
        33
    gender 16–20
        oppression, fighting 35–7
    intersectionality 24–5, 27–8
    lifestyles and sustainability 31
    love 25–7
    power 28
    racism 20–1
        fighting 35–7
    reconstructing everyday life 27–31
    social justice 34–5
post-development 107
post-Fordism 153, 156, 175
    political dynamics 156–8
post-growth 79
poststructural justice 36–7
poverty 84, 99–108
    cash transfers 103–6
    charity redistribution 102–3
    conditionalities 104–6
    income poverty 99–100
    international redistribution 106
        bilateral ODA 106
        multilateral aid 106
        tied aid 106
        untied aid 106–7
    LETS (local exchange and trading systems)
        108
    measurement of 100
    official redistribution 103
    post-development 107
    poverty-alleviating redistribution 103
    public goods 103

redistribution 102
    relative deprivation 100–1
    SDG 101–2
    socialist perspective 107–8
    subsidies 105–6
    taxes, redistribution of 104–5
    universal basic income (UBI) 103–4
poverty-alleviating redistribution 103
Poverty Reduction and Growth Facility 95
Poverty Reduction Strategy Papers (PRSPs)
    96–7
power 7–10, 28, 185n3
Power and the Governance of Global Trade (Soo
    Yeon Kim) 82
power in structures 8
power to change structures 8
precariat 2
price mechanism 17, 30, 59, 61
price takers 79
principal financial centres (PFCs) 128
*On the Principles of Political Economy and
    Taxation* (Ricardo) 81
Principles of Scientific Management, The (Taylor)
    150
privatization 30, 31, 94–5
problem-solving concepts 55–60
problem-solving theory 6
production
    deterritorialization of 155
    global, sustainable 179–81
    see also globalized production
productive economy 17–19
    benefits and additional profits 19
    exploitation of unpaid female work 18
productivity 86
profit 19
progressive tax 105
prohibitions 77
Prosperity Without Growth (Jackson) 39
protectionism 73
Psychic Life of Power, The (Butler) 38
public goods 103
public sector 57–8
Putin, Vladimir 96

Q
Quantitative Easing (QE) 133, 178
queer theory 37
quotas 64

R
racism 2, 20–1
    affirmative action 171–2
    fighting 35–7
ratings 127

re-embedding 61
REACH (Registration, Evaluation,
    Authorisation and Restriction of
    Chemicals) directive 80
Reagan, Ronald 53
real estate 129–31
reasonable aspiration curve 101
Recipe for Chile (Friedman) 53
reciprocity 16, 30, 66
reconstruction
    of corporations 166–9
    of everyday life 27–31
    financial crises 178
    financial markets under socialism 134
    of global financial markets 55, 59, 133–4
    of global production 161–5
    of markets for sustainability 55
    of ownership 134–8
    SAPs (structural adjustment programmes)
        90–6
    technology and 169–71
red tape 94
redistribution 102
refinancing society 178–9
Reform Parliament (1832) 43
regional trade agreements (RTAs) 73–4
regulations 58–9, 124
regulators 5, 124
relative deprivation 100–1
religion, conflict with capitalism 42–3
renewable energy sources 180
repoliticization 140
reproductive economy 16, 18
    benefits for capitalist production 18–19
    feminization of 17
    pool of labour for productive economy
        18
reserve army of labour 21
responsibility 29
responsibility to protect (R2P) 186n1
responsive units 9
retail banking 123
returns to scale 150
revolution 174
Ricardo, David 49, 63
    On the Principles of Political Economy and
        Taxation 82
Rights of Man (Paine) 21
risk perception 146
Rodrik, Dani 58–9, 81
    Straight Talk on Trade 82
Rostow, W.W. 83
Roubini, Nouriel 140
Ruggie, John Gerard 62
rules 34–5
ruling classes 26

S
Sachs, Jeffrey 19, 62
Sachs, Wolfgang 107
safeguards 65
SAPs (structural adjustment programmes) 54,
    90
    adjustments 95–6
        local programme design 95
        poverty reduction dimension 95–6
        time allowance 96
    budget balance 90–1
    bureaucracy 94
    competitive exchange rates 92
    deregulation 93
    devaluations 92
    education 92
    foreign direct investment (FDI) 93–4
    ideological radicalism 95
    international trade 92–3
    investment-friendly climate 93–4
    lessons from 96–7
    poverty, necessity of 100
    privatization 94–5
    reconstruction 90–6
    shock therapy 95
    tax reforms 91
Scholte, Jan Aart 54
Schuurman, Frans 112
science 21
Seattle conference (1999) 68–9
Secretariat (UN) 44
Security Council (UN) 43–4
self-reflection 61
self-regulation 144
self-reliance development strategy 80
Sen, Amartya 112
Senghor, Léopold 36
sexual services, regulation of 5
Shanghai Cooperation Organization (SCO)
    97
Shao, Ibrahim 94–5
shareholders 135, 136
shares 117, 119
Silent Spring (Carson) 87
similarity-equality strategy 35–6
Singapore issues 71
single undertaking 49, 66
Sirleaf, Ellen Johnson 167
sisterhood 27
Smith, Adam 23, 43, 100, 165, 187n1
    Wealth of Nations 42
Smithsonian Agreement 52
social capital 24, 153
social fields 24
social justice 34–5
    and poverty 100